DOÑA MARÍA'S STORY

A book in the series

LATIN AMERICA OTHERWISE: LANGUAGES, EMPIRES, NATIONS

Series editors:

Walter D. Mignolo, Duke University

Irene Silverblatt, Duke University

Sonia Saldívar-Hull, University of California at Los Angeles

DANIEL JAMES

Doña María's Story

LIFE HISTORY, MEMORY, AND

POLITICAL IDENTITY

Duke University Press   Durham and London   2000

© 2000 Duke University Press   All rights reserved   Printed in the United
States of America on acid-free paper ∞   Designed by C. H. Westmoreland
Typeset in Bembo by Tseng Information Systems, Inc.   Library of Congress
Cataloging-in-Publication Data appear on the last printed page of this book.
Frontispiece photo: Doña María Roldán in her kitchen, Berisso 1987. *Courtesy
the author.*

DEDICATION

This book is dedicated to the memory of my mother Chris James, my mother-in-law Verna Di Pietro and my friend María Roldán, three extraordinary working-class women. It is also dedicated to my daughter Rachel in the hope that the history bequeathed to her by them will prove to be a matchless heritage as she struggles to build her future.

CONTENTS

ABOUT THE SERIES

Latin America Otherwise: Languages, Empires, Nations is a critical series. It aims to explore the emergence and consequences of concepts used to define "Latin America" while at the same time exploring the broad interplay of political, economic, and cultural practices that have shaped Latin American worlds. Latin America, at the crossroads of competing imperial designs and local responses, has been construed as a geocultural and geopolitical entity since the nineteenth century. This series provides a starting point to redefine Latin America as a configuration of political, linguistic, cultural, and economic intersections that demand a continuous reappraisal of the role of the Americas in history, and of the ongoing process of globalization and the relocation of people and cultures that have characterized Latin America's experience. *Latin America Otherwise: Languages, Empires, Nations* is a forum that confronts established geocultural constructions, that rethinks area studies and disciplinary boundaries, that assesses convictions of the academy and of public policy, and that, correspondingly, demands that the practices through which we produce knowledge and understanding about and from Latin America be subject to rigorous and critical scrutiny.

Doña María's Story is about many stories: it is a tale about María Roldán's life as a labor activist and ardent Peronist, about the tangles of Argentine politics from the 1940s to the present, about the ways that gender shapes human experience, about the power and malleability of memory, about the craft of writing history. What makes this book so remarkable is the ways these stories intertwine.

Doña María's Story can be read as an engagement between the author, the discipline of history, narrative structures, and the fluidity of the past. As Daniel James presents a landscape of memory that both exalts an urban community's past and silences it, he makes the reader think again about all historical reconstructions. James forces us to confront the limitations that all historians face by highlighting the narrative tropes mediating Doña María's story and by critiquing the assumptions and tools on which his profession rests. But, precisely because of this, Argentina's twentieth century takes on depth and Doña María comes alive.

Doña María, evoked through her words and the author's thoughts, obliges the historian—and the reader—to engage her in dialogue and participate in her world.

Walter D. Mignolo, *Duke University*
Irene Silverblatt, *Duke University*
Sonia Saldívar-Hull, *University of California at Los Angeles*

ACKNOWLEDGMENTS

This book has taken almost ten years to reach publication. During that time I have incurred many intellectual, and more personal, debts. The research on which it is based was originally made possible by grants from the Center for International Studies, Yale University, and the Social Science Research Council. My colleague Emilia Viotti da Costa gave me initial encouragement and much further intellectual provocation. Tom Klubock and Heidi Tinsman offered me valuable feedback as together we charted the uncertain waters of my first seminar on oral history. The final writing was aided immeasurably by the tranquil atmosphere and supportive staff of the National Humanities Center where I was a Fellow in 1997–98.

An earlier, shorter version of chapter 4 appeared in the *Journal of Latin American Cultural Studies.* I am grateful for permission to republish. Some of the material herein appeared in a chapter in *The Gendered Worlds of Latin American Women Workers* (1997, Duke University Press).

Since 1999 I have taught at Indiana University. However, my thinking about oral history and Doña María Roldán's testimony matured in the unique intellectual environment I encountered at Duke University. I have been the beneficiary of a rich interdisciplinary environment centered on the Latin American Studies program. The program has provided me with both a stimulating intellectual setting and firm friends who have contributed to my ability to complete this book. Debbie Jakubs offered her friendship from the moment I and my family arrived at Duke; that along with her talents as librarian, her leadership of the Duke-UNC Program in Latin American Studies, and her passion for Latin America were invaluable gifts. Friendship, food, wine, and a sense of fun have provided the underpinning for my writing. I must thank Jim Roberts, Natalie Hartman, Teresa Vilarós, Walter Mignolo, Anne Wylie, Ariel and Angélica Dorfman, Judy and Tom Coffman, Wendy Luttrell, and Robert Shreefter.

I have also benefited enormously from the privilege of teaching some exceptional graduate students at Duke. Ann Farnsworth-Alvear, Mark Healey, Jody Pavilack, Adriana Brodsky, and Jon Beasley-Murray all contributed to this project by their readings of versions of the chapters and by their intellectual passion and commitment. Mark Healey, in addition, provided the translations of the two poems discussed in chapter 4.

For many years I have participated in the intellectual environment surrounding the Latin American Labor History Conference. Several of the chapters in this book were first essayed there, and I have profited from the critical input and friendship of Barbara Weinstein, Deborah Levenson, Peter Winn, Mike Jiménez, and Jeff Gould. Bill Roseberry was kind enough to read the manuscript and to give me encouraging feedback. His untimely death earlier this year has robbed the fields of Latin American history and anthropology of an important critical presence. A pioneer in the complex task of constructing a fully historicized anthropology, he was a generous colleague to many across a wide range of disciplines. In an academic world all too prone to reward self-promotion he was a beacon of modesty, decency, and humane treatment of others. He will be sadly missed.

I have had the good fortune to have shared my time at Duke with three colleagues who have helped me and influenced me more than they may realize. John French and I founded the Latin American Labor History conference at Yale in 1984. Since 1992 we have been colleagues at Duke. In addition to our shared intellectual project of furthering the study of Latin American labor history, John has provided me with a model both of a thoughtful colleague and of a serious intellectual. Our daily conversations have been an invaluable filter for ideas, honing some of the better ones and weeding out some of the more half-baked. He has been unstinting with his time, his friendship, and his incomparable knowledge of the international labor movement. Jan Hoffman French did me the inestimable favor of finding time in the midst of an outrageous schedule as a mother and a scholar to read every word of this manuscript and to give me insightful critical comments in a spirit of support and friendship.

Alberto Moreiras has been a constant intellectual presence for me in my time at Duke. I have had the good fortune to collaborate with him in the Latin American Cultural Studies program and to coteach several graduate and undergraduate seminars. His restless critical intelligence has been a source of provocation, of excitement, of concern for me. I have learned much from him about Latin America and ways of thinking about Latin America. Above all, I have been challenged by his willingness to question the accepted limits of theories and theorizing, the established boundaries between knowledges. He has been a generous colleague who has taught me much about the politics of friendship.

In Argentina my debts are many. In Berisso I have been honored by the friendship and support of Nestor and Elsa Juzwa; Miguel, Emilce, Mónica, and Lito Sánchez; Jaime Teixido; Dora and Eduardo Roldán. Miguel Sánchez has been a true friend always ready to help me with his time, his car, and his advice. Renzo, Beba, and Dante Anzolini opened their home to me and treated me as family. Raúl and Ana Filgueira also put me up in their house and put up with my questions. Much of whatever understanding I have for Berisso as a community I owe to Raúl with his inimitable passion for life and for the people of Berisso and their history. My stays in Berisso have also been enlivened by the hospitality and humor of the muchachos of the Club del Lote, led by its master of ceremonies, Pocho Aries. In Buenos Aires I have been fortunate to have enjoyed the support of a wonderful network of friends. I have known Jorge Montgomery for twenty-five years, he is my best friend, confidant and surrogate brother. My experience of Buenos Aires is marked by the bars, boliches, and bookstores where we have talked, dreamed, and argued. He is a master of Tai-Chi, an expert on the films of Fassbinder, and one of the few genuine intellectuals I have known, and this book would be simply unthinkable without him. Alberto

Ferrari and his family have always been there for me when I needed their support, as have Dora Barrancos and Eduardo Moon. Judith Evans was also a kind and generous friend who helped in many ways in the early years of this project. Hector and Mirta Palomino were unfailingly good friends who allowed me to share the warmth and spirit of their family. Pablo, Mariana, and Laura were a constant reminder of how great kids make it all worthwhile.

Another friend Juan Carlos Torre is a fundamental reference point for anyone wishing to study modern Argentina and most especially Peronism. While this book may not reflect his own preferences for historical narrative, I trust that he can recognize the influence of the many conversations we have had over the years.

Rosa Achuger transcribed the tapes with a professionalism and an eye for detail that was invaluable. She also became a friend and interlocutor who has contributed greatly to my understanding of Doña María's story.

Alberto and Estela Belloni are my oldest Argentine friends, "companeros de alma y corazon." Although they have lived in Paris for twenty-five years they have remained fundamental reference points for me in all things Argentine. This book is a small testimony to the wonderful gift of their friendship that has helped sustain me over the years.

My greatest debt is owed to my friend and collaborator Mirta Lobato. For the last five years we have worked jointly on the project, "Berisso Obrero." I have benefited greatly from her unparalleled knowledge of the history of meatpacking, women workers, and Berisso. Her own work on the packing houses and the community of Berisso has been enormously influential on me. Many of the ideas in this book were shaped by innumerable conversations with her over the years. I have been truly fortunate to have been able to work with a historian with her passion, talents, and sense of fun. She and Juan Suriano, and Lisandro their son, also opened their home to me and gave me their support and friendship, and for that I am deeply grateful.

It is something of a formality for authors to offer thanks to patient editors. In my case the debt I owe Valerie Millholland goes far beyond a formality. I certainly must have tried her patience sorely, but she has been a gracious, sympathetic mediator who sustained me in this project through some difficult times. I would also like to thank Paula Dragosh for the superb copyediting.

Finally, I owe many things to my family. My father, Morgan James, instilled many things in me, among them a love of books and history, an appreciation of good food and drink, a passion for Welsh rugby, and a capacity to be outraged by social injustice and economic exploitation. His mark is present on all that I write. My debt to my wife, Lynn and my sons, Nick and Daniel, and my daughter, Rachel, is almost too obvious to state. Their love is the foundation for everything else.

I

PROLOGUE

THE TOWN WITH NO PLAZA

Memory and Monuments in Berisso's Centro Cívico

Memory is like a wonderful gift and a relentless curse.
—Aharon Appelfeld, "The Pains of Memory"

In its own fashion the Centro Cívico is the nearest thing Berisso offers to the traditional central plaza found in most Argentine towns. Situated some fifty miles from Buenos Aires, Berisso developed in response to the arbitrary expansion of dwellings and commercial establishments for meat-packing-house workers. Up till the late 1950s it was an administrative subdivision of the nearby provincial capital, La Plata, and would always live in its shadow. It was a growing community of labor that afforded little opportunity for the niceties of urban planning, even after it achieved municipal autonomy in 1957. It lacked the facilities associated with urban centers: a central municipal building, a central plaza, and the other public spaces that embody the status and civic claims of urban elites. Berisso's Centro Cívico, despite its formal title, began as and would remain an unremarkable open, grass-covered space, although it would eventually bear rich and unique testimony to the community's history.[1]

In 1873 Juan Berisso set up a *saladero* (salting house) on a piece of land on the bank of the Río Santiago, itself a short tributary of the Río de la Plata. The land stretched south to a dirt road that headed along the coast. This road and the river itself provided local cattle ranchers access to the salting house that would preserve the meat that they sent to be slaughtered.

With the advent of refrigeration at the end of the nineteenth century the saladero became obsolete. At the same time about a mile away, the Chicago-based Swift and Armour meatpacking houses set up shop on a much larger scale. They used the original site of the saladero as a general depository for the plants and for the burning of animal waste. The dirt road that skirted the open tract of land became the Avenida Montevideo, and the windowless brick panels that formed the sides of the newly built commercial buildings and warehouses framed the area on the north and south.

The space was officially designated the Centro Cívico in 1948, and a large part of it was taken up with the football field of the Club Trabajador de la Carne, though waste from the plants continued to be burned in the part farthest from the road. Over the years there were several plans designed to transform the space into a true commercial, administrative, and cultural center. However, little was done in practice to develop the area. Football continued to be played and the space between the field and the Avenida Montevideo became the designated gathering place for kids from the nearby secondary school.

In the years following the reestablishment of democracy in 1983 the square underwent a more significant transformation. In a space never claimed by the founding fathers and other national icons normally found in the plazas of the republic, the Peronist-dominated council empowered by its victory had free rein to commemorate the heroes who symbolized its political and moral values. The council placed these statues and monuments in the twenty meters nearest to the road. At the same time the community commissioned local artists to adorn the walls of adjacent buildings with its interpretation of history.

The murals, statues, and monuments that the community commissioned reflect an attempt to express and memorialize the elements that make up the collective memory of Berisso. The packing houses had closed by then—Armour in 1969 and Swift a decade later. Poised on the cusp of a period of profound economic and social transformation that carried with it a sense of profound loss, the

The mural in the Centro Cívico, Berisso. *Courtesy Norberto Gullari.*

community attempted to name that loss and to ward off its onset by constructing a memoryscape. This memoryscape, the Centro Cívico, would evoke and validate time gone by. For the older generation it spoke nostalgically of an idealized community. For the younger generation of high school kids who gathered among its symbols it made a claim for the value of a past that was rapidly slipping beyond their reach. The Centro Cívico became a site dedicated to both remembrance and commemoration.

Doña María Roldán's story is shaped by the moral principles, the ideological forces, and the historical experiences commemorated here. A walk through this space can help us establish the context within which her life story must be read.

Some thirty feet high by fifty feet long, the mural on the north wall is a montage of scenes representing Berisso's past. The common thread unifying the fragments of this montage is that of industry and labor. At the top right-hand corner we can see a panoramic shot of the Grand Dock and the quay running beside the two plants.

Ships crowd the waterfront, taking on the meat and various by-products produced in the *frigoríficos* (packing houses), whose buildings reach within ten meters of the water. In the distance stretching out toward the Río de la Plata estuary we can see the canal cut by immigrant labor in the 1890s to link the Grand Dock to the river and, beyond that, the markets of the North Atlantic. It is this trade that underlies Berisso's growth as an industrial community. Immediately below, another wide-angle view of the Swift plant depicts workers disembarking from a train and entering at the start of the shift. Superimposed on one corner we see the carcasses of cattle hanging from the moving line of hooks that form the *noria*, the assembly line that carried the dead animal past the different stations of white overalled workers, each assigned a particular task in preparing the meat for market. Clearly visible, too, in the shot of the Swift packing house is the five-story building that housed the different sections involved in the processing of the meat: the *conserva*, the *picada*, the *tripería*, the *salchichería*. Many of these sections consisted mainly of women workers.

The complex industrial system represented in these images brought together thousands of workers. At the height of production during World War 2 Swift and Armour were said to employ between fifteen and twenty thousand workers. In peacetime they employed less workers, though still significantly more than any other employer in the area. Meatpacking employment was characterized by a high degree of instability. Faced with fluctuations in market demand, and with seasonal variations in the provision of livestock, the companies required a pool of available workers who could be rapidly incorporated as demand warranted. It was these conditions that provoked what was perhaps the most lasting symbol of the harshness of meatpacking work in the era before 1945. At the beginning of the day shift, the hiring manager would appear and select from the crowd waiting at the gate the new workers needed for that day. Local lore had it that workers were chosen for their physical appearance, and when the quota had been met, the remaining workers, who had been straining and pushing to attract the manager's attention and were now reluctant to leave, were often dispersed with fire hoses.

The other images of the mural refer to the community that sprang up around the packing houses. The houses made of corrugated zinc, single story and brightly painted, were characteristic of Berisso's early housing stock. Cheap to build and cheap to maintain, they were also hot in the summer and cold in the winter. Below the houses, we can see an image of a school and children waiting to enter, and a picture of the number twenty-five tram, crowded with workers, as it made its journey along the Avenida Montevideo to the two packing plants. The tram signifies Berisso's geographical expansion. As the resident population grew in the 1920s and 1930s, new lots were opened away from the densely settled area in the immediate vicinity of the packing houses. Taking advantage of the easily available land, contractors and banks divided up and sold new lots, principally near the Avenida Montevideo: Villa Banco Constructor, Villa San Carlos where Doña María would acquire her first house, Villa Zula, Villa Arguello, Villa Dolores were all constructed in this era with first-time home buyers.

Later, in the Peronist era, the number of working-class home owners increased even more, with the construction some five kilometers from the packing houses of the Barrio Obrero, a state-financed housing scheme that made home owners of thousands of workers. Much of this urban expansion was carried out with inadequate infrastructure; few roads were paved, and the sewage system was nonexistent in many of the new barrios. Indeed, to this day many of Berisso's roads, away from the main arteries, are mostly unpaved, reduced to dust in the summer and mud traps in the winter.

Drainage, too, was a problem. Most of Berisso lies beneath sea level; it is, urbanists will tell you, a mistake, an aberration whose foundation and expansion was due to the imperatives of the meatpacking economy rather than the logic of planning. Regular rainfall drains away with difficulty, and the city has few storm drains. Those areas that lie on the river side of the Avenida Montevideo are also vulnerable to flooding from the river. Periodically, large parts of Berisso are victimized by the powerful flood tide known as the *sudestada,* after the powerful southeast wind that drives high tide over the estuary.

The number twenty-five tram ends its journey on the calle Nueva

York. Berisso's most celebrated street, it ran the length of the two packing houses. There are two images of the Nueva York in the mural. In the bottom left we see a long shot of the street, with the plants immediately behind. On the right there is an image of a street vendor offering his wares, framed by a concrete arch that is recognizable to anyone above a certain age in Berisso. At the top of the arch the inscription reads, "Mansión de Obreros, 1920." Originally intended as a reformist scheme to provide decent housing for workers, it was soon abandoned. Instead, its title would ironically mock the reality of densely populated houses and tenements that can be glimpsed through the arch.

The first *conventillos* (tenements) were built here and in adjacent streets. Workers could literally cross the street and enter the plant. The tenements on the side of the street nearest the factories actually backed onto the Swift plant, which was separated from them by only the railroad line. The crowded living conditions on the Nueva York and its side streets are embedded in popular memory in the image of the *camas calientes* (the warm beds), which kept their heat as one body rolled out to start a workday and another, exhausted after a full shift, collapsed into the same bed.

The Nueva York was, until the closing of the plants, the social center of Berisso, with an array of bars, brothels, cheap hotels, and restaurants crammed into the six blocks nearest the frigoríficos. In the recollections of Berissenses the memory of the Nueva York stands out as a location for memories of labor (the hiring gate) or the activity in the bars themselves. Beyond that, the street is a metaphor for a dominant strain of nostalgia and yearning that informs the memories of many older Berissenses.

The memory summoned by the mural is paradoxical. It celebrates the suffering and hardships of a community of laborers. At the same time, it honors the notion of industrial progress brought about by the sweat of these laborers and incarnated in the modern machines of the plants. The Nueva York could embody this tension; it could summon up "camas calientes" and the hiring gate at the same time as it symbolized all that was vibrant and hopeful and modern about the community. The language used to recapture its qualities often, indeed, seems to have a sensuous, almost corporeal quality. The street in these recollections was alive: it hummed, it buzzed, it funneled people in and out of the frigorífico, which consumed people but also produced wealth, and gave money and consuming power. The very vibrance of this memory also transforms the Nueva York into a reference point that Berissenses use to express their puzzlement and sense of frustration at what devastation can be wrought on a community by far-off economic decisions. Today the Nueva York has the aspect of a street in a half-deserted ghost town with boarded-up storefronts and half-abandoned tenements.

Immediately above the shot of the Nueva York, there is a picture of a horse-drawn cart at rest by the edge of a river. In the distance there appears to be a home at the water's edge with a boat dock in front. Surrounding the house is the lush vegetation of tall trees. At first glance, the image seems jarring, out of place with the representations of industry and urban community that have dominated the mural. Yet the juxtaposition of images is a telling one. It reminds the viewer that Berisso is a semirural space, different from the traditional urban, industrial landscape normally associated with meatpacking. The technology of the plants may have come from Chicago, but Berisso as a space was very different from the Chicago stockyards.

The Nueva York ends at the water, alongside the Armour plant, which was perched on a headland constructed with the earth removed in the construction of the Grand Dock. The plant, before it was torn down in the early 1980s, looked directly up the main channel leading to the river. The street, then, points toward the estuary, toward nature, toward the somewhat magical zone that Berissenses call the "monte." People still take the launch to the estuary from the landing at the end of the Nueva York. In the heyday of the plants the favorite destination was the launch's last stop, the Isla Paulino, the headland where the canal enters the immense, muddy waters of the Río de la Plata. It was here that the end-of-year picnics were held by the sections of the plant, where prodigious quantities of meat were cooked and consumed.

There are a thousand different ways into this giant floodplain formed with the accumulated silt of many millennia. All the streets running off the Avenida Montevideo on the riverside end within

The monument celebrating immigrant origins, Centro Cívico, Berisso. *Courtesy Norberto Gullari.*

five or six blocks at the river. Beyond the edge of town begins a world of streams, canals, dense vegetation, and unique wildlife. For many the monte is a space of leisure; for many of the young it is a place of adventure. In the not-so-distant past it was also a place of settlement and cultivation. Many of the immigrant workers from Italy who constructed the canal and the Grand Dock stayed to settle in the monte. With the help of drainage ditches they established plantations of fruit and vegetables intended for the local markets. This area also became a source of cheap wine sold in Berisso. The *vino de la costa* made from the *uva chinche* native to the coastline was sold door-to-door. For more serious drinkers the grape was also used to produce a smooth but powerful *grappa*. Nowadays few of the plantations survive; most have been abandoned, victims of flooding and market gardening competition. The area has been surrendered to hunters, fishers, boaters, and the adventurous.

The juxtaposition of the bucolic scene and the Nueva York is not, therefore, without its significance. The street could lead both to the

The Mural of Immigration, Centro Cívico, Berisso. *Courtesy Norberto Gullari.*

killing floor, and the intense physical exploitation of modern production systems found in the plants, and also to a space of leisure, a place of growth and cultivation of nature.

The Community of Immigrants

Berisso has its face turned toward the ocean. It clings to the coastline, looking out toward the Atlantic. The great shipping lanes of the Atlantic were the lifeline of its economic development. The majority of its early inhabitants had traveled these waters before disembarking to populate its shores. Berisso is the quintessential immigrant community in a nation largely constructed by immigrants. The community's sense of its own history has as one of its crucial axes the image of the immigrant. Approaching the city from La Plata the visitor is greeted by an arch that proudly proclaims: "The Capital of the Immigrant." It is safe to say that nowhere else in

Argentina is there such a wide spectrum of different ethnic groups. Every year on the second Sunday in September these groups celebrate the "Day of the Immigrant" by parading through Berisso's streets, dressed in national costume and playing national music. By the 1930s nearly 50 percent of Berisso's adult population had been born in other countries. They had come as part of the great southern European transatlantic migration that had brought Argentina the majority of its immigrants. But they had also come in large numbers from central and eastern Europe and the Near East, from the Hapsburg, Romanov, and Ottoman Empires as they entered their death throes.

The image of the laborer is inseparable from the image of the immigrant. The calle Nueva York itself symbolized the mass of ethnic groups who made up Berisso. Memories of the street are framed in terms of the *turcos* who ran many of the stores and gambling operations, the *rusos* and *judíos* who were the *cuenteniks* (door-to-door salesmen) offering cheap goods on credit, the Spaniards and Armenians who owned many of the bars, the Poles, Lithuanians, Bulgarians, Ukrainians, and Slovaks who lived in the tenements and worked in the plants.

The Centro Cívico speaks to this memory. Toward the front of the grass, near the street, there is a concrete slab adorned with the flags of nineteen nations who sent their sons and daughters to Berisso. It is a symbol of Berisso's sense of itself as a cosmopolitan community. On the same wall as the giant mural there is a smaller one consisting of three panels. The first panel shows us the immigrant family disembarking from the ship. In the background we can see the factories beckoning. The second panel represents the lives of labor of the immigrants with images of industry, technology, and workers. In the final panel we see an old man representing the immigrant father or grandfather, seated, bowed over by years of labor. He has in one hand a shovel, the symbol of physical labor. He has his other arm raised, touching the shoulder of a young man. The young man is dressed in modern attire, and he stands erect, a picture of vigor and optimism in contrast to the older man. This image depicts the classic immigrant story. The first generation struggled and suffered to "make America," an inheritance whose benefits were passed on to their children.

We cannot only define these immigrants by their labor in the plants. They also founded institutions that encouraged a densely textured fabric of social, cultural, and religious networks. To this day Berisso's immigrant past is clearly present in its urban topography. A walk up the Avenida Montevideo, past the Centro Cívico, soon shows the visitor evidence of this immigrant presence. Opposite the monument to Berisso's ethnic heritage we find the Sociedad Italiana, founded in 1919. Further along on the opposite side of the road lies the imposing frontage of the two-story building that houses the Asociación Ucraniana Prosvita, founded in 1924. The architecture brings to mind eastern European motifs; the massive front door is carved with traditional Ukrainian patterns. A granite plaque beside the door announces in gold lettering the celebration in 1988 of the millennium of Christianity in the Ukraine. A few blocks further up and one street over is an entire city block dedicated to Ukrainian cultural and religious life. The Church of San Vladimir the Great, of the Uniate Catholic faith, is by far the most impressive in Berisso. Next door, taking up the rest of the block, is a convent; attached to it is a school run by the nuns. Rejoining the Avenida Montevideo the visitor passes the Sociedad Lituana Católica "Mindaugas." Beyond this in what is already Villa San Carlos there is another Ukrainian Society, the Sociedad Ucraniana Renascimiento.

Further off the calle Montevideo is more evidence. The Unión Polaca, founded in 1921, is on a side-street near the calle Génova. Around the corner is the white-domed, Byzantine architecture of the Greek Orthodox Church, Saints Constantine and Elena. A few streets further over a modern building with a mildly Levantine flavor houses the social center of the powerful Syrian-Lebanese community. Many blocks further over, far from the calle Montevideo, we could also find a small, all-white domed church in the Russian orthodox style, where in years gone by Berisso's small community of immigrants from eastern Ukraine worshiped.

The imposing nature of many of these buildings is itself testimony to the advancement of the communities they represent. They are icons of the immigrant success story, but it was not an easy success. Most of the buildings were constructed by the sons and grandsons of the original immigrants. In the early days many of the ethnic associations functioned in the houses of individual members, or in meeting rooms rented for special occasions. Their functions were multiple: they were mutual aid associations offering a minimum of security in a harsh and inhospitable environment for the newly arrived; they were also social centers offering sociability in a familiar idiom and cultural centers that aimed to preserve and project particular national identities. They did this in myriad ways—performing plays, celebrating national days, maintaining choirs and dance groups, and organizing schools to teach the language to the younger generations.

The first generation of immigrants lived the tension between establishing a new home and keeping alive the links and identity associated with the old. For some, strong echoes of political struggles in Europe in the 1920s, 1930s, and 1940s intensified these tensions. The struggles of left and right, communist and nationalist, resonated in Berisso in these years, often dividing ethnic communities.

In the mural on the north wall the artist chose to represent this tension in a more intimate register by including a family photo. There are other photographic images in the mural, but this one is explicitly shown as a snapshot. No attempt has been made to crop the serrated edges. It is a shot of a group of two women, one holding a baby. In front stand two children and at the back an older, apparently male, child. It would seem to be a snapshot typical of the type sent by immigrant families. We cannot tell whether it was sent from Europe to Argentina or the reverse. But it serves to register the pain of separation and dispersal families and at times ethnic groups of this first generation felt. At the same time it demonstrates the importance of photos as mnemonic artifacts that helped create and sustain feelings of longing and attachment for this generation.

Another part of the immigrant success story emerges in the Centro Cívico. It draws on the image of a harmonious multiethnic community whose members are integrated into the beneficent *patria,* which offers them shelter and opportunity. This vision is powerfully present in Berisso's folklore today. It can be found in the works of its artists, poets, and storytellers. It is expressed in the frequently told adage that Berisso is the only place where Jews and Arabs can be neighbors and get married.

Certainly, the melting pot was effective in Berisso. In the large mural, the scene of the children in their smocks waiting outside the school is, I think, a deliberate reference by the artist to the power of public education to acculturate and socialize the children of immigrants. Yet for the older generation the melting pot was a double-edged sword. Today very few of the grandchildren and great-grandchildren of the immigrants speak the languages of their ancestors. Other anecdotal evidence points in the same direction. The mass at Saint Vladimir's church is attended by only a handful of elderly women who join the priest as he recites the prayers and blessing in Ukrainian. The only marriage he has performed in recent years was of a non-Ukrainian couple who happened to like the unusual ceremony. A look behind the impressive facades of ethnic associations often reveals a struggle by a handful of older members to keep the institution intact. It is getting increasingly difficult to attract the younger generation to traditional cultural performances in an era of cable television and a global youth culture.

The Cradle of Peronism

The busts of Juan Perón and Evita form the centerpiece of the Centro Cívico. They are placed squarely at the front of the space, a few feet from the sidewalk of the Avenida Montevideo. Evita is several feet in front of the general. The busts are cheap reproductions. Painted in gold, they bear only a vague resemblance to the honorees. Evita is recognizable chiefly by her hair drawn tightly back into the characteristic bun. Perón wears his military uniform, the left shoulder of which is already crumbling away. A plaque identifies Evita as the "Standard Bearer of the Humble." The plaque identifying Perón bears no accolade. It simply refers to his military title, lieutenant general, and bears the date when the plaque was installed, the fiftieth anniversary of the 17 October 1945 protest.

The busts of Perón and Evita, Centro Cívico, Berisso. *Courtesy Norberto Gullari.*

The cheapness of the busts should not be misinterpreted. Berisso is a profoundly Peronist place. It is proud to claim the title of "the cradle of Peronism." The roots of this identity go back to the years between 1943 and 1946, the years when Doña María entered the Swift packing house. These were years of mobilization within the plants, when the boom conditions of the war and the political support of Colonel Perón made these times ripe for unionization. Led by a charismatic leader called Cipriano Reyes, the workers of Swift and Armour began to organize effectively for the first time since the plants were built.

Reyes soon established personal ties with Perón himself. He made frequent visits to see him in the Secretaría de Trabajo [Secretariat of Labor] and on several occasions Perón visited Berisso. Old-timers can point out the open space in front of the Swift plant where Perón first addressed the packing-house workers.

Perón represented a new political identity for the packing-house workers. Within Peronism they found a discourse that legitimized their claims safely within the rhetoric of the state. Encouraged by the benevolent neutrality of the authorities, the newly formed Sindicato Autónomo de Obreros de la Indústria de la Carne struck the plants first in 1944 and then again in early 1945.

It was these kinds of actions, precipitated by Perón, that increasingly led him to be perceived as a threat by the more traditional political parties and by his military comrades. Throughout 1945 Argentine society became polarized around the figure of Juan Domingo Perón. In October 1945, his military rivals had Perón arrested. On 17 October, the packing-house workers of Berisso, Doña María among them, claimed a role as one of the chief protagonists who congregated in the Plaza de Mayo in front of the presidential palace to demand his release. The workers had been on strike since 15 October. Groups of men and women had been marching through the streets of Berisso chanting Perón's name. By dawn of the seventeenth, word had spread through the community that there would be a march on La Plata and beyond to Buenos Aires. By late in the day significant numbers of Berisso workers were present among the hundreds of thousands camped in front of the Casa Rosada (the presidential palace) waiting for word of Perón's fate. Finally, at around midnight, he made his appearance on the balcony. This event consolidated the bond between Perón and the workers of Argentina and Berisso. It was to be taken as the symbolic birth of Perón as the leader of the workers, the beginning of a unique bond reaffirmed every year in the celebration of this foundational event. Buoyed by their success in this endeavor, Reyes and others formed the Partido Laborista, which would play a major role in Perón's election victory in 1946.[2]

These events gave the workers in Berisso a sense of empowerment and a new status in the Argentine community. They moved away from defining themselves solely as a community of immigrants. Peronist rhetoric afforded them a vision of themselves as full citizens invested in a new Argentine nation. This newfound self-image contrasted sharply with the construction of identity of the previous generation. The immigrants of that generation had been celebrated in the community narrative for their hard work and abnegation. Theirs had been a generation largely excluded from the political process. Their political quiescence formed part of the identity of a generation dedicated to physically draining labor and the maintenance of their families, a generation too involved in survival and invested in the dream of "making America" to engage in political or union activism.

This quiescence was reflected in Berisso's collective memory of the era prior to Perón. It was a period defined by corruption and uncontested caudillo politics. Walter Elena, a local conservative lawyer, controlled local politics. At election time those entitled to vote were alternately courted with wine and meat barbecues or intimidated by conservative thugs—one of whom, a legendary figure called "el turco Mustafa," would stand at the door of the polling station and decide who could enter to vote.

The shedding of the purely immigrant identity had another important dimension. It afforded the workers an expanded class identity. They were able to imagine themselves as part of a harmonious Argentine working-class community composed of both immigrant and native Argentine workers. As a rhetorical figure the native worker formed an important part of the national Peronist ideology. The *criollo* worker embodied "authentic" Argentine values in contrast to the "foreign" ideas espoused by some immigrant militants and the forces of the Argentine left.

Interestingly, the native worker in Berisso was also a newcomer. In the late 1930s thousands of migrants primarily from the northern province of Santiago del Estero supplied the labor needed for the wartime expansion of production. They joined the residents already installed in the tenements around the calle Nueva York and the outlying barrios. They were both culturally and, with their dark skin and hair, physically different from their neighbors. Under Perón they, too, embraced the rhetoric of nationalism—a rhetoric that could speak to the workers' exploitation by U.S. companies. It was also a rhetoric that could comfortably accommodate and unify a plethora of immigrants and internal migrants in a new national synthesis overseen by the figure of Perón. This rhetoric could erase the more militant but less safe platform of the communists and anarchists who had unsuccessfully struggled in the years before Perón to mobilize these workers.

The Gaucho, Centro Cívico, Berisso. *Courtesy Norberto Gullari.*

The blending of native and immigrant created a reconfigured national community—a cohesive force that defined Argentine working-class politics for the coming generations. It was founded on concrete improvements in their working lives. Better wages and better working conditions were associated with the union, and the union was, ultimately, associated with Perón and Evita. This association was symbolized in Berisso by the construction of a new, imposing union local with extra room for the many social services the union now offered. Later a union sanatorium would be built to serve the members and their families. These were just two of many improvements associated with Perón during his government from 1946 to 1955.

In the 1980s when the Peronist authorities of Berisso set about populating the Centro Cívico they chose to emphasize these symbols of a national consensus founded and articulated by Peronism. The statue of the gaucho on horseback can be read as an affirmation of "lo nacional"; it is a classic symbol of national identity within the discourse of Argentine nativism. As if in counterpoint to the

Perón's image, Centro Cívico, Berisso. *Courtesy Norberto Gullari.*

figure of the gaucho, the wall that runs along the northern side of the square features a large picture of Perón. This is a familiar, comforting image from the 1940s of a smiling Perón. Alongside, in large black letters that cover the entire wall, runs the legend: "Your spirit of national unity will not be destroyed."

There are several possible reasons why this emphasis was chosen. In part, it reflects the fact that although Berisso may be a mainly Peronist community, it is not exclusively so. The emphasis on national values and unity blends well with other narratives of community harmony shared by other political parties. It is also related to the history of Peronism in Berisso and nationally. Although the years from the exile of Perón in 1955 until his return in 1973 can be represented as years of resistance and struggle, they were also years of bitter internal divisions within the movement. These divisions came to a head during the government of Perón's widow, Isabel (1974–76). In Berisso Peronism lived this state of internal warfare between left and right in a particularly intense fashion. It is not surprising, then, that with the restoration of democracy in 1983 the Peronist authorities would choose to represent the symbols of Peronism least likely to reopen old wounds.

Today there is a final factor that needs to be taken into account. This is related to the issue of the status of Peronism as a basic political identity in this community. Berisso remains an overwhelmingly Peronist community. Every mayor since 1983 has been a Peronist. Carlos Menem enjoyed large majorities in the presidential elections of 1989 and 1995. Peronist "unidades básicas" populate Berisso's barrios like mushrooms. Some fifteen thousand Berissenses are inscribed on the list of Peronist affiliates. In the last internal elections some ten thousand voted. With only a little exaggeration the head of the local Partido Justicialista was heard to comment, "We could put up a dead dog for a candidate in Berisso and we'd still win." But something has changed. The long process of deindustrialization that began with the closing of the packing houses and that has accelerated in recent years has corroded the fundamental basis of Berisso's identity as a community of labor and with it the automatic identity of Peronism and industrial, unionized workers. The union local in Berisso has long since closed down. The unemployment rate hovers around 35 percent. Many Berissenses are now part of the informal economy. In fact, local Peronism itself reflects these changes. Its leadership is largely made up of the local elite: doctors, lawyers, engineers, small businessmen, the educated sons and grandsons of meatpacking workers. All of Berisso's mayors since 1983 have been drawn from these ranks.

In this context, the Centro Cívico can be read as a text that is peopled by fundamentally residual symbols. They have a power to evoke resonances that speak to a past whose traces are sedimented in streets, buildings, the shell of an old frigorífico, the icons of this very square. But viewed in another light, they have a sort of ineffable quality. To the right of Evita and Perón is a monument to Motherhood. An all-white figure, the woman gazes into the eyes of a baby who sits on her knee, head at her breast, looking up into her eyes. The scene evokes the image of woman as mother, guardian of the hearth and family, nurturer of her children. This representation

Motherhood, Centro Cívico, Berisso. *Courtesy Norberto Gullari.*

of women was a powerful element in the Peronist imaginary and the discourse of Argentine nationalism. The woman who gave birth to and nurtured her children also, by extension, gave birth to and nurtured the nation. In a community of factory women this is the sole representation of working women.

Placed alongside the Gaucho and other images representing the hard work of an immigrant community and national unity, these images represent a sort of lowest common denominator, a safe invocation of unassailable virtues. Perón and Evita themselves have an irredeemably bland quality, smiling benignly. Evita is given her most anodyne denomination, the "Standard Bearer of the Humble." We might say that these images are consistent with Peronism's historical meaning, but it is also true that they reflect the crucial sense of unease and disorientation of the movement in an era of neoliberalism and global realpolitik. Perhaps it is too painful to memorialize the strikes, struggles, and militancy of the past if the depleted community of the 1990s represents its legacy.

Monument to
17 October, Plaza 17
du octobre, Berisso.
*Courtesy Norberto
Gullari.*

17 October 1945

There is in fact another memorial space in Berisso. If the visitor
were to walk far enough away from the Avenida Montevideo, she
would come across an open, grass-covered space. It is irregular in
shape, and the grass is rarely cut. It is interspersed with bare patches
and covered with litter. In the center is a white concrete monument. In the front, steps lead up to a large painting that covers the
entire facade. The concrete at the side of the steps is beginning to
crumble away. The image has been constructed on tiles that have
been individually attached to the concrete. The artist has chosen to
take up the bulk of the painting with two, huge forearms entwined
with a thick, black chain. At the apex of the chain the two hands
are shown breaking the link. To the side there is the smokestack of
a factory. At the point where the chain has been sundered we can
see what could be both a ball of fire and a radiant sun. Above the

sun, at the very top of the monument there is a pale outline of a figure with his arm raised and the open hand extended. The figure is unmistakably Perón, easily recognizable by the characteristic gesture of greeting to the masses. In fact, if we search hard enough, we can find the key to this monument. This ill-shaped space is the Plaza 17 de Octubre. The chains being broken are the chains of exploitation associated with the factory system, a familiar symbol of socialist iconography. The breaking of the bonds ushers in a new day for a liberated humanity, and presiding over this new day is the figure of Juan Perón.

This monument offers a different reading of Berisso's Peronist past from the invocations of national unity and the harmonious community celebrated in the Centro Cívico. Here, too, the community of labor is a community of struggle symbolized in the powerful arms that break the chains and the flames that seem to be consuming the old order. This is a difficult story for contemporary Peronism to celebrate. The official celebrations of the fiftieth anniversary of 17 October in Berisso were carried out in front of the busts of Perón and Evita in the Centro Cívico, far from the apocalyptic images to be found in this abandoned plaza. Clearly, the harmonious images evoked by the figures and monuments of the Centro Cívico speak to the needs of many working-class Peronists in Berisso. But, equally, it would be true to say, as we shall see in her testimony, that many Peronists like María Roldán also found themselves attracted to the meanings of Peronism embodied in the white concrete monument.

One further monument stands in the Centro Cívico. This one refers not to symbols rooted in Berisso's distant past but to the relatively recent experience of the military regime that governed Argentina from 1976 to 1983. It is the Monument to the Disappeared. With its militant labor history and its strong Peronist tradition, Berisso was singled out for particular attention by the military authorities. From the late 1960s groups associated with the Peronist left and guerrilla formations had established a notable presence within the community, particularly among its youth. They had in part merged with a bitter set of struggles being waged to oppose the running down of the one remaining frigorífico, the Swift plant. At the same time, they embarked on a confrontation with the more

Monument to the
Disappeared, Centro
Cívico, Berisso.
*Courtesy Norberto
Gullari.*

orthodox currents who controlled local Peronism. When the military overthrew the government of Isabel Perón in March 1976 they set about the task of "restoring order" within the community and the plant with singular ferocity.

Berisso would become one of Argentina's most savage local killing fields. Memories of this time are not easy for the outsider to access; they scarcely form part of daily conversation. Even after spending nearly a decade working in the community, I still find this topic the most difficult of all to broach with Berissenses. Yet some memories are available, offered in brief anecdotes and random comments that tell of the sound of bursts of automatic gunfire breaking the silence night after night, of whispered rumors of a neighbor's child who had not returned, of bodies showing up on the fringes of the monte, of the sick feeling in the pit of the stomach as the military searched an entire block, house by house. By the end of the military regime in 1983 some 160 Berissenses, most of them young workers, had been "disappeared." Many others were arrested, imprisoned, and tortured. Others fled the city, hoping to find safety in a larger city or in permanent exile.

This legacy has been a difficult one for the community to come to terms with, a fact that was symbolized in the story of the inauguration ceremony for the Monument to the Disappeared. The ceremony took place on a bright spring day in November 1995. A crowd of several hundred people had gathered at the edge of the Centro Cívico, near the large mural commemorating Berisso's past. The walls of the hallways of the nearby high school had been hung with the photos of nearly all the disappeared. The photos were enlargements of shots taken from family albums, and the faces almost all wore the smiling expressions of the professionally posed photo. I was struck by the youth of the people captured in these shots. They smiled confidently out on the world and on the rest of their lives, which would surely stretch far into the future. Yet the brutal truth was clearly stated in the text below each photo. Alongside the name appeared the date of the disappearance. The date also left an unstated implication. From the date of the disappearance to the unknown date of death stretched a brutal odyssey of suffering that haunted the imagination and memory of the relatives and friends of these young people.

Later in the afternoon, on an improvised platform, an orator from the human rights commission in Buenos Aires gave a short, impassioned speech. Then, several family members read a list of the disappeared. As each name was read, the silence of the crowd deepened as people listened with bowed heads, searching within themselves to deal with the feelings evoked by this naming. The silence was broken only by the sound of stifled tears, and the call of "presente" following many of the names. Later, personal reminiscences were offered by family members. The most impressive of these offerings were from the children of the disappeared. They spoke movingly of their need to speak of their parents, of how the ceremony and the monument were opportunities they had rarely had to openly express a grief they had not before confronted. Many of them had no direct memories of their parents, and they had often been brought up in settings where their parents' lives and their deaths were unmentionable themes.

It struck me that this ceremony was a kind of public therapy session. However, unlike the analysands of classic psychoanalysis these young people had no buried memories whose uncovering would make them free. Rather than addressing repressed memories, they were, in their words, confronting a gap, a hole, a void. They hoped desperately to fill this gap, to construct through speech and dialogue the memory of their parents they had been denied. This process of prosthetic remembering, which could only be collective in nature, would, they insisted, be their only assurance that their parents' murderers would not be proven victorious in the end. In their insistence that the military's ultimate goal was to erase the ideals of their parents by erasing a memory of them as individuals, these young people were drawing one of the bitterest lessons of genocide in this century.

There was little to say after this testimony. The ceremony concluded with the unveiling of the monument. It is made of metal parts taken from the different trades of the dead; winches, lathes, cogs, cables, levers, and knives form a figure of indefinite sex whose avant-garde form jarred with the naturalism of the other monuments and murals in the Centro Cívico.

The ceremony was an apt metaphor for Berisso's complex and fractured response to the legacy of the military period. It had taken the community twelve years to offer any form of public commemoration of those of its members who had disappeared. The ceremony that finally took place that November afternoon was rich in ironies and absences. The vast majority of those memorialized by the event had considered themselves Peronist, yet no member of the Peronist-dominated city council that has run Berisso since 1983 was present. The official Peronist movement played no role in the organization of the event, and it was not mentioned in the deliberations of the city council. It was the opposition parties who intervened to authorize the raising of the monument in the Centro Cívico. Its position off to the side symbolizes the unease that it provokes among many of the citizens and political representatives of the community. Like the monument to 17 October, it is not easily integrated into the harmonious community narratives that dominate the space.

The reasons for the unease provoked by the commemoration of

the disappeared are, I must confess, still largely beyond my analytical and imaginative skills. Some possibilities suggest themselves, but I would caution against any oversimplistic conclusions that might be arrived at by an abstract logic that ignores the complexity of local, intimate context. In Berisso we might start by going back to the internal Peronist warfare that preceded the military regime. In the intimate context of local Peronism neighbors, friends, and families of one side knew of the threats and violence practiced against the other, and the grudges were harbored well into the military regime. We might also suggest that guilt, both individual and communal, played its part with neighbors and friends who had avoided helping or offering shelter. Berisso was a community founded on an ethic of solidarity and mutuality at work and within the neighborhood, and yet it was unable to protect its sons and daughters, neighbors and friends, from military repression. The Peronist government under Carlos Menem implemented an official policy of "national reconciliation," granting amnesty to those guilty of human rights abuses. Forgetting the past has been touted as an imperative if the nation is to move forward. Within Berisso what sense did it make for local Peronism to go against this ethos? For community leaders the logic of placing a veil over the past made sense. In the end the logic of official community amnesia—the desire to forget—was stronger than the claim of the young speakers who urged the psychic and moral necessity to remember.

II

DOÑA MARÍA'S TESTIMONY

In 1930 Doña María Roldán and her husband arrived in the community whose past and present identity is inscribed in the Centro Cívico. She raised her family, worked in the plants, engaged in political activism, and worshiped her God during the following six decades, all within the confines of the social and cultural space called Berisso. This book is devoted in large measure to transmitting her life story. Although it is one woman's story, it is not a story that stands on its own. Her narrative must be read as one thread within the web of narratives that form Berisso's story. Her unique voice carries within it tones and lyrics imbued with the sharp outlines and the fading traces of the cultural, ideological, and moral context that Berisso bequeathed to her.

The translation of Doña María's testimony is mine. The testimony was recorded between January and September 1987 and in June 1988. I have edited the transcript, shortening, condensing, and at times reconfiguring the order of parts of her testimony. I have also omitted from Part 2 most of the extended translations of testimony that appear in Part 3, chapters 1–4.

Childhood

You could say that I was inclined toward the left from
the moment I was born. —Doña María

Papa came from Rome. He used to work in the Catholic Church from the time he was very little, serving the Mass. He was very

Catholic, something that we, his daughters, were not. We rebelled against the Church. I have been an evangelical Baptist above all else from the time I was very young. I visited many different places, I was very curious from childhood, ever since I realized that Jesus existed. I even visited the synagogues of the Jews. When I was young we used to go to the center, my friends and I, and I embraced evangelical Baptism because it seemed to me that it was there that I really found what I was looking for. I looked for it and I found it, and here I am still.

Papa came over when he was eighteen. He first arrived in Córdoba, where he contracted cholera. They interned him in a hospital called Loreto. He told me that one night he was so thirsty he drank the holy water in the fountain in the hospital chapel. After he got better he wandered all over. He didn't bring any family with him. He came alone as an immigrant, as a young man who was looking to open a path for himself. His name was Agustín Bernaviti. He ended up in San Martín working as a bricklayer. He met my mother, who was an orphan. She was the daughter of Spaniards who had emigrated here and then died. My mother and her brother and sister had been raised by Don Luis Monteverde. She met my father while she was doing a chore at the market, and they became engaged. She was younger than him. He had already spent much time traveling around, and he wanted to form a family. They were married, and they were very happy. And my father had kept contact with his family in Italy, and he brought his mother over, and my mother had my grandmother with her for many years in the house. She was a very big Roman woman; I seem to see her still in a chair, a very big woman, very pretty. Later, the other brothers who had already married in Italy came over one by one. They all stayed in San Martín, forming the Bernaviti family. Papa was the pioneer who came on ahead, like a cabin boy, he got in a boat and came, whatever happens he said, if anything happens to me it will happen to me alone, so he ventured ahead. After eleven years in America, and after marrying my mother he sent for *abuela* and then the rest came.

My father spoke Italian, English, and Latin. He was too well educated to be a bricklayer, he had a lot of talent, he was almost an intellectual. He had taken up bricklaying and made his living that way. When he couldn't make a living putting up walls he used to work in the brick ovens. That paid very well. There was always a demand for bricks in that time, in San Martín and beyond in Buenos Aires and the whole republic. My father was a man with a tremendous sense of rebellion. He helped many other trades, the bakers, the glassmakers. He was a union man above all else. But his principal trade, what he used to support his family and what he did to the end of his days, was bricklaying. Toward the end of his working life he ceased to work with his hands and supervised the construction site. He earned good money then, we lived very well. He sympathized with the anarchists and socialists. We spoke often in my house about social themes because that was his topic and he was head of the family. My father spoke a lot to me about politics. He was a man who had come from another world with a certain experience of life. There were a lot of books in my house. It was a happy house. My mother was very happy with my father. My sister was a high-level dressmaker, she even made bridal gowns. I was a young girl who liked to roam. I was very predisposed to curiosity as a kid, to know what was going on here and there, where there was a political meeting, for example, there I would be, listening. I remember May first meetings commemorating all the blood spilt in Chicago, the taking of the Bastille when men, women, and children fought for their freedom, which is the most important thing in life; without liberty why should we live? I gave my family quite a few worries because I had the rebelliousness that my father had, for me to stay shut up with a needle, sewing and hemming and things like that, was a waste of time, I thought that you had to go beyond that and do other things. Of course, all this caused many conflicts in my family. They used to say that I was threatening the tranquillity of the home, because at times I came home late at night with the other daredevils. Though really we didn't do anything but poke around and give our opinions and talk with people. Why do these workers do this? Why do they earn so little? They spend eleven hours in the factory, and they should only work eight hours. We were thinking about all that, but we didn't find the answer because we didn't have the unions like we did later. I had a lot of friends with the same concerns. Once some friends and I stopped by a button factory in San Martín, listen to this, and we said to the girls working there, "Why are you working for free? Why don't you rebel one day and not come in? Or why don't you have a sit-down strike inside?" We incited them to struggle, and nobody ordered us to do it, it was just something we had here [touches her chest]. We poked our noses in because we felt the pain, the pain of exploitation that was imposed on other girls. Because my father protected me, gave me clothes and food and a place to live, but these other girls, no, they had to go out to give food to an invalid mother, a widowed mother, or a father who had lost his wife. At that time we all knew one another, they [the factories] were like villages, not like now, and everyone knew one another. So we would say to other girls, why don't you strike, give the Japanese boss a fright? It was in this way that there developed in me this feeling that has to do with the purity of youth. I was like the tip of the spear, that others could follow, and I would say to them, do this, do that, but they never struck because everyone was scared. I spoke of strikes and tried to induce those girls to strike because I had inherited that feeling from my father. I had a school right there in my home. It hadn't come straight from me; I had assumed the inheritance. But it had come straight from my father's heart to tell me that. "Look at those girls working for a peso a day, poor little things, and these rich Japanese who come here to make money from Argentines, why do they do that?"

In San Martín in those days there were many different immigrant groups but everyone got on fine. We Argentines have the expression that every foreigner who comes to live in our country immediately assumes the position of the other country—the other country is this one that is now theirs. When they arrive and take possession and Argentine children are born, this becomes their country. We never had conflicts. It is the same now in Berisso, you will see that we have all races here, we love one another. When they have the Day of the Immigrant every year along the Avenida Montevideo we are all brothers.

I went to school till sixth grade, and after leaving school I spent time at home and on my street adventures. I was a great wanderer. I didn't want to learn a trade, I didn't want to tie myself down; there were girls who already had their *novios*. But I felt that there was a profundity to life that had to be sounded out, to be entered into, to be taken up. For example, visiting an orphanage, or some hospital. I had that gift. Many of us girls had it.

Early Years in Berisso

I met my husband in the mid-1920s. He lived in Brandsen and came to San Martín to do some business in the local courts, to fix some papers. I went to do something for my father. I was still a minor; I couldn't sign papers or anything. That's where we met, in the San Martín tribunals. His name was Vicente Francisco Aberastegui Roldán; Aberastegui is a Basque name. Though they had had money, his family had lost it, and he was a poor man when we met. He worked as a foreman in a small frigorífico in Brandsen. He always dedicated himself to everything to do with meat. So when we were a little short of money in San Martín, after we married, he said to me, "Let's go to Berisso; there are two big frigoríficos there and we'll be alright." It must have been in 1931. We didn't want to always be tied to my father, because my husband belonged to the butcher's trade so he wanted to be in places where they prepared meat, in his own atmosphere, doing what he wanted to do, what he knew how to do. He came on ahead and spoke with people when they were leaving the plant. Berisso already had a reputation. The bars, the diners, the women ate there at midday because they didn't have time to go home and come back, they only gave them an hour. Whoever came to Berisso knew that they would have to pick up a knife and work with meat. So he didn't think twice about it. He went there, presented himself, I'm Argentine, I'm this old, here's my civil registration card, I want to work.

He was taken on in the Armour [plant] as a *despostador* [deboner]. The animal is hanging from the hook, and the *matambrero* comes along to take out the *matambre*. He separates the whole matambre from the leather. They pay him well to do this because you have to take the matambre off whole, without cutting it. And after the matambrero is finished, while the carcass is hanging, the despostador goes about separating the parts. First he takes off the front quarters, then he takes out the ribs; he throws them on the table and then unhooks the carcass and takes off the rear, which is the heaviest, and throws it on top of the table. When these three parts are on the table, with a fine knife he separates the meat from the bone and throws them in metal bins. This is the despostador, and they are well paid for this work. My husband used to earn good money. After he was taken on as a despostador he sent for me.

When I left San Martín and came to Berisso I was very happy because people welcomed me. Many people said to my husband, "What a good wife you found, what a pretty wife." I was young, more or less pleasing, and I have always got on well with people. This mass of people, people in overalls, friendly people, affectionate, from all nations. There were also many Argentines, there were people from Corrientes, Santiago del Estero, Formosa, Río Negro, Entre Ríos. There were people from everywhere, though there were also many foreigners. When they landed in the boats here in the port they were greeted with a fiesta, because the frigoríficos needed people. When the foreigners arrived they were happier, because the companies accepted them better. For example, if thirty men went one morning to seek work and if twenty of them were foreigners, twenty foreigners would enter.

But I didn't feel afraid when I first arrived, because when you arrive with your children and you find a neighbor who says, "Whatever you want, I'm here, if you need anything don't be shy, that's what we are neighbors for," then you feel encouraged. You leave your intimate family there in San Martín, but you have the other big family here, the one that isn't your blood but is also your family. And this is still the tradition in Berisso. When I had an operation four years ago a woman came and brought me a chicken, another came with six eggs, another a packet of pasta. This is still the custom here. There is a lot of solidarity.

My first home was a conventillo. A tenement took up a whole lot, let's say, and perhaps four families live in it. Each has a room and a kitchen. We had to sleep with the children. The two kids had a bed and we had a bed. And we had to cook in a kitchen that was so small that when you turned round you banged into the pots. This was in the calle Nueva York. Others came with a little money and bought lots, and they put an already built house on it, made of wood and zinc. But I couldn't do that. I came to rent. I had married a poor man. Life in the conventillo was nice. There were many turcos, and the fact is that, well I don't know, they are a little slow, they hadn't been educated in the finer points. They might enter a room and not ask permission and you could be in your underwear, things like that. Nothing too bold. I always say that the woman who knows her place never lacks for respect. Nothing strange ever happened to me, but then it never happened because I never went around being cute, joking with the men in the patio; I waited for my husband, gave him his food, cleaned, stayed with my children. Finally things improved. My husband got more money, and we rented a house of our own in the calle Hamburgo. It was a big change. I was alone in my house; I could have a little garden, a hammock for the kids. I was on my own. I remember that I bought a radio with a magic eye; at that time having a radio was like having a color TV today. After the calle Hamburgo we moved around renting, until one fine day my husband says, "Look, I am going to buy a lot, it will be this one and we're going to get a house, near the avenue, you and the kids will be comfortable." That's how I brought my kids up. The three of them went to seventh grade. The oldest son has secondary and my daughter, too. They were educated in Berisso for elementary school and in La Plata the secondary. And a son who died, from the same disease that Franklin Delano Roosevelt had, polio. He became ill when he was ten and died at seventeen and a half. We were at his wake when a package of medicine arrived from North America. We used to bring medicines from there; we hired two massagists, imagine the sacrifice. We did the unimaginable to try and save him. We sold a house that we had bought. Well, that year many kids died; it was a plague, a calamity. So we were left with Mario and Dora.

Berisso was nice in the 1930s. That rambla was full of people, young people, dances. They were beginning to set up the societies: the

Greek society, the Spanish, the Italian, which had been in existence for a long time, the Czechoslovak, the Arab, the Bulgarian. In all these societies on Saturdays and Sundays there were dances, Berisso was very happy. The Avenida [Montevideo] was developing, with houses of two and even three stories. The immigrants did that, because no Argentine built two stories overlooking the street. No, the immigrant did much to advance the country; perhaps these words are a little harsh but it's that way. But there was never a problem with the immigrant. They might speak their languages at home, or among their *paisanos,* but if I'm going to the market and I meet a Lithuanian, he says, "How are you, María? How is the family?" he says this however he can but in Spanish. They have a lot of respect for the country they have moved to, for the nation to which they have given sons, who were born here, for the nation that gives them bread. They are very respectful, especially the turcos. They are a little distracted and things like that, but a turco is never going to speak to a fellow turco in front of someone who doesn't understand the language. He tries to speak Spanish even if he destroys it, but he makes himself understood. No, the immigrant has respected the Argentine Republic a lot. He has contributed a lot to it. If you go to the Barrio Obrero the houses occupied by immigrants shine out. You can tell where an immigrant is: painted doors, everything tidy. For me the immigrants are in general very good people. There's a pharmacist here in front, he analyzes blood. He's Jewish, you should see what a nice person he is. There were a lot of Jews in Berisso. I know that they had a synagogue in the center. Once my husband took me to a viewing. They don't allow flowers; they have candles on the ground. It was the relative of a man who worked in the frigorífico. They have a big black cloth on the floor, the dead one is lying there, with golden crosses, nothing else. The crosses are different from ours. But everything was with the greatest of respect. They await their messiah and we ours. Here we have all the races; for this it is the city of the immigrant.

The 1930s were years of great misery in Berisso. I recall that they were difficult years, just after my husband had started to work, and he would say to me that we had to watch every little coin in order to keep on going. Getting work and keeping it was everything. You had to present yourself in the personnel office, and there was an Englishman, Señor Wacking, an English Jew they said, who was chief of personnel. You know how he chose people to work, professor? They used to choose the tallest, the strongest, the one who seemed on sight to be the strongest, and then there were the doctors to check them out. . . . They had to pass the medical exam and then the X-ray and only then, "yes, you can enter" or "no, you can't." There might be some defect in the hands, the fingers, and that would exclude you, so that later you wouldn't give any trouble to the company. Someone of my stature, a man of my height, if there was someone taller that would be better for the company. They wanted flashy and shiny personnel. They chose the women on the same basis. My husband's work was hard in some ways and not in others. For a man who knows how to use a knife well and knows where to place it it's like cutting cloth to make a suit. Later, as well, there came the norias. Instead of two or three men having to hang up half an animal on a hook, the machine did it. When the despostador cut a piece weighing twenty or thirty kilos, a machine would pick it up and take it to another part of the shop. Then it wasn't so much the forced labor of the man as of the machine. But that was later, long after my husband started. He liked the work because he earned decent money. At times there were ten or more despostadores working, and sometimes they worked eleven or twelve hours. One of his big complaints was the way the company treated the peon. There was a great difference between the skilled worker and the poor peon who, for example, might sweep the floor. Because the company always treated the one who gave them profit better and treated the other one worse. It's obvious. If I am an unwilling benefactor of the company because I'm preparing an animal, and working on the animal is already a profit for the company and the other is sweeping the floor, I give more profit to the company than he who sweeps. There was a tremendous social difference. They had only a few minutes rest; they didn't used to provide clothes at that time. You had to buy the white blouse, white pants, boots, white hat. Later they started to provide all that stuff. But before when my husband started working the skilled man got good money and could buy them. The others earned little and they had to go to the store, because the grocery stores had work clothes, and they had to ask for the clothes on credit until the next payday, or ask to pay it off in two or three quotas.

For me a man who works with his head and gives the best years of his life in an office is just as much a worker as a factory worker, with the difference that the physical toll isn't the same. It's not the same as the rural laborer who at times because of the great heat of the day has to open up the heart of the land at night, plow the earth at night, sow at night, with a light on a tractor. So you can't compare the man who is in his office, can go to the bathroom when he wishes, who they treat like a human being. A man who takes over a field has a great responsibility, and sometimes puts his family to work, to work the harvest, and no government, nobody, has taken into account the fact that this man puts his children and wife to work to improve Argentine agriculture. I have seen with my own eyes that are now a little aged, a viewing of a little kid on a *chata,* a chata is a cart with four big wheels used to carry thousands of kilos of wheat. They were viewing a child, six candles. It was the child of a tenant farmer. They were viewing him on the cart because the *estanciero* had evicted the father after he had failed to produce the required number of kilos of wheat. So he was thrown off. The man had the chata and four horses, his wife and three children, and at this time one of his little sons dies from one of those illnesses, and they had to view him in the street. This I saw myself. My family saw it, my husband saw it when we went to La Pampa to see if we could make a peso in those times when there was nowhere to find a morsel of food. It was in the thirties. We went for two years. They had told my husband that you could work very well there, that they would give land to the people. At that time things in Berisso were very bad. When he first entered the plant he wasn't a skilled worker. He used to work two weeks and they would fire him; he used to come with the yellow card. I would be watching out as he came home to see if he were carrying the yellow card. It meant that you were laid off. He would be two months without work. He even became a traveling salesman to try and put food on the table. I have no shame in telling you because he wanted to feed his children in an honorable way. Things were so bad in Berisso that you had to leave your kitchen in the conventillo locked, or they would break in and steal the *yerba maté,* sugar, potatoes. So one day we said, "Let's go, let's leave the odds and ends of furniture with a friend and let's see what happens in La Pampa." Many people in Berisso were doing it at that time. They would leave, come back, leave again, seeing wherever they could find a bit of bread. My husband assumed a contract for corn, he hired some peons, we rented a house in the village and he went to the fields. He had to harvest the amount of crops laid down in the contract. But it didn't work. We thought, the children are growing, here there is no school, no anything. We wrote to friends in Berisso, and they said that things had improved some in the frigoríficos. So we returned to Berisso.

There was a Radical Party committee in Berisso. One day my husband says to me, "Look María, go to the Radical committee, they say that they're going to give out clothes, blankets." So I went. The poor person seeks help wherever he can. I went with another woman, a neighbor. You know what they gave me? Pants that didn't fit me and a kilo of sugar. I took it because I was already there. My husband said, "Why did I send you there? What a disgrace." It was propaganda because it was election time. That was politics in Berisso before Perón.

There was a lot of social life in Berisso in the 1930s. Dances in the societies, barbecues at home. In the summer people used to go to Palo Blanco to fish; there was a tram that left you there. There was a buggy that would take you to the beach right up to the place where you could fish. All the societies began to mobilize themselves to improve the culture of the people. You can see now how Berisso is. It has poets, it has culture, professors, all that sort of thing. But work dominated everything. They came, they worked, and they stayed. The husband, the wife, the daughter, and the son would work. Whoever arrived home first would throw a *bife* on and then go back to the frigorífico. I used to pay a woman to take care of the kids, and we both used to work. Or do you think that they gave us this? All this cost a lot, to pay for a plot of land and begin to build a house you have to have pesos, and eat, live, buy shoes for the kids, education, medication. So life was dedicated to work exclusively.

DANIEL JAMES: There wasn't much time for amusement, for relaxing?

DOÑA MARÍA: No, and people didn't demand so much in the way of amusement. What people wanted, because the truth is they had arrived starving, many had suffered, many had been victims of wars, what they wanted was to have a piece of bread in peace, buy their plot, make their house. The frigorífico absorbed all their energy and exhausted them. For example, someone who didn't have a skill would have to push a *zorra*. A zorra is a big thing of iron with handles that could carry up to five or six hundred kilos of meat. One man had to push it from one section to another, till they installed machines to do that. So if you were pushing a zorra with five hundred kilos all day it took all you had, do the job and home to rest, eat and rest, get up at dawn and back to work. To be frank, it was a form of slavery. Sometimes you had Saturday afternoon and Sunday off, but if there was a big contract to meet then you worked. Whatever they said you did. The frigoríficos of Berisso, and all those of Gran Buenos Aires, have carried many people off to the cemetery. Our dream was that our kids wouldn't have to enter the frigorífico, that we could educate them to a trade to get them to university. My husband used to say, I hope that my children don't have to enter the plants.

I went to work in the plant in 1944 above all because the medicine for my son was so expensive. So with my husband's fortnightly paycheck and mine we could afford it. It came from North America, and a specialist here had told me that it could help him, so I made the effort. I said to my husband, "Look, *querido,* I'm going to work for a while," and that while turned into ten years. You had to continue and continue because we were improving our house and though it seems not so, an extra pay packet every two weeks, improves the home, buys you sheets, an extra bed, a mattress, eat a little better. I think that all the women who went to work in the frigorífico . . . because it's a place, well, it's like a monster when you go in there, in that darkness and dampness, in that situation of lines of men with knives in hand. I don't think that that was very nice, you felt bad, but necessity obliged you to get used to it.

It made home life very difficult. There was little time to be with the children. It separated us a little from them because the parents had many hours of work to put food on the table and buy clothes. The children matured very quickly, working. Because I said to my son, Mario, "Look, little one, peel these potatoes, clean the squash, cut the tomatoes, and when mama gets home she'll make the stew. My son helped me cook; he couldn't go and play while I was at work. Only someone who has worked, worked outside the home, the mother of the family who has worked outside knows what it was like. Some women went to La Plata to clean houses, but most, if they could they entered the frigorífico because it was better paid, and it wasn't cleaning the mess of others. However dirty and bad it was, it was a job.

Health conditions in Berisso in those times were very bad. One of the worst things was the "fiebre malta." It's a fever that goes up and down. First you get chills, then you get fever, sometimes a month will pass, and then it comes back, it's incurable. A person who gets the fiebre malta from an animal does not get cured. Here in Berisso we had many cases. It's like AIDS is today. In the final stages they interned you in the San Juan de Dios infectious diseases center in La Plata. They say it comes from the animal; you can have a small cut and it comes in contact with the blood of an infected animal.

Even today we don't have sewers in Berisso. We have the "black hole." There wasn't any drainage either. Running water and thank you. We have an abundance of running water, which is good water because it has never been contaminated. We live cleanly because we are clean, we have our black holes, we bathe our children, we have a shower. Whoever built a home always put in a nice bathroom. So we were always clean.

In the 1930s we lived a little isolated from the outside, from La Plata. Now we are just as much citizens as the people of La Plata, as

ple of North America, we are human beings, but, of course,
/as a gap. For the majority of the people La Plata is a univer-
ty par excellence. There were some tremendous resentments.
October seventeenth we shouted, "Alpargatas sí, Libros, no!"
and they shouted, "Books yes, alpargatas no!" and there were conflicts.

There were attempts to organize a union in those years, but they
really weren't more than conversations. There were fifteen communists in the Nueva York, they had a local and they wanted to do
something, but as I say that was all there were, fifteen, they didn't
do anything. Some worked in the plants, others no. They handed
out leaflets, made speeches. They might put up a soapbox and then
run off because the mounted police came. They were tough times.
The police wouldn't let you speak like they do now. If I stand on the
corner on a box and give a speech, they'll let me. There's democracy.
But then the police were tough. I'll tell you. When I was a delegate
and they were taking us off, they took away nursing mothers too,
with their breasts full. They wouldn't let them feed the babies. That
tells you everything. The one who changed everything and gave us a
concrete example of how we should all work organically for a union
was Cipriano Reyes. That's undeniable. He was the main motor who
moved all the gears so that the whole republic would come to realize
that without a pure and well-managed trade unionism we wouldn't
get anywhere. Capital would continue to screw us, paying what it
wanted and sucking our blood and keeping its foot on our neck
so we would drown as soon as possible. Because, there were always
workers to spare to work in the plants, there were always people
asking for work, let the one who is dying of exhaustion die, let him
stay in his house, bring on the next one. Here in Berisso Reyes was
the one who opened the way for politics and unions, no one else.
Anyone who says differently is talking nonsense. It was Reyes who
came to speak to me in the Swift, he was working in Armour with
my husband. He said to me, "I know your husband, Señora Roldán,
and I've come to speak to you." I was working there with my knife,
at my position, where you had to prepare one hundred kilos of meat
an hour and you were going and going because you had to always

be working, and he said to me, "I want you to be a delegate because you have the talent."

Work in the Frigorífico

I started work in the picada section of Swift in 1944. You cut the meat and separated the nerve, and then you put the meat in one vat and the nerve in another. You had to do one hundred kilos of clean meat an hour. It was an enormous section with about twelve hundred women. It was like a village, an entire city block. You could look across it and see a mass of people in white working; it was beautiful, a real spectacle. When I first started working, the meat used to arrive at your table with men pushing huge zorras. Later, a mechanical line [noria] brought the large chunks to each table. The line used to hang from the ceiling, and it passed in front of each table. You had to grab it with a hook and then use the knife. It wasn't difficult to learn. Hunger, necessity, and the desire to take home a peso forced you to learn it in two days. It was tough work. For one thing, you could easily cut yourself. I cut myself on this finger, and the mark has stayed with me my whole life. There were also fatal accidents, slips, broken bones. The workday started at six in the morning. We stopped at midday, back at one, and we finally left at seven or eight. The lunchtime break hardly gave you time to do anything. Many just ate a sandwich in the *boliches* of the Nueva York. But some would take the opportunity to go home and see the kids. The end of the workday depended on how many animals they had killed that day. At the start of the day the foremen and women were already there, your bin was beside your table all clean and waiting, there was the checkweight man and the *anotador* who registered the weight of everyone's bin, how many kilos of meat everyone had done. The goal was fixed at one hundred kilos an hour. If you didn't reach it you were in trouble. Once a foreman said to a woman, "You are useless"; I was the delegate and I said to him, "Watch your mouth, señor, here no one is useless, the woman can't do anymore than she is doing, watch your mouth señor, each day she will work better, each day she will produce more, but don't insult her, don't offend her, she is a woman." You are useless, he had said to her.

You couldn't talk while you worked. The most that you could do was when you saw that they were some distance away, you could say, "What time will we get out today?" But under your breath; you could never talk while they were walking around. It was like being in a church at Mass. It was a tremendous slavery, that's the honest truth. In the twenty-minute break for *maté cocido* you could take a drink from the water tank, eat a cracker, a piece of bread to have something in the stomach till the evening.

DJ: What did the women feel toward the foremen? Were they afraid?

DM: Afraid of the human being, the foreman, no. Fear of losing their job and the bread it represented, yes. So because of this fear of losing the job and being without food they treated them like gods. If you saw a foreman coming you would lower your head and work as hard as possible, because everything depended on them. They sent in the written reports upstairs, such and such a worker is doing well, this one is all right, this one is doing badly. Now, behind their backs they spoke terribly of the foremen. They would say they had a mind to beat him up. We had some very tough foremen and forewomen as well.

I immediately began to be respected by my fellow workers, to be a sort of leader in my section. I don't know why, God knows. We made up little cards, sent them to a printer, which said, "Member of the Sindicato Autónomo" and "Member of Partido Laborista." The two went hand in hand. Most of the women in my section signed up. It was fifty cents a month. "If you can't pay up, don't, but join the union anyway, sign here, sign the card." We got over three thousand signatures. Some we had to tell, "If you don't join the union we'll make them fire you." A lie, but some of them didn't know any better, the *rusitas*. Later the women would even shout in front of the foremen, "Viva el sindicato de la carne," but at first we would whisper quietly to those who wouldn't join, who had said they were afraid, "You have to be afraid if you're not in the union.

We'll make them fire you," and they would sign up. I used to hide the union cards in my bra and I would sign them up in the bathroom. Not just me, all the women delegates, because the union resulted from the collaboration of a large number of men and women; a single swallow doesn't make a summer. There were others, too, who with their words and actions helped this thing of beauty, which is the city of Berisso, to progress. This weeping shawl, which is today Berisso, where today we have such troubles, lack of industry and where we have to emigrate in search of food, was also a place where we have experienced great satisfactions, great happiness. We Berissenses have been very happy. We used to get our money every fifteen days, along with all the exploitation that existed, it's true, along with all that anarchy of the bosses, there was happiness because every fifteen days we would see some fresh money to keep on feeding our kids, buying some clothes, so we could live poorly but happily. Some would say to us, "You are going to expose yourselves and end up in jail, or dead or rotting away in Patagonia because no one can do anything against the oligarchy, be content with having a job and don't say anything else." But we insisted with our rebellion, that we had to struggle for a better tomorrow, that these wages were wages of misery only fit for survival, not for living. And we were successful over months and years. We achieved concrete realities.

The most important of these realities at work was the respect of the boss toward the worker. They no longer treated us like an animal, like a piece of furniture, like something that you use. We were treated as you should treat another human being. Once the boss respects the worker he has achieved much more than wages are worth. Respect and morale of the people are above all else. These changes we were feeling gradually, but we definitely noticed them after 17 October 1945, when the Argentine people and well-intentioned foreigners went into the streets to demand the liberty of a man imprisoned by the armed forces, who was called Juan Domingo Perón, from that moment we noticed the difference. From that time when we went into work we weren't overbearing, but we did enter the plants with a certain cockiness, a certain pride, which was as if to say, "I'm going to work content because I have someone who will defend me, in Trabajo y Previsión there is a man we can rely on to defend us." From that moment we were more respected. But we also made ourselves more respected. There were hundreds of stoppages, of two hours, of five hours. Every time that there was a firing for reasons of health, or for anything else, like someone couldn't meet the demands of the company, in those situations when they fired a compañero we would have a stoppage because so-and-so was fired unjustly. We would notify the management, "If this compañero, who has a family to support, returns to his job we will continue to work." And sure enough this compañero would return, and we would stay on the job. It always worked.

At that time we worked under the Standard system in the plants. It was like the alms that the rich give to the poor or the powerful to the needy. There were bonuses for those who produced more kilos, or worked more, to such a point that the foreman would say, "Hurry, señora, because that way you'll get the bonus." The bonus was a stupid thing, "una tontería de monedas." It worked like this. If instead of producing 100 kilos an hour I managed 110, I got a bonus. If I produced only 90 I got no bonus; on the contrary, it was marked down against me. In my section the standard was 100 kilos. Most of the younger workers could make that, but it took a lot of effort. You couldn't alter the rhythm because that was determined by the way the meat arrived at your station. So the meat itself keeps on piling up, which means that you have to keep working. Basically the worker had to work at the speed of the noria, which keeps bringing meat, so it mounts up, and eventually the moment arrives when one of the supervisors has to say, "Stop the noria," because you would be drowning in meat. "There's a surfeit," they used that word, surfeit. When they had got rid of the buildup and only two or three big pieces of meat remained for each worker, they would start the line again. If a worker couldn't reach the standard, they ran the risk of being fired, because the company and its technicians said that a man or woman had to reach this standard. The technician who really controlled all this was the anotador. There are balances between the tables, the workstations, and they count what each person produces and mark it down. If today I do 110 kilos, why can't I do that tomorrow? If I have a headache, a stomachache, I've arrived feeling bad or I've slept badly, well that day I lose the bonus and they bring it to my attention. So everyone works in one way or another as if under the gun. And it was very difficult to help anyone else. It was an era of "help yourself if you can, and hurry because if you don't they can throw you out." Of course, when the union had taken off and we said, "We're here and if this woman can only do 60 kilos, it's because her lungs can do no more," then things started to change, they couldn't fire her. But before the union they could just fire her.

Now this led to problems among the workers because we used to say to some women who were really good with the knife, and very strong, big women who came from Yugoslavia, Lithuania, Poland, Russians, we would tell them not to work so hard because we couldn't keep up with them, that they were doing us harm even without wishing to. But they wanted the bonus, and there would be serious problems between compañeros because he who worked too hard damaged the other worker. Later when the union had taken hold we explained to these señoras, these compañeras that if the company had set the standard at 100 that was already too much. Why did they reach 110? I, for example, had three children and wanted to help my husband, and wanted to buy some clothes, live a little better, I also wanted to earn a decent wage and that's why I was in the struggle, but I couldn't do 100 per hour. When I reached 90 I was already exhausted, and there were many women like me because of our physiques, the body of the criolla woman is always slimmer. Those were women some of whom had been through a war, and all the trials and suffering. They were more prepared for the battle of work than we were, who had perhaps come straight from our homes where we had spent most of the time preparing meals, looking after kids and entered that cold, brutal frigorífico. The ones who could reach 110 kilos an hour were these big Russian women. Lithuanians, Ukrainians, as tall as you. I used to look at them in amazement. With the steel in one hand and the knife in the other, they were like another race of women. They were different with a different work discipline. They were afraid that they would be thrown out. They would arrive before the others and leave last. They are made to work; you could tell that they had come from their country where they had worked hard. They had tremendous arms and hands, hands like the hands of men, and compared to them we Argentines were like dolls.

This system remained, but with Perón we were able to make some changes. It became more of a sectional bonus than an individual bonus. If there were 600 kilos in a bin, perhaps you did 100, another woman 80, another 120, another 130, because here were people who had got really skilled with the knife. It was like weaving. So they would calculate the standard jointly, and I would get a bonus sometimes though I never reached 100. But this cost us dearly convincing people of this. Because it seemed to people that working more was better. It cost us a lot, the internal struggle with our own compañeros. I will tell you, professor, at times it was tougher than struggling against the boss himself. It seems incredible, but I have to say it. The same as trying to get the people to go out into the street to get a few cents more. It was very difficult to get someone to go on strike when he says, "I cannot lose this job, I'm not going to go hungry because you want the union."

"No, it's not that we want it, we *need* it. It is a necessity of the twentieth century and you have to accept it and leave the plant."

So we had to force many people to stop, and it's important to say so, so that everyone knows. It's very important. That one man used to do the work of two, and that can't be because he is taking work away from another, hours of work from another father with a family who is outside the plant with his ID card waiting for a day's work so that his kids can eat. Because the one who works for two is doing the work of that man who is unemployed on the street. No. Do what you're obliged to do, feel happy that you're being paid every fifteen days, but don't take the bread from the mouth of another poor person like yourself. We had this struggle constantly in the union with compañeros and compañeras. They would say: "No, I like to work hard, work quickly, who is going to prohibit me from doing it?"

"We are! You have to work if you come into a factory, but not ruin another's life or ours!"

So our struggle was a little unequal. We had to struggle with our compañeros and compañeras and with the company. But that's the way it was.

DJ: But you gradually succeeded in convincing them?

DM: Well, they ended up convincing themselves when they saw that from thirty-seven centavos an hour for women and fifty-five centavos an hour for men they reached ninety cents for women and a peso five for men. So when they began to receive a double-wage packet, they saw that we had said that they shouldn't work so hard, normally yes, but not to kill yourself, no worker could last a year working at that rate. They saw that they didn't have to do the work of two people. Those big Russians used to come to me, for example, and ask me, "María, what should we do now? What should we say?" Because, for example, we had won the point that if any woman had to go to another section she was paid the half day she worked in the section she had started off in and a half day for the section to which she was moved, even if she didn't start in that section until the next day. So that at the end of the fifteen days, they had much more money than they expected. When they got their wage packet they would say, "Look, how much I earned," and I would explain why, and they would say, "Ay, it's a good job that you people are struggling for us." They were very grateful. They were very good people. However they could express themselves, in their language or half in Spanish, they were very educated people. I respected the foreign women a lot, and they respected and loved me in return. The big change came with Perón. The standards stayed the same, so much work for this task, so much weight per hour, so many yards of tripe. But the reality was that you didn't have to always meet the standard now. Everything was gradually toned down. There came a time, for example, when one of the chief bosses came, Don Pepe, I remember him, and told us, "Well, I understand that this is pretty hard work for you women, so if you can't do a hundred kilos do ninety, but I want clean meat." We were really pleased, and when we reported it in the union the men said, "See how soft they're getting." So it was becoming more humane. With the arrival of Perón and open unionism things changed a lot, though, of course, you still had to put in eight or nine hours a day.

Being a delegate was a great responsibility because all sorts of situations presented themselves. My compañeras were always very grateful for my work as a delegate. When I was younger I was a very activist sort of person. For example, a woman would say to me that such and such had happened to her, that only this much money had been included in her pay envelope, and she would bring me the packet. Immediately I would put down my tools, take off my overalls and go to the management. "What's going on with this woman, because here there is only so much money, the señora wasn't absent at all, why only this much pay?" And when she got the right amount, "Ay, María, how lucky we have you." I would have to march out in the rain sometimes, walking along the passages to the offices while my compañeras put meat in my bin. I went to demand justice for a compañera. They gave us lessons about how to do this in the union, how to act when you're a delegate. It wasn't, "I'm the delegate, I'm in command here." No, no, one moment, there are many things involved. You had to do things the right way, be motivated by love. And at times foremen would come up and say, "I have a cut of cloth in my house, my wife has it in the closet and she wants to give it to you, if you only could see this cloth."

"I thank you very much, señor, but I already have various dresses and that's more than enough for me."

It was an attempt to buy me off.

Someone might arrive late because the tram had not come on time and the company would want to dock half an hour from the pay, something that as delegates we couldn't allow, and we had all the arguments ready, about how often we would work half an hour extra and they wouldn't pay us, so why if we arrive ten minutes late should we lose half an hour's pay. Especially if it was because something happened in the street, and I don't have a car and I have to come by tram and once I'm inside the plant I have to still negotiate four blocks of passageways and buildings because inside the plant is like a city and you have to be careful of the trucks and containers. So if a person arrives ten minutes late and explains why, you know that she isn't going to arrive late every day, the delegate has to make sure that they don't steal that half an hour from her. And we did it by following certain procedures to take our complaint to the sectional chief once the anotador had marked down that so-and-so had arrived late by ten minutes. This was a very important part of the delegate's job. Also the delegate has to ensure that there is humane treatment of the worker in all things. If there is some problem the bosses have to talk to the delegate that such and such has happened; then the delegate can call the woman over and can say, "Look, señora, when you go to the bathroom don't take half an hour." We have to respect our work because it provides the bread of our children. All this was the work of ants. It took time. Because the worker also has to be educated. I always defended the worker, but I have also to say that educating the worker is a very difficult task. Many thought that having a union meant that they could do many things inside the plant that they couldn't before. If there was a work stoppage they might throw meat and bones around, as if to say if I'm not working let's play. "No, señora, that is sacred. That piece of meat you're throwing is going to end up on the plate of your child. So please, señora, let's keep our arms by our side, our mouths shut because we are dealing with the bread of our children, our work, and there are many people who want to work." So for the delegate who really knew what her obligations were it was very special work. And it cost us a lot to educate the worker. There is one part of the working class who are educated in union terms because they were born educated. And there is another part that thinks that having a union and paying dues at the end of the month means doing what they want, and I used to explain to them in terms we had discussed in the union, "No! Compañeras, if we don't respect our work it will not respect us. So let's not shout or sing or throw bits of meat. If we act correctly we'll win and be respected." Imagine, professor, in a section where there might be three or four hundred women: Poles, Lithuanians, Russians, Turks, Spanish, Czechs, from all the nations of the world and each one with their customs, and this made it difficult for us to make them understand. I would explain things to them, but there were some things they might not understand. I used to say to them: "We are here to work, if we don't work what will we give to our children to eat, how will we pay the rent? We must respect the boss, and we've come here to work and not to play around. Everything you do outside the gate is your business, but the only thing I ask you is that here inside you are respectful. I will defend you, but you must respect me." After Perón things became more liberated, but one thing is liberty and another is *libertinaje,* one thing is to spend ten minutes in the bathroom and another half an hour. In other words, it was a process of education, many workers didn't know what the word *union* meant. Perhaps the word *educate* isn't the right one, because the poor person who came here from their country in search of a piece of bread was educated. It was rather to make them understand what a union was, what a union was truly for.

The Strike of Ninety-six Days

The strike of ninety-six days didn't come out of nowhere. In 1944 we had already won the fourteen points. The fourteen points included many demands, including the reincorporation of workers laid off in strikes. Many communists had been thrown out of the plants, and they went back to work. Another demand was the so-called law of the chair, which said that women who had varicose veins in their legs could have a chair that they could push under the table where they worked and work from that just as they would, only seated. We also demanded that we get maté cocido at 3:30 in the afternoon and that we had to make it, not them. We were afraid that they might put something in it. These were all very important things for us. Like when a woman felt ill they should let her go to the company doctor, nobody can fool the doctor, and if she wasn't really feeling bad then, all right, she could be suspended for a day, but she should have the right to see a doctor. And, something that was very important. If I start to work in one section, let's say *graseria,* and they move me to tripe, they have to pay me the half day in graseria and the half day in tripe, even if I don't start work in tripe till the following day. They still have to pay me for eight hours.

The eight-hour day would be implemented as well, if they asked you to work overtime you could, but you weren't obliged to. The other thing that we won at this time was the *garantía horaria*. In other words, if there wasn't sufficient work in a section, you still got paid for the eight hours of work. For example, if on a Friday the word came down that there had been no slaughtering that day on the killing floor, it meant that all the other jobs in the plant were affected. If no animals were killed, then the worker who cleaned the meat couldn't do her work, so you stayed home and got paid for it. Now it rarely happened that way, but it was a very important conquest. Do you know what it represented to stay at home and get paid for it? It was a thing the company never imagined we'd win.

The strike of ninety-six days happened because we knew how much meat they were sending out, the union knew how much profit the companies were making, fabulous profits, millions of dollars. And so we said they can't keep paying us ninety centavos an hour if we are the prime factor that moves this whole tremendous enterprise. You've seen the size of the frigorífico, professor, the colossus that it is. Men who were working on the killing floor were earning a pittance. We had to strike for everyone, for the men who killed sheep, the men who gathered up the wool, the men who loaded the ships. It wasn't a question of stopping just for the picada or for María Roldán. We had to stop for everyone. So we launched a strike. We launched it after we had presented a petition to them claiming wage increases to the level we should have been earning at that time, but they wouldn't receive the petition.

It happened like this. We were taking a list of demands to the personnel office, asking them for an increase of fifteen cents an hour for women, and I think that it was twenty to twenty-five cents for men, because the work of men is always tougher, heavier. They wouldn't meet with us.

"We don't recognize any union or commission, here in the plant there is no commission," they used to say to us.

There was a door that by luck had a crack in it, so we used to go like this and push the petition under the door. We would go back the next day at the same time, ring the bell.

"We've come to talk to you gentlemen, to hand over a petition."

"We don't receive anyone here," they would say through a gap, "because for us there is no such thing as a union and commission." Bam, they slammed the door.

Once again we'd do it, seventeen petitions we pushed under the door. So one night Reyes said, "Well, enough is enough, we're going to begin by stopping one line [noria] for a short time." The frigorí-fico was already becoming mechanized, modernized. After that, if they don't give way, we're going to stop two, then three, then if they still don't give in four, then five for longer. We'll go to the plant but we won't work."

So at first we tried entering the plant and not working, but after a set of meetings we decided that we couldn't continue to send people in and expect them not to work, just standing by the line, by their tables. Meat was being wasted because a packing-house strike isn't like a metalworking strike. The meat rots. So we let four men in to maintain the machines. So in secret meetings we decided that everyone had to be out on the streets. We're going to stick it out hungry, or maybe not, whatever, but we were going to all bear it together outside the plant. In the end we managed it, it ended hap-pily, the compañeros and compañeras ended up understanding us. It's as I said to the police chief, Dr. Marsijak, after they arrested the delegates: "Look Señor Marsijak, every Argentine worker at this moment, though you might not believe it, is now a delegate, they know their obligation. And you know why they know? Because it makes them very sad to send their kids to bed at night with a maté cocido and a crust of bread, because it is very sad to send a child to school without an overall, it's sad to see a child hungry. A child that we have carried here in our bellies for nine months, that he's hungry and we can't do anything about it. That's why they are all delegates, because they are struggling for a better tomorrow, for a bit more bread. So do what you want with us, but be absolutely certain that this time the company is going to have to give way be-cause we are not going to go to work, we're not going to give in." Where were they going to get seven thousand workers from?

The strike was so beautiful in some ways. It was like a kid's game. We had won the fourteen points with smaller stoppages, two or three hours. Because a stoppage [*paro*] is a shorter thing, depending on what the union has decided, it could be two or three or five hours. But a strike [*huelga*] is something else, it's to go out on the street, where nobody works. So after so many short strikes, after the bad faith of those people who always had us dancing to their tune and the wages still miserable and the work ever harder and the hours ever longer, we reached the end of our tether and launched the strike of ninety-six days. This was something that had never happened before, it was almost unprecedented in the world. A strike of ninety-six days was a tremendous thing if you have seven thousand working. It's not like a strike of a hundred people. It's seven thousand who stay in their houses and don't go to work, and this is very difficult to do. It's very easy to talk about but very difficult to pull off; to keep in their houses all these people who are yearning to go back, who are saying we are going to be hungry, they're going to fire us, what will we do with our children? It's tough. It involves a tremendous struggle inside the plant with your own comrades. There were people you would persuade to join the strike by charming them, "Look, compañera, let's go, let's go outside," and you'd be stroking their shoulders. They were scared of losing their job, of losing their bread. There were others that you would take the steel and place it against their backs, saying, "Come on now, get out of here," making them leave. Whoever lived that era knows it. Nowadays they don't understand. They arrested all the delegates. That's why we formed the first commission, the second, and the third. When ten delegates were arrested there would be ten more to take their place in the leadership commission. There was always a backup. We were always well up on union tactics. You always had to have consistency in the leadership group. If not, the mass of the workers will be dispersed because they get confused. The rumor starts, "Tomorrow we go back," and one says it to another, and another repeats it, and they get ready to go back and just like that the strike is broken. So we always had to be ready, sometimes with some odd tactics, which were unfortunately necessary. You always had to have leaders to counter the rumors, to say, "No, lads, you can't go back." It was a constant job of convincing, because they would come to consult the union, they had learned something of union discipline, and that's very important. But even so, you have to think that when you're on strike, one, two, three days, then a month, then two. Some workers tried to get in the back way to start work again. They would put on grey overalls that management wore. They thought that by doing this when the strike was over they would be made foremen. There are always these sorts of snitches. Well, when the lads discovered them they grabbed them by the hair, by the ears and dragged them out, "Go back to bed, querido, and stay calm because this isn't a joke, it's deadly serious, here we're playing with the bread and happiness of everyone." So at times we had to contend more with our own compañeros than with the company. But in general the workers of Berisso showed great discipline in this strike.

DJ: Where did that discipline come from?

DM: Some brought it from Europe, some came from the speeches of Cipriano Reyes and others, like me, that provided a certain guidance. But there was also a force, I don't know, it seemed that God put his hand on us, something beyond human factors, and told us that we had to hold on, hold on, that everything would turn out fine, and it did. Things changed. You still went to work and to sweat, but with respect, with love. So that, for example, they would ask me if they wanted to move a woman from my section to another: "Señora delegate, can I send the señora to tripería?"

"Wait while I ask her, because she is a human being."

"Señora compañera, do you want to go to tripería for a few hours?"

"Yes, why not."

"Yes, señor, the señora will go."

So it wasn't any longer, "Go there!" or "Come here!" They no longer acted in that way. You can see how important the respect of one human being for another is.

17 October 1945

Before 17 October it was all just talk, but Perón appeared that night in the Plaza de Mayo and everything was different.

The idea of 17 October was growing because Reyes went by plane, by mule, by bus, however he could, visiting all the unions and all the factories, cooking oil factories, textile factories, every sort of factory, arguing that there had to be a strike, that there had to be a 17 October. This started before they imprisoned Perón. We knew definitely that there was going to be a seventeenth on 12 October. On the twelfth Reyes disappeared. "Where is he?" we asked his wife. "He's in La Rioja, he's in Tucumán, he went to Catamarca." He was talking to all the trade unionists so that they would strike the seventeenth. They had to get to the Plaza de Mayo however they could, and everyone who could come somehow got to the plaza.

You know why we went that day? Nobody sent me the seventeenth of October to the Plaza San Martín to ask for Perón, but I felt a tremendous pain, I saw pregnant women crying, asking for help in the streets. In October 1945 there was still awful poverty here, as God is my witness. The union used to ask for meat in the butchers, to give out. "How many kids do you have?" Three kilos of potatoes for you. Then the next, "How many do you have?" Well then four kilos of potatoes. We lived liked that, making do here and there, as best we could. So the seventeenth arose from our pain. Let me repeat it, it came from the great poverty. There were conventillos in the Nueva York where seven or eight families lived, twenty kids playing on the sidewalk, the only yard they had was the sidewalk. What sort of men were they going to be tomorrow?

We set out from Berisso on that day with an old flag, torn. We had already heard from Reyes, that we had to go out into the street with the people, and nearly all the women had been told to be in the calle Montevideo at such and such a time. We went to Los Talas on foot, that's about twenty blocks along the calle Montevideo, and from there we came back with the flag. That's when we met the mounted police. The police didn't let us pass so easily like they say now. No, there was gas, they chased us, a little of everything, they wouldn't let us shout "Viva Perón." We got to the Sportman bar at the corner of Montevideo and Río de Janeiro, two blocks from the Swift. When we arrived there the streets were full of people. We were some seven thousand souls. We formed a caravan on foot. We went to La Plata on foot. Some women who couldn't walk, they got rides in a truck, a car. We arrived in the Plaza San Martín in La Plata. In the Plaza San Martín there seemed to be almost the entire province of Buenos Aires. The plaza was full and the crowd flowed over into the diagonals. I spoke from a stairway leading into the government house. From there you could see more. There were people in the side streets, up in the trees, on the balconies. It was like the taking of the Argentine Bastille. I never saw the French Revolution, but for me it was the taking of the Argentine Bastille. Everyone was happy, nobody fought, people didn't insult each other: "We're going to win. Peróncito is going to come."

DJ: I read that there were some fights that night.

DM: Well, when there are men who drink. You know there are people who drink. There were some who broke windows and took beer, wine, those sorts of people are never absent, then they get into fights. But this is a very small part of the people that has nothing to do with decent working people who get up at four in the morning to be in the frigorífico at five. But you're right, there was a little of everything that day, you can't deny it. But people were happy, especially when we heard by phone that Perón was going to be in the Plaza de Mayo at midnight. In my speech in the Plaza San Martín I had said that if Perón wasn't in the Plaza de Mayo alive and well by midnight the workers would continue with arms crossed, that we wouldn't work. Then we went on to the Plaza de Mayo. We went in a truck. I don't know how many of us, forty or so. The truck driver said, "I won't take children, I don't want problems, I'll take adults," and even so Ricardo Giovanelli, who was a man from the union who was worth his weight in gold, was telling everyone who got on the truck not to bring sticks, arms, not to bring anything, we were going in peace, we were going to wait for Perón, that night we would have Perón with us, and that's the way it turned out.

When we arrived at the Plaza de Mayo, we pushed our way to the front, rubbing up against the people, we lost buttons on our clothes, there were so many people. We had also taken a lot of our clothes off. It was so hot. Imagine it, spring, and yet it was so hot. The people, euphoric, they were throwing shoes in the air, hats, they were taking their shirts off, the men were naked up to here, all of them. Later, several of us from Berisso spoke, Ricardo Giovanelli, myself. Reyes wasn't there. He didn't appear all day. When it was my turn I said that the moment of the social demands had arrived, that the people have their moments, their dates, their day, their hour and their minute, and this is our minute, twelve o'clock on the night of 17 October:

"The colonel has to come here because we in the Sindicato de la Carne have sworn that if he isn't here by twelve midnight among us, we will continue without working, as will all the Argentine people, come what may, we offer our lives for Perón, and we will take inspiration from the statue of General San Martín, that man who gave everything for freedom and received nothing, and who is carved in stone and in bronze by great sculptors with his finger raised in the air warning us, "Beware Argentines, so that the gains that we have made shall be eternal." And I say this because what is in play here is the future of Colonel Perón. Because here there is talk of a Señor Braden whom we do not know. He may be a great man, a great father, but he is not Argentine. May those who are not Argentines forgive me, but I as an Argentine must say this. Let us remember San Martín at this moment. Let us ask above all for liberty, peace, and work, but this work must be rewarded with salaries that allow us all to live in peace and love." It was more or less with those words that I spoke. It was spoken spontaneously, without preparation. On all the walls, wherever there was propaganda there was the shape of a pig, and next to it they wrote the word *Braden,* and then alongside an image of Perón and a flower beside it. That sort of thing that the people invented, the people is extraordinary, there were little songs that really were like small poems, incredible, with just the right words, they were very well received.

Well, when I finished, Edelmiro Farrell, General Farrell, the de facto president, asked me who I was, because my husband and Ricardo Giovanelli were supporting me with their hands.

So I said, "I am a woman who cuts meat with a knife that's bigger than I am in the Swift packing house."

"But who are you, señora?"

"My name is María Roldán."

"Pleased to meet you, señora. Please be patient, Perón will be here." It must have been about eleven o'clock.

In fact, when Perón arrived Farrell was speaking, and the people started to applaud, and he says, "One minute, please, I am still the president and I'll speak first, then Perón will talk." After his words he and Perón embraced, patting one another on the back the way military men do. And then Perón started to talk, and he would have to stop, and he would start again and then have to stop, he couldn't communicate with the people, they wouldn't let him, they kept interrupting. Then there were the *bombos* [big drums], beating away. It was something so tremendous. It was almost four in the morning, and when they let him talk for a moment he said, "Muchachos, if you let me I'll talk, if not I'm going to leave because I am very tired." When he said, "I'm going," they finally got quiet. And the speech he gave that night was for us the most memorable, the most sublime that we could have experienced as trade unionists. That night in the Plaza de Mayo, when he arrived all tired, all agitated, the speech was for us who knew that our country was in a bad way, that working people were completely defeated, humiliated if you want, by the bosses, not only in the frigoríficos here, but all the bosses, the words will remain ingrained in my mind until the day God calls me to him. Because he delivered the speech as if he were transported outside himself:

"I am a mortal, I may be here and in a short time cease to exist. I feel very bad, but God will know how to give me the strength to continue with what I have determined to do. I promise you nothing, but I know that you need me."

The people were almost beside themselves.

"You need me, and I will join you in this project. I will follow what my heart of an Argentine citizen tells me to do. I have very good intentions. I am going to work first for the workers who are those who keep the nation moving, and then I will work for all the Argentines. But first I will work for you. I know how you are living, because I have seen you weep in the Secretaría de Trabajo, because I have seen you on your knees say to me, "Please, colonel, do something. We can't bear anymore." I have never allowed a man to go down on his knees before me, but you did so. I know that

Berisso is like a weeping shawl, I know that since 1917 you have struggled, because I am no neophyte, I am old enough to know. I will fight first for you, who suffer most. First, I will raise up the weakest, then I will see if I can raise my country up. I think I will be a good leader, but you will have to accompany me muchachos and muchachas, because we have to rescue the Argentine people from the pain in which it is submerged."

When he finished speaking we started to leave. The people went back to their homes, to work, half naked some of them, without shoes, without sleeping. We got back to Berisso about seven in the morning.

I think that Perón, without the support of the people, wouldn't have been Perón. Let's start with October seventeenth. If we hadn't been in the plaza on 17 October and all the people in the streets, Perón would have stayed in prison, and I don't know if they wouldn't have killed him. Perón's life was hanging by a thread, because the armed forces had already realized that the Argentine people were with Perón, and that he had a majority of the people. It wasn't just a gift. Nobody gave us anything. It's the people who did everything.

DJ: Because that is a very common idea about what happened. That the people just passively received everything.

DM: I know, and that's what I want to explain to you. The Argentine people needed a man to follow, and Perón was that man. Semana Santa [Easter Week, 1987, a military rebellion against the Radical Party government] in the Plaza de Mayo was not like the 17 October for one basic reason. The people went to the Plaza de Mayo this time because they were frightened for themselves and their families. But we went into the streets because we were afraid that they would kill a man, whom we already wanted for president. Look at the difference. The people went into the streets for a man. You have to analyze that. Because at 7:50 I was on a platform in the Plaza de Mayo, and we said that if Colonel Perón doesn't appear there was an order from the union, tomorrow nobody works and we won't work until they give us Colonel Juan Domingo Perón. And Perón was there at twelve midnight. That's what people don't realize.

Doña María Roldán speaking at rally of Partido Laborista in 1946.
Courtesy María Roldán.

Perón, Cipriano Reyes, and the Partido Laborista

The first time that I saw Perón in Berisso was at the funeral of Cipriano's two brothers. They had killed them in front of the Cine Victoria. The communist leader José Peter had come to speak there. Cipriano had told us not to try and stop him, to stay home, but, you know that these things sometimes get out of control. I spoke in front of Perón at the cemetery, and I said to him:

"Look, colonel, today we take our leave of two brothers who fell under enemy bullets—I didn't say communist, in that place, in a cemetery—men who don't think, who don't suffer, who don't love, who don't cry, because there have not yet sprouted in the garden of their soul the flowers that perfume their heart, because they have not yet felt the suffering of others, these men have left a family and children abandoned. We are going to struggle so that someday you will occupy Rivadavia's chair, and be our president, because we love you a lot. But we also must tell you here in this sacred place, colonel, that just as we struggle so that you will arrive at the presidency of the nation, so we will struggle to bring you down if you do not fulfill what you have promised us, because the Argentine people, and especially the working people, are tired of lies, tired of disgraces, tired of being picked clean, tired of being tricked, tired of the foreign companies sucking their blood and giving them four cents to subsist. We don't want anybody's chimneys, we don't want anybody's dollars, but we do want to live with dignity and love, we want to send our children to school well dressed and with shoes, so they can be protected from within and without, we want to live with dignity and love, so that our spouses live in happiness, so they work contented, singing, because our country is one of love, happiness, and freedom, and we hope that an Argentine president, a military man, a man like yourself, may understand us. I will say it again, colonel. If we feel that you are cheating us, we will fight to bring you down. Nothing more."

DJ: Have you always had the ability to speak in public?

DM: Since I was fifteen I have had the ability.

DJ: And it had flowered in those years, in the union?

DM: No, words just came out for me like that, I said much more, I spoke for something like a half hour, because Reyes told me, "Speak all you want to," because there was only two speakers, myself and the intendente; Cipriano wasn't going to speak because he was the brother.

We already knew of Perón. He used to say to us, "Strike and then let me know, I'll support you. You struggle and I'll be with you with money and with my words," and that's why there was always a special relationship between the meatpackers' union and Perón. He used to come to talk to us at night so that the whole population wouldn't follow him. He'd take *maté amargo* with Cipriano, and the delegates would be there. I used to make the maté for him. He would come to talk man to man to inform himself. He'd ask someone who was in grasería what happened in their section, another in tripería what happened in theirs. He came to converse with us to see how we could solve our problems. He could talk to us in our language. He used to *tutear* with Cipriano, he could tell jokes. He was very criollo. I remember that when we used to try to hurry him with, "Look, colonel, this is taking a long time, how long do we have to wait?" he'd say, "Let's wait until morning arrives, then we can unsaddle." He wanted to say that just as if we were riding a horse we need to be patient and wait for light to reach our destination.

We had already begun to talk about forming a political party. I remember we were in Cipriano's house, and his wife had just bought shoes for the daughter, and we used the box to draw up a chart showing how we could organize the national party. And you know that the Partido Laborista was like a contagion, we'd sign up people in the plant and they'd bring friends the next day. There were people who put all they had into opening a local. It was like the first emancipation where the worker discharged all his pain, his complaints, his wish to live better. The first struggles were some of the most dangerous, the most risky and perhaps the most beautiful because one threw oneself into the struggle without knowing whether what we were trying to do was possible; we were going forward like a boat without a rudder. Of course, we were always strong numerically, but we still didn't have strong unions, the union force was only gradually establishing itself.

Our idea was that with a strong union it still wasn't enough. We needed a political party. All the peoples who have truly progressed have done so with a workers' political party to defend them in the parliament. Because we knew that in the union we could discuss our problems and have all the right in the world and still only get as far as the ministry of labor where Perón was, and there everything stopped. But we knew that in the chambers were the laws in question and that it is law that really runs a nation and that really could manage the worker by improving his economic situation. So for this reason we wanted a political party not to do politics but so that some man would advocate in the chambers for a better life for the worker—at first this man was Reyes—and defend us and create laws to protect us. In this sense the union and the party went together. We had read in books on unions that unions couldn't have even a picture of the secretary-general on the wall, or of the president of the republic because politics is one thing and unions are another.

But we were so bound to Perón because we had fought to free him from prison, perhaps from death. But be careful! We didn't do just anything that Perón ordered. He consulted us, but there was never a time when Colonel Perón, or later President Perón, sent us something, and we just adopted it without a quorum or a small congress to discuss it. We would say yes if it was in the workers' interests or no if we thought something was bad, if it didn't suit us. So there was a contact, a tie between the political and the union, the two had to march together, in parallel, not united because one thing is the union and the other is politics.

When we went to see Perón in Trabajo y Previsión to tell him about forming a new party called the Partido Laborista he said, "Very good, I'll be the first laborista." But he told us that we had to be serious. We had to know why we were forming it, we had to start with a founding charter, founding principles, why the workers of Berisso need a party, what is the fundamental fact that leads us to create a Partido Laborista. And we created the doctrine of laborismo. It was created from various books that taught us many things. It is a doctrine very similar to that of Jesus Christ, that is to say, always help the weakest. Later that was embodied in national labor laws. This doctrine was the basis of everything.

DJ: Of course, but what importance did it have for the ordinary member? Did they identify with the doctrine or with Perón, with the concrete improvements in the factory?

DM: The workers, even those who are illiterate, understand that they are working for the boss, that they live miserably with their wives and kids, that they are renting and they can be thrown out at anytime because they have no legal protection, so the workers understood perfectly well, perhaps the most ignorant knew it better than the best read, that there had to be men in the chambers to defend them, to create national labor laws. So it wasn't so difficult to understand. The worker needed support, but support from above. When we got to Trabajo y Previsión there everything stopped. What happened there with Perón was good, but it wasn't definitive national law because it didn't come from the chambers. So it wasn't difficult to get them to accept the doctrine. We would read it to them, reread it, there were pamphlets, we would read it to them again. Some got to repeat it almost from memory and they accepted it. With some compañeras it took more convincing. With the death of Reyes's brothers there was a lot of tension. They said that they hadn't fired on anyone, and we said they had, and it got very tense. There was some sympathy for communism, especially among certain Slav compañeros. We had to explain with great patience and very calmly that the Partido Laborista was a thing that was created purely here in the Argentine Republic simply to put in the chambers a man or woman who would defend us, so that they could pass laws so that the oligarchy in our country, the powerful, would not mistreat us. And we were able to convince most of them.

Well, professor, the first time that I spoke in public was in front of the Sansinena packing house during the laborista campaign. It was in La Matanza, and a man—those busybodies are never lacking—wrote out what I had to say, I don't know exactly what his post was in the chamber, I think that he used to clean the floors with a brush: "Here, I've brought it all written out for you, more or less you say this here . . . ," as if to say, this idiot what might she say, I took it and had it in my hand, and I was on a platform pretty high up, they gave me an arm up there, like up a ladder, and it was beside a river, and this paper was bothering me in my hand. When I got up there and saw all the people and they knew that it was a worker from Berisso who was going to address them, they started to applaud and to shout, that's already enough, an encouragement, an injection of optimism, and I took the paper in my hand and threw it in the water. I didn't even remember who gave it to me because at that moment I revolutionized my brain as I was about to start to speak. . . . So, I throw the paper in the river, I see all the people looking at me, that they're applauding me, and I see some women right in front of me with some flowers and I revived, because I said, "God is with me," so I began to speak, I heard a person say, "This señora must be a communist," really clearly I heard it, when one is young you hear more, and I said, "No, compañera, I am a laborista." . . . so I began to speak, and I think that more or less it came out this way:

"Today is a special day for we women of the laborista movement, which was born from the very heart of the people on that memorable 17 of October 1945, on that day of happiness and of greatness that we could call the taking of the Bastille—but I gave it everything, not like I'm doing now—that movement that is marching forward with enormous strides and that nobody can now hold back, because it is capital and labor that are in struggle, because it is we who want to live better, because those who have the power and greatness live better from the moment they are born. So compañeros and compañeras, I am a meatpacker from the Swift plant in Berisso, and I have three children, I have my husband here with me, and I want to say only one thing to you. The laborista movement is a movement of the people, a movement that was born from the heart of the people one 17 of October, and that nobody will be able to forget, because we the Argentine people did not go out into the streets, Argentines and well-intentioned foreigners together, to demand the presence of a man just for the fun of it. We went out in the streets because we were drowning, because we needed the lifesaver, we came out because we could no longer live in misery, we came out because we could no longer bear the infamy of the powerful. We don't want either the chimneys or the dollars of the powerful, but we do want decent wages so we can live with dignity and love. We do want to be respected, that's why we are here, so that the earth will belong to he who works it, so that the farmworker, just as now Colonel Perón is already doing with the Estatuto de Peon, will be respected and not given the fruit that falls from the tree, the rotten fruit. And they will not any longer pay people with tokens in the north of Argentina. And women will give birth not in a tent in the middle of the street in the presence of a *comadrona* but with a doctor. These are Argentine women, Argentine mothers. We are here so that all children can go to school, so that we have no illiterates or semi-illiterates, so that we are all happier . . ."

The people responded to that with the same enthusiasm, the same emancipation, the same tenderness. That's why at times I ask myself, Professor Daniel, with all that we did and all that was spoken about laborismo, and for all that we loved laborismo, how could it cease to exist from one moment to another? That was a full stop that should never have happened. Well, the true history, because you can never erase history, is that Perón created the Partido Único from laborismo. We the laborista women tried to keep laborismo going, but it was betrayed, we don't know to whom. All we do know is that we went to our locals one day and found them all closed up. We gave the best of our lives, and not only María Roldán. We won by a large majority on 24 February 1946. We won in places where the conservatives had never lost, and we won by ten thousand votes, not just one or two hundred. We went to the frontier with Bolivia, with Cipriano we stayed in each province fifteen days. When all this was wound up there were people who were weeping. Reyes had left the union in Berisso and gone to live with his wife and daughter in La Plata. He was traveling a lot to Buenos Aires and lost sight of us. I don't know if he was to blame or if Perón made him do it, but the bottom line was that the Partido Único was declared, and Reyes attacked it, saying that it would be interred with four horses, attacking Perón, wounding him. As his own daughter said to me, "If papa had not been so hurtful, María, and not offended Perón, you and I would be millionaires." Because in practice it separated us from Perón. Well, not in my case because for me he was still my president even if he didn't think exactly like me. But Reyes offended him deeply.

Perón, the Working Class, and the Oligarchy

In Perón's time Berisso was one of the happiest places on the face of the earth. I have seen the people happy, shopping, going on their vacations because we got paid vacations, too. We got almost free tourism, to Mar del Plata. There were thousands of people who had never seen Mar del Plata. There was also support for the old, with pensions and other things. They say that Palacios had already done it. Well, fine, but those laws were yellow pieces of paper on the shelf. It was Perón who effectively sanctioned the law. We got civil rights for women, too. The union had extensive social services, too. With Perón we had it pretty good, we had tourism, geriatric in-stitutes paid for by the government. Everyone was happier. There were dances every Saturday and Sunday. There were two cinemas in Berisso. People could dress better. There were people who didn't even know Buenos Aires before Perón. With Perón we discovered many things. A pair of nylons, a nice dress. Life changed. We could buy things like refrigerators. I bought my first in 1947. We could buy sheets, mattresses. You could buy on credit at low interest, especially things for the kitchen. We also had tourism, the right to vote with your husband. Do you know how it feels to have the freedom to choose your own president? In Berisso four schools were built by Perón's government, and the possibilities for our children improved. Every year they gave us two overalls, two pairs of shoes and food for the poorest children at midday. So our kids had a better chance when they left school. Most of us didn't dream of sending them into the plant. I wasn't going to send my daughter there, into that hell. Most women fought so that their kids didn't go into the frigorífico, to save them a little from that which we had experienced in flesh and blood.

Berisso was really a thing of beauty in those days. They were like white doves, those women dressed in their white work clothes buying things with their children in hand, happy with their wage packet in hand. They would buy a whole lamb; you could buy meat in the frigorífico at really cheap prices. When Perón began to go into action things changed, it was as if all had been sterile land before and then everything turned green. Do you know what it means to enter a packing house and say, "Keep me two kilos of *asado,* one kilo of flank steak and two of stewing steak, I'll pick it up when I leave work." We had defenses now. You would leave work at six tired because packing-house work is tough, but you'd leave with your packet of meat and your wage packet.

DJ: But even under Perón there were still conflicts. The strikes and conflicts didn't end?

DM: There is something I always said in my speeches. If we struggle against capital for a hundred years, we the workers of the world, they will be watching us, waiting for a hundred years to step on our necks and choke us. So that oligarchic capital always reemerges to tighten its grip on us. Faced with this, the worker has reason to think that striking is the only weapon that he has left, and it is a right that the constitution guarantees. In the case of the strikes of the meatworkers under Perón, what happened is when it comes to defending the bread of the worker he who is on top, even the government that is our friend and thinks like us, is still in a better situation than the worker. The cord is always cut at its thinnest point. So the worker defends himself with what he has at hand. The powerful can screw him with the stroke of a pen, overturn a law that protects us. But at the same time, by crossing our arms, we can paralyze a people at any moment as we did the seventeenth of October, whichever government is in power. Because though it seems a lie, the real strength of peoples lies in the workers. So the strikes under Perón were justified. The poor have always been oppressed, even with governments sympathetic to us. To this day this is the case. We have children living in the streets today, girls of fourteen and fifteen having babies. This is the Argentine Republic, the land of the fat cows, the country where you can make asphalt out of wheat, the country where we could feed the world, God has blessed us with four seasons so we can grow something all year round. And yet we suffer from hunger and poverty while a few are the owners of all this land. Until when? How did the big families get this land? Did they buy this land with money earned from the sweat of their brow, or did they acquire it just because they wanted it? And this always seems to be the same. "The land belongs to he who works it," said the man from Galilee when he saw the villagers suffering and unable to pay their taxes. And Jesus said to them, "the land will belong to the poor," and two thousand years have passed galloping by on our backs, and still the land does not belong to the poor, the land belongs to a privileged few. I don't think that it is only in my country that the land belongs to a few, but in many parts of the world. All these hungry families that could come and settle in Argentina to sow, to open up the heart of the land to sow wheat. We could say to them, here is a tractor, here are four horses, work! this land is yours. If the owner of this land can make do with two meters of soil, why is there so much injustice? How many immigrants can fit into Argentina?

I criticize all governments for this state of things, including Perón's.

DJ: Do you think that he could have done more?

DM: I don't know, because he had three presidencies and three times he was strongly opposed. I am very grateful for what he did. I am enjoying a pension thanks to him. I adore Perón and Evita, but all the same all this dead land, why does it exist? I have traveled by train, Daniel, and seen that for mile after mile there is nothing, no animals, no people. Why does this happen if there are people living in squalor, sleeping ten to a room, who could leave with their families and live in the open fields, sowing, harvesting, living, eating fresh vegetables? Why are we human beings so negative? I think that the owners of these lands should talk to the government and negotiate the access to the land for others. After all, in this world we are all equal, the color of the skin and the hair doesn't mean anything, we are all human beings, we all have children, we all know what pain is, what happiness is. I have a very good memory of Perón's government, but it seems to me that however much poor Juan Domingo Perón struggled against capital, one needs many years of government because capital is very powerful, very strong. It isn't so easy. To me it might seem easy because if I had all that land the first thing I'd do would be to measure it out and give to each family so many hectares each. But it isn't so easy because capital is cold, it's hard, it's negative, and that is the suffering that humanity has. The problem is that if the land belongs to them, how are you going to convince them to give it up? But it is a tremendous injustice. Argentina is immense, but it seems that it belongs to four or five landowners, the Anchorenas, the Alvears. And I buy a plot of land, I pay two or three quotas, perhaps I can't pay more, I lose the money of the three quotas, and I now have to rent, and I'm an Argentine who gives children to the patria, who may have to die for the patria at any moment. So much injustice!

So with Perón we had it pretty good because we didn't have time to think of the things I'm talking about. Because the lands are ours after all, they have fenced them off and they have the titles, but they are ours, they belong to all Argentines. We had tourism, so we didn't have time to think about this sort of thing.

DJ: But what about other issues? What about anti-imperialism, was that an important issue for laborismo? For example, the national-ization of the packing houses, was this a demand of laborismo?

DM: Yes, but it was never achieved. Even now they won't give us that sleeping monster, that they keep down there for what reason, I don't know.

DJ: Why do you think it wasn't possible to achieve the nationaliza-tion of the packing houses?

DM: There is a lot of capital concentrated on a piece of our land, and this capital is British, or from wherever, it isn't ours. We have a perfect example of this: they stripped the Armour of everything, they took it apart and tore it down, only the land is left.

DJ: But that is now. What about in Perón's time, he did after all suc-ceed in nationalizing the railroads, why not the packing houses?

DM: He struggled a lot. I always said and I'll repeat it that he needed to be younger and have ten more years in government to accom-plish all the things he wanted to. He couldn't manage to get to many things. Because he could be the most competent president and the one who loves the workers most, but if you are the owner of a packing house, you say "this is mine" and that's that. "I pay my workers, they'll earn this much today, and this much tomorrow, but the frigorífico is mine." And who's going to argue that the packing house is theirs? The big powers have always dominated us, Daniel, and they were a power that Perón couldn't overcome either, and that's a fact.

DJ: Do you think that the workers had some of the blame for that, because they didn't support him enough?

DM: On the contrary, I think that the worker always got up at dawn, went to work, left the best years of his life for a meager pension and sometimes got to give his opinion. But the opinions of the workers were never taken into account. I think that the great powers and the great powers of the oligarchy can always do more than any government, no matter how good the government may be for the workers, however good the intentions of the president of the nation. The power of the dollar is stronger and wins, it wins out. It is a very big obstacle in carrying forward a nation like ours that is still in diapers. Because, in the era I'm talking about, from 1945 to 1955, there were workers who didn't know what a union meant, why a union had to exist, and why they had to go and pay monthly dues and why that union defended them, and what happened when there was a strike. I remember that at times the union speakers would get up on a table and spend two hours speaking and then when they had finished the workers would ask them what they had just said, ask them to repeat the explanation. Because it was necessary to educate the people both politically and in terms of unions as well, because the two things were born almost together, the Sindicato Autónomo de la Carne of Berisso and the Partido Laborista. So you can imagine, and I say this without wishing to offend anyone, for the man who is used to leaving the packing house tired, exhausted, to have a drink in a bar, to go home to eat, to go to bed with the stomach full, tired, completely beat, to get up once more at four in the morning and sometimes go on foot to the plant, you can imagine how much it cost that man to understand what was a union and what was the Partido Laborista. It was terribly difficult to educate the working masses with respect to the union and politics. Now, it's different. You ask a kid of fifteen now about politics and he'll leave you dumbfounded, he knows more than his elders. But not back then, those were different times. This was one of our big problems, and a problem for Perón, too. How to get people to accept the philosophy that we have to struggle so that the bosses are softer, that they give us a little more, a few more dollars. That we have to do it gradually, without picking up a knife, or an ax or getting angry, but with papers and with struggles. It was with this philosophy that the most talented in our ranks got to be senators and deputies. Convincing people that you had to create a political party to take people to the chambers, who would then say, well, lads, here is this law that is going to defend you. We didn't attack the concept of private property, on the contrary. We said that we didn't want the smokestacks, the dollars, the wealth of the landed oligarchy, we didn't want their wealth, we wanted to be respected, to earn a decent wage so we could live like Christians without being exploited.

DJ: In other words, you weren't in favor of the class struggle?

DM: We didn't want anyone's capital. We wanted to work with capital and respect it, but we wanted to be respected as human beings and to be paid what we merited as men and women who work. But we get back to the same thing. There weren't national labor laws. So they paid women thirty-seven centavos an hour and men fifty-five. There weren't laws to protect us. They did what they wanted. We come back to the same thing: we had no one to defend us. Ninety-six days of strike, with animals rotting inside, the bosses coming and going with sailors, and we held out till we won the strike. We won it with our rebellion, but we didn't win it with a law. Let's be clear, because we didn't have the law.

Our struggle was to obtain the laws while we respected capital. Because we understood, you don't have to be very bright to see that if there is no capital there is no work. Right? If two packing houses hadn't been installed here, there wouldn't be seven thousand men and women working. And this is where we differed from the communists.

DJ: Communism wasn't a pragmatic, realistic demand?

DM: No, it was a dream, something that on the other side of the globe might be very good, but not here. They may be very happy over there, but as an Argentine, over here, I don't accept it. I respect them because I consider them to be very capable, but these are things that don't apply here.

Evita

I simply considered her to be a perfect human being, who loves the other, though she doesn't know her, she is another human being who suffers, though she doesn't think like her.

Evita visited Berisso; she gave out clothes, sewing machines, mattresses, sheets, sweetbread, cider, little packets with money. She came with Perón to choose the site for the Barrio Obrero. She marched along with him, stride for stride, like a man, through the debris and the earth. Very bold. I spoke with her many times. She came to Berisso once when they struck the plant, she made them go back to work because they were wrong, she was right, they were earning well then. She gave out gifts from the number fifty-two school, nice things, but she also spoke to them harshly. But you could talk to her easily, she liked funny stories, she had a real sense of humor. She referred to everyone as "che," she was like a woman from the barrio. But here in Berisso they loved her. When she was in the streets people went crazy. She was like an idol.

I once went to the prison in Mercedes, this was when she was ill, or maybe after she died. I was like an official visitor, inspecting the food, everything, and one says to me, "Could you go and buy me a pack of candles?" This was a prisoner.

"What do you want candles for?"

"To light them for Evita," inside the prison.

I saw them weep and fall down on their knees and light the candles.

In prison I've seen women lighting candles to Evita. Among the prisoners they insult one another and say anything that occurs to them to say.

One prisoner says to another, "Light a candle for your mother." "For my mother who abandoned me, who threw me out?" replies the other prisoner. "Evita came to see me, she said to me when I leave here she's going to give me work, while she stood here behind bars."

This was very important, very important. It shows the warmth for the people that that woman had. She was like an imam, she had a thing that swept the multitude up. It's difficult to explain. Supernatural; to tell the truth I have never seen anything like it, because there was one moment in the Argentine nation in which she almost, almost surpassed Perón. People were forgetting their leader, because she was leading such splendid humanitarian campaigns. She didn't want to be president or vice president so that she could be Evita, the protectress of the *grasitas,* the *negritos,* the dirty ones.

Evita's life, which you can read in that book over there, you immediately realize that it was very sad from the day she was born because she was born out of wedlock, her father was an estanciero called Juan Duarte, who had five children with her mother, Doña Juana. From her childhood she was hard done by. Doña Juana had a boliche in Junín where she was raised. The other little girls didn't want her chores with them because she didn't have a legalized mother and father, things like that. So that she was despised from the time she was very young. So much so that when Duarte died the book says that they blocked the girls from getting down from the carriage when they went to see their father dead in the coffin.

"This was the first blow of my life," she says, "the toughest experience I had in my whole life."

She was seven years old. In the end a man intervened; it seems he was a military man, and they were able to see her father. Later they returned home in the carriage, a wagon for carrying goods. They went back to the business that the father had set up for them to support themselves, and they cried a lot because their father had died, but a father in the house they had never had, which means to say that Evita was already a woman who suffered many blows. Perón, on the other hand, already knew everything; he knew how to box, to fence, to ski, to ride. He came from wealth. She wound up marrying the man who would become president, for those things that happen in life; I think he went to get something at the radio station where she was working. He met her there where she was working in "La Cabalgata del Circo." She was an artist; they fell in love and later they married.

Eva was different from Isabelita. We respected her as Perón's wife, but as a president, please! She might know how to dance the zamba very nicely and other things, but you can't compare her to Eva. Because Eva, with all her ignorance as a bastard child, as a woman who suffered during her childhood and everything, had something very great, very pure, very noble that only the great ones have. She loved the poor; she used to enter the shacks without having them disinfected first. That is very important. She would go up to the bed itself.

Once, they say, the girls who worked with her told her, this is an anecdote, about a family and a man who was dying. She sent the women who were in charge of the cases out on the periphery of Buenos Aires to a hut where there was a man in a very bad way. The man said to his wife, "If the people from Peronism come, don't let them in."

So the girls, the social workers who were sent, say, "But how can that be? Why won't the señor let himself be taken away and cured?"

So they left, and they said to Evita, "Your Excellency, this man rejects us, anything that comes from Perón he rejects."

"Oh, yes," she says, and she called a police truck and called an ambulance with three or four doctors and a stretcher, and they went to the hut, she too, she took off her fine clothes, and put on a light blue overall, and went to the hut. This was on the outskirts in La Matanza, I think.

She entered the hut, and he says to her, "What do you want, señora?"

"I am the señora de Perón." They say that the man almost died.

"What do you want here?"

"I have come to take you."

"What do you mean, take me?"

"I've come to take you to the hospital. You have to come now, if you don't come of your own will, we'll put the cuffs on you, but you are going to get cured because you have four children and you have to raise them."

"Come in," she says to the police; they picked him up from the bed, put on his pants, shoes, into the ambulance and to the hospital. It was very serious. Four children and the señora crying, and he doesn't want to go and be cured. She gave work to the wife, put the three kids in a day care, they were half tubercular, bought him a piece of land with a little house, and when he got out of the hospital gave him work. Later he was Perón's shoeshine, poor man, speaking badly of Perón.

These are the anecdotes that Evita has left. She used to go and visit the huts, she didn't have them disinfected as Isabelita would do before entering them. She would touch the pus, with her hand she would remove the pus, that's why I admire her, for no other reason.

This is what Evita did, but it doesn't get broadcast, the bad is all you hear about. That she was an artist, that she sang on the radio, as if it were a bad thing to sing on the radio.

On another occasion, this is another story, a young man went and says to her, "Your Excellency, for some days I've been wanting to speak with you, and I couldn't get in."

"What's up with you?"

"You remember that you gave me a chalet, and in five or six months I'm going to be married, but a married couple with several kids have moved in there."

And she said to him, "And when are you going to get married?"

"Well, within five or six months."

"Very well, I'm going to make you another even nicer one, because a new batch of tiles has arrived, new mosaics, beside the other chalet, leave them in there. How are we going to throw them out with five kids?"

The young man said to her: "This is the social justice that you practice?"

She pressed a button; two guys came from the rooms behind, took him away, and he wasn't seen again. Evita was absolutely single-minded, that's for sure. They must have arrested him or something. He was rude to the president's wife; if she told him, "I'm going to make you a better one, in five months it's done," how are we going to throw out a couple with five kids on the street? Think about it a little. He insulted her, he said to her, this is the social justice that you practice. She was tough, a little violent, but just.

There was a story about when Evita went to visit some boys in prison. It was in Olmos, near here, because the mother of the boys had written to Evita a letter asking her to please, if she could, go to the prison and speak with the boys, that her boys had never stolen anything.

So one day Evita with a little free time went to visit them and said to them, "I promise you that while we are in government you will have jobs, you'll be well paid, but you must also promise me that you aren't going to steal anymore."

But at that time, some tremendous things happened. I'm going to show you a chest, a thing that means a lot to me, this chest was given to me by a prisoner in Olmos to put my deputy's ID in, it's made by hand. This man who gave me the chest is called Juan Pica, he's still alive, I don't know where he ended up, *pobrecito*. He stole two bolts; he worked in a company, which made things to keep houses secure, and he wanted the bolts to keep his house, which was a prefabricated one, from flying away in the wind. And it was just at this time that Lopez Frances, the minister, had stolen the rails of the railroads and sold them and then escaped to Europe, but they locked this man up for stealing two screws. As I had emerged as a candidate for deputy in the first list, he sent for me. At that time women didn't have civic rights, but he didn't know that, pobrecito, in his ignorance, that I couldn't be a candidate.

But he called me, and I went; when he saw me, "You are Señora Roldán?"

"Yes."

He says, "I've been making you a chest for more than a year."

The things made by hand are amazing, the things he had made.

"I swear on my children and my wife, my mother and father, that I stole two bolts, nothing else, and it's the first time in my life that I stole anything."

They had given him six years. So I went, and sometimes it was very difficult to get to see Evita, and I couldn't get near her, the gang who are there with their things don't let you in, you had to see the iron circle they maintained around her. So I sent her a letter with my name and address and all the details of the man, that he had sworn by his family and mother and father that he had stolen two bolts, and please if she could try, that it was going on two years that he was inside. She set him free that very month, Eva. When they arrested me in 1955 they took all that material. I had a letter—if you had seen it, it would make you cry—from him, Señora Roldán, you are my mother, what you did for me, you are like my mother. He wrote to me because he saw my name on a list. I went to see him, I went with my husband to the little window they have there. Pica, yes, a lad, I didn't steal anything but two bolts and the other good-for-nothing, who made himself a multimillionaire, he went to one of those places with a lot of snow, with all the money that he stole from here. The Alps.

"With two screws I pay for all the robberies of the others. You believe me that I'm not a thief," he told me, and he cried.

So, in this way many things happened, many injustices because he who stole a lot was able to pay for justice, and get a judge to keep quiet, while he who stole a little went inside.

Evita went to see him in prison, and visited Pica. I know all this because he told me.

She saw as many thieves as she could, "I'm going to help you, come to my office, I'll get you out of here, what did you steal?"

Then she went to see a woman who had stolen a pair of stainless steel pots, and Evita asked her, "Why did you steal that?" And she said that she didn't have money to buy diapers for her baby daughter, she would sell the pots and so buy clothes for the girl. Think of that.

DM: Eva was the sun of the poor.

DJ: She was very personalist, she personally fixed all the injustices in these stories. Don't you think that it would have been better if instead of this marvelous woman, the system had been changed, and then there wouldn't have been injustices to fix?

DM: If her reforming works had continued . . .

DJ: But once the person dies, all her initiatives go with her, the injustice of the system remains, and what Evita did was to make less harsh the injustices of the system.

DM: The pains of the people . . .

DJ: But after her death, the pains, the griefs remained.

DM: But Daniel, we are human beings and we have a journey to run on this earth, and she lived thirty-three years, she died while she was still almost a girl. So she died leaving a trajectory that was so luminous, so divine, so exceptional. Because though she was the wife of a president who could have lived surrounded by shiny things and gems, and all the comforts of life, she gave her life. For her last speech they had to prop her up so she could talk, and she wanted to talk with her people, and tell them, "I am going but I will return as millions," because she knew that she was leaving a work that was so great, so enormous that I believe that on the periphery of all the towns of the republic there isn't a humble shack that doesn't have a memory of Eva. Valuable memories, pensions for the elderly, wheelchairs, beds, mattresses, houses, plots of land, even a mobile home for women who had nowhere to go, women who sold themselves to men. Even this she thought of, the *mujeres de la vida,* as they say. She said that they were women who gave their bodies, and we have to help them, make sure that they don't sleep in the street. She thought even of these women.

She said, "If Jesus Christ did not despise them, why should I despise them?"

Once in a speech she said, "Who am I to look down on a woman? When I should cover the failings of another woman with my skirt." It was marvelous. Nobody who hasn't dealt with her, who hasn't seen her close up, who hasn't followed that trajectory for the short time that she lived so intensely can fully realize what Evita was worth. It seems that she was something sent, something that was told, "Stay here in Argentina and do this." There are people who eternally grateful.

That woman had a tremendous human value. Imagine, she must have had, for her to go to the Vatican and the pope kisses her hand. The pope followed the life of this woman, and he didn't do this with any other woman, not Señora Roosevelt who did so much good, nor Madame Curie who struggled against infantile paralysis, nor the great wise men who would sooner struggle for war than for peace. She always struggled to go to the poorest place where everything was full of pus and where she used to clean the pus and cure the wound. This is what is important, to arrive in time.

It is undeniable that when she died it was like Perón lost his arm. A woman who struggling until dawn in her office so that she could get the time to deal with all the tremendous pains of the republic. In fact, she didn't have the time to cover but a small part of the good that she had to do, because after her death the Argentine Republic has remained in a very bad state. She managed to fix many things, but as you say, Daniel, the system collapsed with her death.

The Death of Doña María's Husband

My husband was always a man who belonged directly to the left. He died in 1953. He had been ill for some years, but they were tough years and we had to eat, so he continued working even though he was ill, sometimes with the aid of painkillers. Because in that time the attitude was, "You're no use anymore, crawl into a corner and stay at home." There was no talk of pensions. This was mainly before Perón. So my husband must have worked for a good ten years sick. His illness came from the frigorífico, without any doubt. In the early years a man had to lift half a cow on his shoulders. Later came machines, there was what they call progress, but at first it was all done by a man's labor force. With Perón things improved some, especially with the introduction of the noria. My husband said, "You don't know how much better the work is now that we have the noria." The piece of meat would arrive in front of the despostador on the electric noria, and with his fine knife he would take out the bone and send the meat on its way to the picada.

DJ: The noria came with the arrival of Perón?

DM: With Perón's arrival came everything. Mechanization, everything. Soon there were norias all over the packing house. It was demanded by the union. A man could not be expected anymore to carry half a cow on his shoulders. There had to be norias; the work of a despostador was already heavy enough without the man having to bear the entire carcass. So before they had to do everything. The carcass would arrive on a cart, hanging from a hook, pushed by another man. The man had to take it off the hook and place it on the table. There two despostadores would work on the carcass with knives, one at the front, the other at the rear of the animal. But everything was done with muscle power. The despostador had to do it all, and all the time with a dangerous floor, greasy, covered with water. They had to use big rubber boots. There was always the risk of falling over with the carcass on top of you. My

husband was a strong man, but he was a man, not a beast. The electric norias helped him, the work was more human, but even so his
health got worse. His kidneys, which were already bad, got worse
because the work was still heavy work. Once the carcass was on the
table he still had to move it around and be on his feet. His job had
to be done on his feet, he couldn't sit. It's easy to talk about it, but
it's another thing to do it. The ideal thing would have been to have
left the job, but who was going to pay him compensation for the
illness?

DJ: Even with the labor conquests under Perón?

DM: Well, but the labor conquests weren't such that you could leave
work and receive money to live on at the end of the fortnight. No,
the doctor used to come, he would see him a little improved and say,
"Well, Roldán, you can go back to work the day after tomorrow."
It would be very rare for them to give you a week off work. You
could say that you would have to be in a coma before the company
doctor—who was always a pimp for the bosses—would say, "Well,
this man has to be interned because he is sick."

I'll tell you about a case that shows this perfectly. It's imprinted
on my mind. It involved a man who lived in Villa Azul, just beyond
Villa San Carlos. He called the doctor because he had a temperature
of forty degrees, a raging fever, one of those awful influenzas. So the
doctor from the frigorífico came to see him. He had already been
examined at the local first-aid post. They had given him injections
and told him to stay in bed because he had bronchial pneumonia.
So the company doctor comes, checks him out, makes him stick
his tongue out, a little small talk, and then he says to him, "Well,
friend, you can go to work tomorrow, because this fever is going
to go down." With that the man, who was desperate because he felt
so bad, got up from the bed and gave the doctor such a blow that
the two ended up in the hospital, the sick man with an attack of
nerves and a viral flu and the doctor with his bones almost broken.
They ended up in the hospital with the police involved. This is a
true story; he had such a fever, he felt so bad, "How am I going to go
to work tomorrow, if I can't even go to the bathroom, you animal,
what are you doing to me? You want to kill me. How can you want

me to get up at four in the morning?" These things happened, they shouldn't be passed over, they should be recorded, they happened, they're real.

DJ: But what about the conquests under Perón, the unions after 1945?

DM: Well, things got gradually more humane. The unions always pulled this way and the bosses that way. So that the struggle continued. Sometimes we won, sometimes we half won, and at times we lost. For example, a person who had cut a finger with one of the knives had to still go to work even if it was only to pick up trash, because they weren't going to pay for him to be at home with his finger. That bosses' pressure existed. The struggle existed even under Perón. Time off with pay for injuries received at work was something we achieved later, but it was a struggle and the benefits came too late for my husband.

They finally had to admit him to the hospital, and he got worse and worse. They would let him out, then take him back in. Finally, Dr. Mayovsky told me that they were going to have to operate. It wasn't cancer, but the kidney didn't work anymore. Well, Mayovsky took the kidney out, and afterward he placed it in my hand. It was the kidney of a ten year old. It was shriveled up, consumed. And that was the end. He got worse, and then he died. I never received a cent of compensation. I fought it in the courts. The outside specialists said it was caused by the work he did. The company doctors denied it. I lost the case. We had converted our house into one made of building materials, we'd put in another bathroom, we'd built an outside shed, there were rose trees. Because the fact was that in his last years, even as he was getting worse my husband was earning quite well. But when he died, I couldn't stay in that house.

My husband was, how can I explain? a pure soul, one of those souls who see what is negative and what is positive. It is very difficult to meet a husband or wife like that. He used to say to me, "It seems to me that if there are so many women working they have to have women to defend them. There are things that a woman can't say to a foreman, like it's my time of the month, I can't do anymore, I feel bad. The woman delegate has to go and tell him." He led me by the hand. My husband said to me, "Look, they talk a lot about an army colonel called Juan Domingo Perón," it was one day while we were having lunch, "and you know there's this man Reyes, who came from Zárate with his family; well, he wants to meet you because he says that they tell him that you are a woman who is fighting a lot with the bosses." I didn't have any position, I was fighting because I saw them mistreating an older woman, "Why are you treating her in this way, don't you see that she could be your mother?" I couldn't keep quiet about it. So word had got around the plant about a woman, a small chubby little woman, and Reyes came and spoke to me and that's where my career started. But the basic truth is that my husband took me by the hand. I didn't go alone.

The Coup of 1955 and Perón's Legacy

The coup that overthrew Perón in September 1955 wasn't a surprise for the people. We knew to expect these sorts of coups because we knew that there was resistance against Perón. So we weren't awaiting the coup, and we didn't want it, but it didn't take us by surprise. For this reason we were ready to go out and defend Perón. I was working in the plant when the news first came through, and we poured out into the streets and marched to the Plaza San Martín in La Plata. The bus lines here immediately offered to drive people there. We swore to never abandon Perón. There was no strike the next day because the leadership of the union said that we had to go to work next day. We had already received some wonderful lessons in union affairs and we were disciplined. We knew that we had to follow the power of our unions. If we made a mistake then we would all make the mistake. There would not be one group taking the left road, the other the right. We would take the road to proclaim our faith in Perón, to ask that he always be physically and spiritually with us. We proclaimed out loud the favors that we had already received from Perón and that we would always struggle for him. Now when it became clear that Perón had fallen, that the military had won, then the situation changed. There were those who said that we had the obligation to continue working, that things would work out just the same. The union said no, that the working class that had always struggled, and now was in a better situation, had to show its grati- tude to Perón in the streets, that he was in danger and we had to stay out until the union declared the end of the strike. Those who wanted to go back to work were those who, as always, were afraid to lose their jobs. They were the illiterate, or semiliterate who thought they would lose the bread of their children. Of course, it wasn't that way at all because there was already a tremendous union force that encompassed the whole country. There wasn't only the union in Berisso. There were unions in all parts of the Argentine Republic.

The strike lasted two days. The authorities sent two tanks at the intersection of the Montevideo and Río de Janeiro, the main road into Berisso. They didn't do anything. They were there to maintain the discipline of the people because there will always be some people who are violent, and those two tanks were as if to say, "We are here, keep calm." There were women running with their children, shout- ing "Perón, Perón," and they stopped at that point because there were the tanks. The men, too, and the cars. It was all done with great calm, almost a family-like courtesy. In Berisso at least we can say that no police mistreated any citizen. They would gradually push us back, but nothing more. Nothing at all happened. The people in Berisso stayed quiet because of those two tanks. It was a necessity of the moment, because if they hadn't been there maybe a column would have formed and marched to La Plata and who knows what would have happened. So everyone stayed by their radios, this will be settled, they will return to work soon. The union loudspeakers in the cars spread the word throughout the city letting everyone know that this was going to be settled in peace.

We felt a very great grief. More than that, we would speak and cry at the same time because how could it be that after all the things that had happened to us, after the conquests we had obtained with spilt blood. . . . it was not so much now to defend a piece of bread, it was the dead who were saying to us, "Do something." . . . This is what we felt, but it was necessary to retreat. The following day we went back to work. By order of the union, always by order of the union.

Inside the plant it was strange. They treated us with the greatest of respect—the foremen, the section heads, the subforemen, the timekeepers. If there were groups of more than four talking a sailor would come up and disperse them quietly. You can understand the precautions. I think it was correct because inside a frigorífico there are many armed people, people with guns and pistols. You came to work, you worked, and you left. No meetings and conversations were allowed.

DJ: But didn't the bosses try and take advantage of Perón's fall?

DM: No, because the company, the people who give the orders inside the plant, had realized that the blinds had fallen from the workers' eyes, that he was no longer the blind worker. They allowed us the delegates to continue, and we were guided by the union. Because, Daniel, the union school is beautiful. It's much better than politics. Above all, it taught us to respect capital and to be respected in turn by capital. And to do this with discipline. So in general everything happened with rectitude. There was a change, no discussions about what was happening were allowed, and so nothing happened. There were arguments. Young people who said we shouldn't be here working, we should be out on the streets. So the delegate was obliged to tell them that it was a union order, that they should stay quiet in their places of work and that at night we would discuss it in an extraordinary session of the union, but until then the union had said to go back to work, and we had to work and keep quiet. It was a real struggle. They thought that being out on the streets they could do more for Perón, and it was the exact opposite. You can't just decide to strike a whole country, its labor force. The seventeenth of October we could, but not at just any time. The union force knows what it is doing, that's why it has books and reads them.

Even after the fall of Perón, we saw that our pay envelope at the end of the fortnight had more money, the treatment was humane, and the months and then years passed, and we remembered those years when we worked like mules, and so we were accepting of the situation, if not completely then at least semi-accepting. The chance for an adjusting of accounts, for *revanchismo* inside the plants, was limited because everyday in every section someone from the union came to check on conditions. So that person would inform the union in writing that at such and such a time in such and such a section they spoke with the delegate and everything was all right, there was a control. And this existed after the fall of Perón. They knew that that person could enter any section because they had the union seal, the union was an authority, that ultimately came from the ministry; it wasn't a vague thing where you rent a house and put up a sign, the union was a government and the boss had to recognize it even without Perón.

DJ: So why did the Peronist worker in the frigorífico in Berisso continue to dream of the return of Perón?

DM: Because the worker, the Argentine male, the Argentine everyman, who gets up in the morning, has some matés and has to go to work, he has to have his idol, though we say that all idols have feet of clay, that they break and fall, we have to have this idol because it is like a spiritual necessity. It's like many believe in God, but if they don't have a cross hanging here on their chest they think they aren't with God, and it's really only a piece of metal that they have here. Well, Perón is a myth, he's already a myth. I have seen them light candles to Evita in the prison in Mercedes. This is a grateful people. Because if you give the people a file they will not forget it, and these people had received a bed, a mattress, or a sewing machine, or a house or a plot of land, or a stay in a clinic. This is a grateful people, and thank God that it is like that. So what was missing? It's as though in this house there is everything, there's milk, food, but papa is not there, Perón is not there. Why isn't Perón with us? If Perón is an Argentine, why isn't he here with us? And there was this pain in the heart of the people, simply that. Even now he is dead, we know that he is dead, and yet the other night I saw people crying, if Perón were here this wouldn't be happening to us. You'll just have to accept it, Daniel, that is the people.

Doña María Leaves the Frigorífico

I left the plant in 1956 or 1957, I don't remember exactly. I stopped working there because my husband had said to me that our daughter was at the age where she needed a mother's care. She was starting to have boyfriends, and boys also need a refuge, and with mother and father absent the home is half empty. The kids can be very good, but those who should oversee them are not there. And on top of that, Daniel, I had the misfortune to lose a son, who died of infant paralysis when he was seventeen. He died in 1945, shortly after the death of Reyes's brothers, when I spoke in the funeral in front of Perón. He was sitting up in bed when I got back from the funeral, and he asked me what I had said to Perón. So I said to him, "Well, querido, I said this and this." He said, "That's great, mama, never stop doing this." It was something that he asked me to do, "Never give it up, because papa likes that you continue on this path, you have to continue, I ask you to do this. If many people do what you and papa do, then you'll see how beautiful Perón will make the nation." He was half a politician like me, he'd talk politics to the doctors. Well, when he got ill and we could see how serious it was and that the mother had to be at the bedside, at the side of his wheelchair, talking to the doctors, traveling in search of things, it became clear that I couldn't stay working in the frigorífico.

DJ: But your son died in 1945, and you stayed in the plant until about 1956.

DM: But I had to look after the other children, and my husband insisted on the responsibilities of home. Because the girl, Dora, was already a young lady, well, in a word, the home could not remain uncared for. We had to think of the other two, young people can go off in any direction. That's why I left the plant. And in his last years my husband was earning good money, and after he died I got his pension. Even though I stayed working, I was often absent. When I lost my son, I lost my rudder a little. It seemed to me that being in the house I was, in a way, paying homage to him, after his death, because I thought of those years that I had been gone from the home and my child stayed with a neighbor. But I know that it wouldn't have made any difference, infant paralysis would still have taken him just as it took another child, just as it affected Roosevelt. So I gradually stopped going to the plant. I still used to show up at the union when I could. Also in the 1950s I got a job working some days at the race track in La Plata, selling tickets; it was easier, and I could work as I wanted. But the basic motive for leaving the frigorífico was to care for my two children who had lost a brother and a father. Now after they were grown and responsible for their own lives, when Dora had a novio and she said she wanted to marry, then the role of the mama is different. I threw myself into politics then. But until then it's not nice to go and leave an adolescent for eight hours a day.

Doña María, Politics, and Peronism after 1955

After 1955 I joined Reyes again when he relaunched the Partido Laborista. It cost me a lot to unhitch myself from laborismo, and after Perón's fall it seemed that we might have a chance. There was tremendous enthusiasm. I joined Reyes in campaigns, all over the country like in 1945. I had never been able to accept that Perón could simply erase the party with a single stroke, after all the sacrifice. Dorita, my daughter, had a clearer vision of all that, she told me not to go with Reyes, that I shouldn't trust him. We had big fights over that. And she was right. Reyes was elected deputy in 1957, but it was losing force, and so we returned to the Movimiento Peronista, which is the mother of all this. What other remedy did we have? We only had one deputy, our main leader, who finishes his mandate, speaks viciously against Perón and Evita; we couldn't stay at the mercy of a single man. We had no real power. We tried in one more election and that was no better, and one fine day it's obvious that he too realized that this wasn't working, so he wound it up. What he did exactly we don't know, whether he sold it to someone or whatever we don't know. All we know is that one fine day, we found the party closed, our local shuttered up, the house sold. He bought himself a house in La Plata, received his very nice pension as a national deputy, and we were left dumbfounded. So we returned to Peronism.

I met Arturo Frondizi [former president, 1958–62] in 1957, and Don Arturo Frondizi said to me, "What need we have of a woman like you in my party," and I said to him, "What need we have of a man like you in our party." But I also said to him, "I cannot be a militant with Arturo Frondizi, because, you will forgive me, but many times I went to bed at night with an empty belly, I do not come from an oligarchic cradle, so by definition I must be Peronist. We the poor and downtrodden give our allegiance to that great military figure, Juan Perón, we don't know why but it was a thing that simply happened, he was our salvation." I, for example, could never be a Radical Party militant, even if they offered me the world. Radicals are white-collar people, they are different types, I belong to a different set. . . . Evita called us the grasitas, the *cabecitas, el populacho.* So I said to him, "I belong to another breed. The Frondizi's are multimillionaires, the Roldáns and the Bernaviti's are poor, look at the difference, so thank you Don Arturo, but no, I only came to greet you." I continued in justicialism because that was my path, I was right, no? I was initiated with Perón, and I'll continue with Perón, alive or dead, that's our destiny.

DJ: When you returned to Peronism, weren't the years until Perón's return in 1972 tough for you Peronists?

DM: No, because he left us a luminous star, an open road. There were people who perhaps didn't know how to take advantage of this or to understand it. It was a very beautiful lesson that he left us. Many understood him, others didn't want to grasp what he was saying. I always tried to pursue the mission of a poor orthodox Peronist woman. I never associated with those groups that wanted to change, add things to Perón's doctrine. He left us a declaration of principles, a founding charter if you like, a doctrine that for me is very similar to that of Christ, and we must respect it. Simply that. When we have a problem we can search for the answer in the doctrine, and reading we can find where we are. For example, he even dictated a basic municipal code. The workers have to know this because it's very common to use water and not pay for it, to throw away the water bill, water that the state pays for. They thought that because Perón was there they didn't have to pay. But Perón made them understand, no, señores, the water you drink, the light that shines in your home has to be paid for. In a word, he was civilizing the people, making the workers enter into the circuit of decency, because the state is an entity that exists because the people help it. Sometimes I hardly have money to pay Obras Sanitarias, but I pay because I consume the water and because Obras Sanitarias lives from the people. Perón set about enlightening the people in all these issues.

If a father dies, he is gone, absent, but how many beautiful things he leaves as an inheritance for his children, simply by having spoken with them. Though he leaves no capital, no material inheritance, he leaves a spiritual inheritance, which is the best there is. I remember things of my father that have served me so well, just as if he had left me land, an *estancia,* because I have the grandeur of the counsel that my father gave me. Perón left us well positioned, and the majority of the people have understood him. Perón always said save a peso because hard times are going to come, black days, many things will happen, don't waste things, take care of your work, take care of your health, care for your children, educate them, don't make them miss school, vaccinate your children. A father, just that.

DJ: What do you like about politics?

DM: I like what happened on Sunday. Where the different candidates talk about what they will do. It's easy to talk, but how to put things into practice is very difficult. There are many problems. For example, here we have the program of meals for infants, because there are many kids who don't eat at home. There are children who have no books, who have to copy from the book of a schoolmate because their parents can't buy them the book. There are kids who live a long way from the school and who don't have the money for the bus, and they have to walk and it rains. There are sick kids who don't have access to doctors. All of these problems need solutions, and that is what politics should be about. For me politics means being a benefactor of the people, especially the young and the old, as Perón said. These are the two sections of the population that suffer most.

DJ: So for you the Peronist politics that you practice has a strong ethical content? It's a way of behaving, of relating to people, and this seems to me to have a lot to do with your religious faith. There's a link between the two?

DM: Well, for example, if I'm at the table in the voting hall telling them where they have to vote and a woman arrives all dirty, with her belly out to here, with three or four children, black and abandoned, I say to her, señora, take a seat, where do you live; I speak to her as I would someone who just got out of a car dressed in furs, because for me it is a human being like any other, I have that advantage of having the sensibility to treat my fellow human beings the same, whether they have one aspect or the other, for me they are human beings, that is very important. . . . to love the people is to love everybody, it's to love a kid covered in snot, it's to love a drunk and help him cross the street so he doesn't get hit by a car, it is to love, that is what Evita did, that is politics.

I am not a Catholic, I'm a Baptist. I believe firmly in Jesus, I believe that he died on the cross for us, I believe that we are all mortal, but that while we are in the world we shouldn't harm or wound anyone whether the other is black, red haired, or is white, or is half naked, or is dressed; he is a brother of ours, he is on life's path to die in the end like us. That is the way I see humanity, and it seems to me that this, too, has to do with politics. Never to hurt anyone.

I had my first role in local politics in the early 1960s, as a municipal delegate. I initiated a program where adults who wanted to be godfathers of children could be assigned a child and take responsibility to give them every month some food, clothes. The children who went to the local clinic to get treatment were put in the program. Over the years a sort of network was established. I was also a school delegate to the municipality. I could go and inspect any school, inspect windows, see if they had heaters, broken seats, or if they lacked notebooks. I did this sort of thing for nothing, I didn't get any money, I felt happy, it was very satisfying.

I think that social justice was Perón's grand goal. But what we got is only a relative social justice. Perón could not solve all the problems of a people that was so castigated in ten years. He was president three times, but that's not much time, and things can't be changed from day to night. Alfonsín [Radical Party President, Raúl Alfonsín, 1983–89] said he could change the country overnight, and he couldn't change it. The suffering of the people continues. Children die of hunger, and mothers keep asking doctors to operate on them, tie their tubes, after having six children. They don't want more children. But they don't get the operation because they have no money. I know cases in Berisso of mothers with many children who have pleaded for operations so that they wouldn't have more children. But, no, señora it's forbidden. But if you can pay it's not forbidden. So it's only a partial social justice that exists. When Perón wanted to reach much further, when he really wanted to reach the worker, that's when Perón had to go to Spain, they ran him out when he really wanted to achieve social justice.

Social justice, these divine words, are part of life itself. From the moment he is in the womb man is involved with these two words because he needs good food to be born strong, healthy, and happy, and the child feels the reflexes of the mother. If the mother cries and says that tonight there is no food for the children, the child in the mother's womb will feel the anguish and suffering of the mother. This is a medical fact. The human being in the mother's womb can already sense happiness and sadness. Coming into the world is not equal for all babies. It's different to be born in a sad hospital where the birth is free because they have to attend a pregnant mother but where there is not the happiness associated with a woman in a clinic who has flowers, a family that brings her everything. So the words *social justice* were crucially important, but we only partially got there. Part of the problem lies with political parties. Here the Radicals and the Peronists have spent three months discussing divorce, and they haven't said anything about the social security of their people. It's true that divorce may be a relatively good thing, but it brings no benefits to the poor, the worker, who has to search for a piece of bread. And this sort of behavior is the same for both the main parties, the Radicals and the Peronists, and it leads to a lack of real interest in politics. The man who goes to work, who has a boss, he has to wait till the end of the month, he has a thousand things he needs in his home, but he has to wait till the end of the month to get a peso, and meanwhile the politicians blather. And this man will have very little interest in politics. He'll vote because he has to have the stamp that says he voted, any municipal paperwork, even to register a bicycle, he has to show his ID card. Did he vote? The vote is obligatory, so he votes, but he votes and goes back home, perhaps even more sad than before on election day because he's thinking, "Whoever wins, will they do something?" Because the people are tired of lies. I know politicians here in Berisso who tell twenty or fifty men they can work on the municipal payroll in such and such a place, and if we win, they say, you can keep the jobs, if we lose you'll be out of work. This is to play with people; it's a terrible thing, it's very dirty. Many ordinary people go along with this sort of thing. But they do it not because they are bad, they do it because they are desperate, without work, so they think if these people win the elections I'll keep my job. This is how they gather votes. And this is against what Perón taught us. He said that everything had to be aboveboard, that each citizen should vote as his conscience dictates. A person may not be a Peronist but may be a better man than a Peronist, he may look after his family, work hard, be honest, never have shed any blood, he doesn't need to be a Peronist, said Perón. But they haven't learned that lesson. How can I as a political leader buy these people's consciences, tell them that if we win you'll have work and if we lose you'll be out on the streets? I am using them like they're a piece of furniture. The person who allows himself to be used is drowning; he thinks, "I'll go along, I don't have any work, my wife is washing floors, taking in clothes to wash so the kids can eat, perhaps they'll win." And so we succeed in making politics something filthy, like a shady business deal. And this leads to disillusionment, people understand the garbage these political criminals commit, they're political dwarves.

The caudillos are the only ones who gain from this. Caudillos have always existed in this country. The conservatives in the 1930s and 1940s used to have asados for two thousand people at election time. Once I had a discussion with a well-known doctor who was also a big political figure here in Berisso, and I said to him, "Look, doctor. You can't go around feeling someone's liver to see if they have stones and speaking to them about politics at the same time. A doctor should stick to his oath and save people, and a politician is something quite different." So when Francisco Manrique told me that if I didn't go with him, I would never get to be a deputy and that I was trapped in something very sentimental, I said to him: "I, Don

Francisco, am trapped in my own convictions. In this thing that my parents bequeathed to me, of the importance of being cut from a single cloth and obeying a single truth; so I cannot sell myself to the highest bidder, neither I, nor thousands of other Peronist compañeros. We need an honor guard to defend justicialism."

The truth is that trade unionism is much better than politics; the union struggle is more beautiful than the political. Politics has corners where they can hide things. In a union everything has to be open to view, and when everything is exposed you can tell where the fault lies. Like in my case, when I was dropped from the list of candidates in favor of a rich woman. I'm going as deputy, a woman with a lot of money shows up, I don't know anything about it, I'm a woman who is struggling for her family's welfare, of course, we all want to be better off in life, but I carried within my soul from the time I was very little the desire to struggle for the weakest, because that's what my father taught me, because that's what the university of life taught me, what doesn't appear in books but that beats in your heart. On the other hand, there is lying, there is betrayal. There is the person who destroys her soul shouting and saying things, and there is the one who is there behind the scenes saying, "Let her speak, after all, I'll end up on the list of candidates, because I'll put up the money." In unions no one puts up more money than the union dues. In unions the books can be checked and controlled by the members. In politics no, in politics there is a room and then an entrance hall, while you are here below believing in those above you, there above you they are cooking up a candidate. It's all very dirty. The unions represent something more noble. The union struggle is much closer to Jesus, because Jesus was a worker, and everyone who works for a piece of bread is dignified by that fact. The man who works may be bad in some way, of course, we all have some defect, but he is never treacherous and evil like the politician. The man who works has to be basically good by the very fact that he works.

Peronism, and I say this as a woman of the Peronist movement, was just as bad in this. Those who surrounded Perón all wanted to set themselves up and make life comfortable for their descendants; all those people are obsequious because they want to fill their pockets, not because they love the president, not because they want to keep him in Rivadavia's seat. Those who really loved Perón were the working people.

DJ: But if that was the case, didn't you ever think that it would be better to have a different sort of Peronism, a more working-class Peronism?

DM: That's what we wanted, but unfortunately it was becoming more bourgeois, and the case of María Roldán and the señora with money is very clear, it's a fable, perhaps in a century there might be four, the person who comes with money passes to the chamber and goes to legislate. What? If she never lacked for food for her children, if she always lived with two or three servants, if that woman had goods, rents, a car, a palace, if she had everything, can she tell of what I can tell, can she speak of the miseries that I experienced with my kids in the frigorífico, or in my childhood? So, was it becoming bourgeois, or not? Because they installed in the legislature a woman with money and not a working woman from Berisso? There you have the why. Because she brought with her dollars, and Señora Roldán had nothing but reasons, rights acquired with the nobility and capacity that was hers as a poor working woman. That's why Peronism became bourgeois.

DJ: Why did Perón let this happen?

DM: Things just happened like that. If you check on all the figures who are at the head of Peronism from La Quiaca to Tierra del Fuego, they are nearly all very well off, there are no poor people.

DJ: So why did you keep having faith in Perón?

DM: For the reason that we are going to keep on having faith probably. Because thanks to him we have civil rights for women, pensions so we don't die in a plaza of hunger like an old horse. I cashed my pension check today and that of my husband. I'm not going to be rich, but I can buy a bife, a liter of milk, I get by. Perón left me that, because it didn't exist before. They say there were laws before Perón, but they were stuffed in a chest full of cockroaches.

DJ: The sort of criticism that you are making reminds me a lot of the sort of criticism that people on the Peronist left used to make in the 1970s. Does this identification bother you?

DM: Well, I'm content with what I say, because it's the truth. Now it tends toward the left, yes. I don't want to be identified with the Peronist left if that means extremes, violence.

DJ: But words like *left, revolutionary* have meaning for you?

DM: Our movement is revolutionary.

DJ: And in some way Peronism is of the left?

DM: It has to be, because it cannot be on the right. I am not going to support the extreme left, but of course I am more of the left than the right, we must tend toward the left. We do not want to kill or be killed, we want the will of the people to be respected.

The Closing of the Frigoríficos

DJ: I've heard various people, older people, talk about frigoríficos, and often the impression that they give is that in some way they blame the workers themselves for what happened to the plants, that the workers took advantage, the companies didn't want to continue with the losses.

DM: Well, of course, there were some people who acted badly. But that's to say something that has no sense to it. The company never lost money; it always came out well. What the company paid the workers was a joke in comparison to the tremendous profits that they took from here. Does it seem likely, Daniel, that when they're making us work eleven or twelve hours that we're working so that they lose money? Thousands of calves for export. At times they ran out of animals to kill. How could they lose if they were still killing animals at that rate? They should have nationalized the plants. To this day we're still fighting Swift to take over the land that the building is on.

DJ: Well, but they denounced that as communism.

DM: I don't see it that way. I see it as a process whereby nations advance, and if that is communism, welcome to it. But why bring politics into it? When an Argentine or foreign company is seeking men to work it doesn't ask them how they think, if they're Radical or Peronist, communist or laborista. What they do is inspect them to see if they'll produce; they check the eyes, the ears, the blood pressure, they take blood samples. They don't care how you think, to what party you belong. That's obvious. Here what happened is that the companies got tired, almost you could say they got tired of earning, of such profits. So one fine day they said, "Basta, Argentina." For us that is the sad truth. The fact is that all things have their span, if in such and such a year the profits were so much, what does the frigorífico matter to us. It's bricks and mortar. The dollars are already safe in the bank. For us this is the crucial factor. Nobody bothered about the poor Argentines, the poor negritos. What are they going to do now? Here the English interests—some say English Jews—were in command, they closed it down. As an Argentine I see a tremendous cruelty in that. In addition, they tore the Armour plant down. But of course feelings don't count in this. There was a tremendous ingratitude, not only here. They are closing down factories all over the place. The oligarchy, the arrogance, the ambition, the desire to achieve a position count for more than sincere feelings. Satan's tale is at work there, touching them. And Satan says, "Basta! let the workers go and eat grass if there is any, the frigorífico is closing." So don't let's go blaming four idiots who behaved badly in the past. My husband told me that in 1917 it was terrible here, too. He told me what his father had told him about the strike of that year and how the company acted. They put up machine guns in front of the plants and fired at the people. Many went back to work with their heads down. If you didn't go back they came to your house. Some they killed and put the bodies in the furnace inside the plant to burn. At least that's what they say happened. When they had succulent profits they didn't close, they'd kill people to stay open, they demanded more and more people to work, they worked night shifts. So the company didn't lose, what happened in the end is an oligarchic phenomenon.

The killing floor has a very sad history. It often happened that they would tell a worker, "You're going to work on the *playa de matanza*." And the man would say no, "I'm no good at killing animals." Because you had to hit them with a hammer on the head, until they introduced the electric prod. My husband said to me, "I'll do any job, but I won't go and kill an animal, any job but not that." So the life of the meatpacking worker has been very sad. Full of blood, of grease, with the *fiebre malta* that comes from the contagious boil that can infect you as if you had been bitten by a snake. So in many ways it was a sad life. And now they say that they closed because some workers acted badly. No! They closed because the fabulous profits had peaked. We'll get by in some way. But it was a tremendous ingratitude. I knew that black hell from inside, I went through all its sections. . . . I'm not going to say that it was always hell, but there were years and years when, God is my witness. What about the chilling chambers? The men who went inside to work had to wear bags on their feet, some froze. The doctors told us delegates that when a man enters the *camera* his heart rate changes dramatically; they come out with purple faces, and if you touch them they're all white underneath. Purple from the shock of the cold. So losses for the company? What losses? My God, losses? We are the ones who have endured losses, my husband lost his life there inside. Perhaps if he hadn't gone in the frigorífico he would be alive. So, I don't know, it's upsetting even to think about, a living filth . . .

DJ: A filth?

DM: Blood on the floor, bits of fat, men with brooms cleaning, but no matter what they did a frigorífico is always ugly. It's not like other industries, like textiles, which produce dry, clean things. There in the frigorífico one is continually in contact with the blood of the animal, with the fat, with the nerves, with the bones. It's a continual contact with something cold. Meat is cold. And to make it worse they brought chilled meat. Do you know what it's like to work with a knife on chilled meat?

Doña María on Evangelicals and Priests

DJ: Why did you become an evangelical?

DM: Well, my mother influenced me. She was an evangelical. It would take a long time to explain. The Catholic priest in the Barrio Obrero of Berisso is a pure soul, but the Roman Catholic Church contains many awful things. Don't let's forget that the Inquisition was forged by the Catholic Church in Spain. They've killed many people. Jesus didn't kill anyone. On the contrary, he said to Lazarus, who was paralyzed, "Get up and walk." There are some priests and nuns who give their lives for their fellow creatures, but the majority are there to have a good life, to not have to work.

We evangelicals know that Jesus died on the cross to save humanity, that the blood of Jesus cleansed us all. But to be with Jesus, really with Jesus, we must be good, not harm one another. We must be against anything that will harm the human species. This is what makes us evangelicals. This belief comes from my childhood, where I sought out the truth about many faiths. I learned from the synagogues that Jesus was a Jew. I accept that. But what I can't accept is that a daughter of mine has to go to a man dressed in black up there in a pulpit and tell him all that happens to her and that he asks her about the secrets of her body, that innocence. I believe that the only one we have to confess our secrets, our sufferings to is to Jesus. Man is a sinner. Our pastor cannot speak to us in church unless he is with his wife and children. There are so many bad things in the press about priests who abuse young boys. I read these things, and I reason. I've always tried to seek out the truth and reject injustice since I was young.

Once, I was about fourteen, I went to see a friend who was paralyzed with his mother and my mother. . . . we passed by a woman who was sitting on a stairway crying, and when we asked what was the matter she said she didn't have the money for the bus. And a nun passed by with a bronze figure of Christ, a large bunch of keys, a load of ornaments. We said to her, "Sister, this señora doesn't have money for the bus. Nor do we, we've only got enough to get home. She came to see her son and now doesn't have money for the return trip." And the nun says, "Let her ask the people passing by, people will give, they are good." But she didn't give us as much as five cents. A little later in that same hospital they bought a bronze bell, which must have cost a lot. My fourteen-year-old mind was working away, I was thinking about how the Catholic Church acts, and this taught me things. The Church had money, but not for the poor. This is why a little later I became an evangelical. I thought that the Salvation Army did much more good than all those ornaments, black clothes with crosses everywhere. I knew the moment that I was baptized that I had changed. My mother said to me, "María, you've changed, you're another girl," and I answered, "I didn't change, Jesus changed me because I gave myself to him." Because I was searching on all sides for something better, for something I felt I needed.

DJ: Did your Christian faith ever conflict with your union activity?

DM: No, because when you speak in public and name Jesus it is the Jesus who said to the villagers with scythes who told him they had worked and not been paid, "The earth will belong to the poor." In the end political issues and religious issues don't mix that much because Jesus is above humanity, he is the profound force that humanity has to sustain us to go on living. When we die, we die with "Jesús mío" or "Dios mío" on our lips.

The Catholic Church is a large worldwide business, and people are starting to reject that. You notice it in Berisso. We are having to expand our church to accommodate all the people, and the Catholic Church is half empty because people have noticed the social differences in the Church. When a servant gets married, some poor girl who washes things for wealthy people, the priest makes the sign of the cross, blesses them and declares them man and wife, and off to their home. But when a rich person marries who can pay, there are fancy carpets, flowers, lighting, and a soprano to sing Gounod's "Ave María." In other words, if I am a rich woman Christ gives me all this luxury, and if I have washed floors I can't hear the "Ave María." And I'm as much a Catholic as she who entered the church with a gown that had a ten-meter train carried by children. Jesus didn't want this, Jesus wanted equality. It's the same that happens with communion. Some take communion with their school overalls on, all stained, and other girls taking communion seem like brides with white crowns. Why the difference? Why does my daughter with a school overall on waiting to receive the host on her tongue have to look at the others all dressed in tulle? Why don't the priests say all the girls will be dressed in their school clothes, all are equal. People are beginning to reason about this, to see that equality doesn't exist in the Church. In Berisso the daughters of the merchants take communion in dresses as fancy as if they were brides, and they spend money as if it were a small wedding. And the other girl goes home, takes her overall off and says, "I took communion." I think that that is an insult to society and to innocence. But the child already notices the difference between the poor and the powerful. Right there, we already have a union force. They don't realize that they are helping inculcate a rebellious humanity. The girl goes home and says to her mother, did you see so-and-so, what a dress she had, and the mother has to shut her mouth and say drink your milk and eat, and she stays silent and perhaps the overall is the same that she wears to school, it was given to her at school, she didn't even buy it. So there you have the embodiment of those who suffer and those who are all right. It's present even in the act of communion. On this side the union with the school overall, on that side the powerful with tulle and silk. It's very easy to tell them apart.

Doña María on Machismo, the Family, Abortion and Divorce

DJ: You speak of respect of the bosses for the worker but what about respect between workers, between men and women, did men respect women?

DM: No, there was always the domination of the men, but we used to make ourselves respected. Now, of course, in politics it's very difficult. In fact in politics you could say that the woman is completely dominated. Don't we see that on a list of candidates there are twenty men and one woman?

DJ: Among Peronist compañeros was it difficult to make yourself respected?

DM: They respected me a lot. I was loved by my compañeros.

DJ: Thinking of my experience in England, even with union militants, the men, it could take a lot for them to take a woman militant seriously.

DM: No. On the contrary, I was accepted to such an extent that shop stewards came to ask me questions to clear up problems. For example: "María, what do you think, there is a worker who did such and such, what should I do, shall I take action, because he arrived late and every time he comes he gets mad"; "now leave it alone, at work you don't argue, later outside tell him to come to the union and we'll all talk about it" . . . No, I got on fine, they liked me a lot, I have no complaints.

DJ: What about the machismo you just spoke of?

DM: Well, but that's more to do with the political side now. For example, recently we were at a meeting and someone says that señora Roldán has the ability and power of making speeches to merit a deputy or senator's seat, not to be wasted here among us. It's a luxury for us to have señora Roldán here among us. And I know that it didn't please some men there. The man is always the man. I have no unwarranted ambitions. At this stage of my life, I don't want anything, Daniel, I swear it from the bottom of my heart. At times I do a little politics to ward off boredom and because I carry a Perón here, I loved Perón very much, when Perón died I almost died, I cried so much.

DJ: Do you think that your husband was a little exceptional in terms of the normal behavior of men of that era in that he was really understanding, there seems to have been a really equal relationship between you two? Normally, a woman who worked still had to deal with the fact that the man of the house expected her to make the dinner at night.

DM: But these are trifles, not things to be taken seriously. How can I explain it? In that time you made a bife, a salad, a glass of milk for the kids. I think that every man who took his wife to the gate of the frigorífico to ask for work, and if they gave her work and she too brought home a wage packet every fortnight, that man has to lend a hand too, they have to go fifty-fifty because the wife should not have to work in the frigorífico and do all the housework too.

DJ: I agree, but the question is whether the typical, average man . . .

DM: There might have been some cases, but the cases that I know, of the women in my section, no. On the contrary, all the husbands pitched in: "Vieja, what are we going to eat tonight? What shall I do?" "Well," the wife says, in haste because the foreman is always looking, "peel some potatoes, an onion, get some wine, some bread, ah and some milk for the kids." So the man would have done the chores and when the wife got home there would be a meal on the table. So there was cooperation. It was easy. I think that every woman who goes out to bring a peso back home wants this. Because the woman has been born to be at home with her children, to raise them, take care of the home, clean the house, but now the woman works a lot, 70 percent of women go outside the home to help their husbands, and I'm talking about all walks not only meatpackers.

DM: . . . . and one thinks of divorce, there comes a moment in a relationship when divorce threatens, and the children end up in the hands of the juez de menores because the husband struggles to keep his kids, the mother fights for them. I can get divorced at any time from my husband, fine, my husband can divorce me, fine. And the children? The problem is always the children.

DJ: You are against abortion as well?

DM: Yes.

DJ: In England and the United States it's struck me that in the past abortion was common in the working class, the only difference was that people with money could pay for a hospital and the working class woman had to do it in a shack, all hidden.

DM: Yes, and with the danger of infection and death. It seems to me that as science has even reached the poorest shack, the condom can reach there too and prevent the child being conceived.

DJ: In Berisso in the 1940s were there abortions among your work-mates?

DM: Here, all the doctors in Berisso have been abortionists, almost all the doctors, and the midwives, and there have been deaths of young women as well. I've had work mates, pobrecitas, who wanted to end a pregnancy so that they could keep working, or a man abandoned them pregnant, and if you reach three months you can't get rid of it, so they had abortions. That meant asking for help, money,

collecting it from the compañeras because I'm going to the midwife and get rid of it, I can't have a child, I'm single, how can I keep
working, how can I help my mother, who will take care of it after
it's born? Of course, it was understandable.

DJ: In England and the United States it was common for married
women who wanted to keep working and who already had three
or four children . . .

DM: That seems very reasonable to me, when the woman already has
children, to keep on having them and having them. Of course the
problem is that sexual education is not organized, the man and the
woman, so the woman becomes pregnant at any time, but there's
no reason for it. Of course, it's difficult to talk about, it's very deli-
cate because it isn't legal to do these things. But when a person im-
plores you to help in such a difficult moment, you help, because
they would do it one way or another, there was always some doctor,
some midwife, or even a quack who would lend themselves for this,
so on pay day nobody refused to contribute a peso. You would do it
for all your friends or compañeras. It was very dangerous. There was
a woman in Ensenada who was left pregnant by the boss himself, a
very rich man, and she a poor girl, very pretty, and he had promised
to marry her, and the pregnancy went on and on and when they
did the abortion they damaged her and she died of a hemorrhage.
But as she was a poor girl, one of those innocents who come from
the north, who believe that because they gave themselves to a man
the man is going to marry them for the sake of the baby, nobody
said anything. Of course, it's forbidden by law, it was always forbidden, but it's done, it's done everyday and every night in all parts of
the world.

I think that in many homes this has changed. I know of many
homes in Berisso that stayed at two children, and they didn't have
more.

Doña María on War and Peace

This is something that I wrote the other night. I'll read it to you.

We are in a world full of armaments, a world full of hate in which arms rule the day. Love died a long time ago. Disarmament means above all to root out hate from the human heart, from the heart of the people so that love has a space. Love. Here is a word, a theme that is superhuman in a world full of egoism, where a few have everything and others have nothing. This is a world where they put up walls to separate people because love is for them an empty notion, an enterprise with no future when one lives on the basis of greed and egoism, when one's conscience is silenced with inflated words deriving from some crumbs that have fallen from the table of the powerful for the needy and the poor to gather up.

If only we could destroy our atomic weapons, destroy the insults and lies, the self-interest and hatred of man. If only we could bring hope to the hearts of thousands of people who have lost their loved ones, their work, or who are going through a period of personal crisis. If only we could have decent housing for families who live on top of one another, for the mothers who have neither food nor a roof for their children. This is the message of Jesus that has not yet reached the powerful, who have carpeted their palaces with all the conveniences. We the poor know that despite this they feel themselves to be prisoners of a world without meaning, in a world that they themselves have built and that cannot lead to a respect for the pain of those who suffer.

Men and women of our time, especially those with money, are full of compassion, but we need to ask them how they behave toward their father and mother. They speak of them a lot, but they do not speak with them. They complain about their illnesses, their antiquated opinions, their pensions, the cost of their health care, but they don't think about the effort their parents put into raising them. For many children their parents are strangers, or even enemies. They treat them like beings who no longer serve for anything, who are already played out. But we know that he who forgets his parents is stamped forever with the stigma of ingratitude. The fact that they can no longer work means that they deserve the respect first of their children and of all young people and then of all humanity. Or have young people died of cold from within?

We must combat this society, we must change these structures, but the fact is that society is made up of people, and the structures are in the end made by people. We know that there are thousands of elderly separated from their homes, many die of hunger, and there are millions of people who have no roof over their head and no bread. We know that there is hunger, horror, pain, and war. We know that there is ignorance, sickness and misery, catastrophe and fear. We know that we are frightened to sweep hunger from the planet, but if we all work together and demand the security of nations and unite for disarmament, we can abolish hunger. As a start the peoples of the rich countries and the wealthy leaders have to open their hearts and concern themselves more for humanity and less about interplanetary travel. While people die of hunger it will be as if there is an open wound from which blood and tears are pouring.

We want the arms race and the atomic race to stop. We want scientists to work for humanity and not for war, to work for peace, to cure incurable diseases. The whole world is demanding peace, love, and work. Let us remember the pain of the explosions in Hiroshima, where children are still born with defects. We demand an end to this in the name of children and the elderly and in the name of the whole of humanity. We ask that these owners of other people's lives think again because there is a power greater than theirs, and that power belongs to Jesus. Let them rethink their ways because they are going to pay for all this evil just as these pirates of exploitation and owners of the dollar will have to pay.

Doña María, the Peronist Left, and the Meaning of Peronism

DJ: I'd like to go back to something we talked about a while ago. Being a Peronist of the "old stripe," *el peronismo original,* how did you react to the youngsters who seemed to take over the movement in the 1970s? Did you feel bothered, offended by these youngsters who were so loud and aggressive?

DM: Well, in a way, yes. Because in my mind it isn't with a bombo [big bass drum] and shouting in the streets that a nation progresses. A nation progresses when you get up every morning at dawn and go to a frigorífico to work. To move a nation forward is to get up at dawn, put on a leather jacket, and open up the heart of the soil and sow wheat. To help a nation to advance is to study in a laboratory and cure a disease.

I knew many of those kids who were Montoneros. They would come to meetings where I was talking and shout, "Si Evita viviera seria montonera" [If Evita were alive she would be a Montonera]. At that time in the years of Perón's return I spoke at a lot of meetings in Berisso and La Plata, and there were always Montoneros there.

DJ: How would you respond to them?

DM: I would ask them to be silent, tell them that I was speaking of justicialism, that they should calm down. But all those kids were crazy, what with the bombo beating away. I would try and speak to them with respect, with calm, as a mature woman who had been down the torturous paths of politics. Basically, I told them that with love of the patria, love of the family one can go very far, but with accusations, insults, bombs, and threats you could go nowhere. They would stand in the meetings with a banner and chant, "Si Evita viviera, seria montonera." It was like a dirge. We knew that Perón had had trouble with the Montoneros, everyone knows that. They spoke of the *patria socialista,* and Perón spoke of the *patria peronista.* They weren't bad kids, but from time to time they made bombs, and you know where that can lead to if it isn't brought under control. Once we went, a group of Peronist women who had formed a sort of *unidad básica* in Evita's name, to speak at a Peronist local in Berisso. There was a sort of counter and a curtain, and the kids innocently lifted up the curtain. It was full of bottles with liquid to make bombs. So one of our group said, "Señoras, take your children by the hand and let's go because we can't stay here." And this was a Peronist local. The leader of this local was later killed by the army in the north of Argentina. They killed him. He was very tough. In fact, many of the youngsters who were Montoneros in Berisso later fled to the countryside. There are two kids on this street who were mixed up in that all their lives; they were on the run until Alfonsín came in. Their mother had no idea where they were. Many were taken by the *milicos* [military], others escaped. It was a "save yourself if you can" situation.

Thinking about it now, I think that it represented a tremendous grief for the Argentine family, for Berisso, for the mothers, and for themselves. Many of those kids were still in secondary school, many were in universities. They could have had decent careers, but they were unfortunately drawn into all of that. I saw it almost happen in this house, with my grandsons Eduardo and Guillermo. A boy called Karabousian who lives one street down, Carlitos Karabousian, who is now in Sweden, came over, and they were drinking maté. I picked up a shopping bag and was going to go to the store, and I see a suitcase outside the door with a load of bottles and strange things. So I went back in and said, "Carlitos, that suitcase outside, is it yours?" "Yes, Doña María," he says. "If you would be so good as to leave the house, take your suitcase and go." Because I understood what was going on, I read the labels on the bottles and packets. Carlitos was one of those who blew up the Mercado Total in La Plata. There were three of them, a girl of fourteen and another boy. He asked me why I was throwing him out and I said, "Because that which you have in your suitcase, and which is in the doorway to my house, compromises me and my grandsons." I said to Eduardo, "What that boy has there is to make bombs with." And in fact within a short time they came looking for him. He managed to escape across the roofs. The next things the parents hear from him he is in Brazil. From there he went to Sweden, married and is still there. He had been making bombs in his father's shed. He had told him not to go in there, that he had secret things in there. The milicos beat up the father, the daughter, they made her swallow her own teeth; it was so bad to make her tell them where her brother was, but she said she didn't know. I don't know if he wanted to teach my grandsons to make bombs. But thanks to God and to music I was able to save them.

That was a formative experience for many of them. Many of the youth who experienced that gave up on politics after that. Nowadays politics is dominated by the ambitious and the incompetent, the really capable stay at home.

DJ: That's what I meant by them being a lost generation.

DM: They felt offended by Perón when he threw them out of the Plaza de Mayo in 1974. They couldn't understand that it was a very difficult moment in national life and that they had to give up on the bombs. Youth doesn't want to understand that rebellion, the suffering caused by putting a bomb under someone's bed, they don't want to think that that violence shouldn't exist. What should exist is love, faith, hope, the desire to forge ahead.

DJ: I suppose their response was to say that in order to combat a violent society they had to use violence.

DM: But we have many examples in the world that show us that when violence confronts violence wars occur. And what do wars bring for humanity? And we shouldn't forget that in all those confrontations where people die, they all have a mother, brothers, children. I know kids now who are friends, who love me, grandma this, abuela that, Doña María the other, and I know that they are Montoneros, or were, and I know that they are right.

DJ: In what way?

DM: Well, in the sense that they felt obliged to take up a weapon to defend themselves. But I still say that this leads nowhere in the end.

DJ: But in some way you sympathized with their motives?

DM: Well, they are the citizens of tomorrow, we must think of how we can regenerate them so that they can serve the needs of the nation.

DJ: When you were speaking just now I thought that really there isn't that much difference between that slogan, the patria socialista, and the ideas that you espoused, it's perhaps more a play on words.

DM: There are differences. People like me, who really love politics as a process of emancipation of peoples, are different. Because politics is necessary the world over. If it weren't for politics, dictatorships would exist. No, it's good that parties fight one another in congress and a law emerges. That's politics. Politics isn't dirty, it's men who make it dirty. Politics is a necessity of nations. I think that the younger people understand this, but at times being young and impatient they think that going directly and physically removing someone in their way they will advance their cause, but no, they go back, crime is never democracy.

DJ: I remember asking people at that time what they meant by the patria socialista, and they said, more social justice for the poor.

DM: But isn't that what we Peronists always demanded?

DJ: Exactly, that's why I suggested that this struggle between the patria socialista and the patria peronista was in some way a play on words. I'm not sure there were that many differences.

DM: One moment, please! Not so much of this play on words business. . . . they were armed up to here, they were protected, they had a whole secret apparatus. So there were differences. I as a Peronist didn't have any of that. You would not find so much as a carving knife on the table of most ordinary Peronists.

We are not the saviors of Argentine politics, but we are a great political party that originated in the emancipation of one man, a man who continues to be our leader. For us he didn't die; on the contrary, he's more alive than ever. There are every day more Peronists. When we try and ask ourselves why, we turn back on our own history and end up time and again at 17 October. What were we on 17 October? Slaves, and nothing more than slaves. What are we now? You've just seen the receipts for my pension. Have we become more dignified or not? Within the overall bad situation that we suffer, of course. But I think that the whole world is in a bad way.

As workers, as people who struggle we can't belong to the right. By definition we have to be on the left, but not the extreme left. That isn't a play on words. Let's be clear about what we are talking.

DJ: All right, let's say that you don't so much criticize the goals of those lads who shouted "la patria socialista." You are critical of the methods they chose to attain those ideals.

DM: Let's hope that one day, one fine day, when I won't exist any more, socialism will reign triumphant throughout the world. No more radicalism, laborismo, conservatism, or Peronism. Let socialism reign. God willing. Because socialism has a founding charter that anyone who has read it knows they were talking with Jesus as they read it. And if this comes to pass, it is what humanity needs. More work, more bread, more peace and quiet.

DJ: And this is socialism for you?

DM: Yes, sir! A world where scientists don't study for war, they study for peace, because of every five scientists four work for war and one for humanity. As my father used to say many times to me, "Let's hope that we all get to be socialists."

DJ: What would this socialism be?

DM: Equality. Not equality in the sense that if you have estancias and thousands of cattle you are going to be the same as María Roldán, who has a shack to lay her head in. But equality in the chances of life, equality of treatment when you get ill. Dignity. I worked for almost twenty years at the racetrack, and I have seen much suffering in my life, and I've seen the arrogance of the rich, the evil way they treat the poor and the unfortunate. And socialism will not permit this. You can keep so much from your estancias, the rest is to help the poor, the invalids, the insane, that is socialism. Equality in the conditions of life at least, so that a single mother has the right to have a family and nurse her child and is not forced to give it up, the child of her love. God grant that socialism comes. But, I insist, one thing is to say the *patria socialista,* another is to prepare bombs. Wishing for socialism to come and preparing bombs are two totally different things. We consider ourselves by definition to be a revolutionary movement. The seventeenth of October was a peaceful revolution, the taking of the Argentine Bastille, but that's something very different from putting bombs everywhere, walking through the streets with the Peronist flag shouting "la patria socialista." Socialism as a word is almost blessed by God, we all suffer the same pain, we all have the same desires. So what I'm criticizing is the attitude of these young people in certain moments of insisting on the slogan "la patria socialista."

That's the distinction we always made in our meetings. We were with the boys when they spoke of a political socialism, not when they advocated the patria socialista. Because they had to understand that that could lead to a situation of war. If we are a hundred years with our eyes watching out against capital, struggling so that capital respects us, they will also be waiting a hundred years to step on our necks and oppress us. My father used to say to me, I have always carried it in my mind, that there are two parties in the world, María, no more than two. And I would say, but how are there only two, Papa, as I devoured the papers and saw that there were thousands of parties of all sorts. "No," he would say, "there are just two, capital and labor," and for that reason I speak of socialism. Let us pray that God helps us, and, at least in Latin America, socialism may come and put an end to these useless parties.

III

INTERPRETIVE ESSAYS

I

LISTENING IN THE COLD

The Practice of Oral History in an Argentine Meatpacking Community

The trick is not to get yourself into some inner correspondence of spirit with your informants. Preferring like the rest of us to call their souls their own, they are not going to be altogether keen about such an effort anyhow. The trick is to figure out what the devil they think they are up to. — Clifford Geertz, *Local Knowledge: Further Essays in Interpretive Anthropology*

I believe that we can promise to tell the truth, I believe in the transparency of language, and in the existence of the complete subject who expresses himself through it. . . . but of course I also believe the contrary. . . . "In the field of the subject there is no referent." . . . we indeed know all this. . . . we are not so dumb, but once this precaution has been taken, we go on as if we did not know it. Telling the truth about the self, constituting the self as a complete subject — it is a fantasy. In spite of the fact that autobiography is impossible, this in no way prevents it from existing. — Philippe Lejeune, *On Autobiography*

I first met Doña María Roldán in August 1985 in the house of Cipriano Reyes. I was beginning to study the origins of Peronist unionism in Berisso and had made Reyes's acquaintance. He had introduced me to several of his old union and "laborista" colleagues, and

Shell of the Swift meatpacking plant seen across the roofs of the conventillos of the calle Nueva York, Berisso, 1996. *Courtesy Norberto Gullari.*

one day he announced we would be meeting the "first female shop steward" in the Swift plant, and someone who had played an important part in the emergence of the union in Berisso. The meeting in Reyes's front room was a little formal. Doña María evidently had been told about the English professor who was researching the old days of Berisso's golden past, the emergence of the meatpacking union, the mobilization of 17 October 1945, the formation of the Partido Laborista, and, of course, the role of Cipriano Reyes. Although I don't think that there had been any formal prior arrangement of an appropriate script, it was clear that during our meeting Reyes, as he was in other similar meetings, was very much the master of ceremonies, and Doña María willingly, and convincingly, played her role. The meeting lasted perhaps forty minutes, and I filed it away as an interesting encounter, and I filed Doña María away, too, as a potential future source of information on Berisso's social and labor history.

I next met her eighteen months later when I returned to do a

more prolonged stretch of research and began to seek out informants who could provide me with oral testimonies about Berisso's
past, in particular its labor history and the history of work in the
meatpacking plants. Although she had clearly kept to Reyes's script
in our previous meeting, I had been impressed with her articulate-
ness and apparently well-tuned memory. The fact that she had been
among the first group of shop floor representatives in Swift drew
me to her. She had been an active participant in the struggles of
the 1940s, a militant in both the union and the Partido Laborista.
I first went to her house in Berisso in January 1987, with the aim
principally of obtaining from her empirical information that I was
missing in my attempt to reconstruct the unionization drive within
the plants. There was also a hope on my part that I would emerge
with the difficult to define but always sought-after commodity—a
"feeling" for the period by way of some appropriate anecdotes Doña
María might be able to recall for me. I assumed that our conversation, which I intended to record, would last a few hours. As it turned
out, I ended up recording some thirty hours of interview over a
nine-month period, visiting her house on average once a week to
tape conversations, though I was frequently there more often.

One reason for the change in my intentions was clearly the self-
evident one that I found Doña María's testimony of great interest.
Yet this was not primarily for the reasons I had initially intended to
interview her. The testimony, which came to over six hundred pages
of typed script, is a rich, multilayered, often puzzling narrative. It
does contain passages that add considerably to an understanding of
many basic issues that I wished to document and understand better.
Doña María's account, for example, of the difficulties encountered
by the activists during the unionization drive of 1944–45, or her
recounting of her experiences, and those of other women in her
section, of the Taylorist system of work organization, the "Standard," adds considerably to our objective knowledge of these issues.
Indeed, the collection of oral testimony can be of enormous help
in constructing the history of a working-class community such as
Berisso.

On the one hand, oral history can provide access to basic empirical information unobtainable from more traditional sources, such as

newspapers, municipal archives, and company records. In Berisso, for example, knowledge of the early history of the union movement in the packing plants is difficult to obtain from sources such as union newspapers for the simple reason that until the 1940s there was no such thing. It is only in the 1940s that a union newspaper appears with any regularity. Many of the sources traditionally used for historical research in working-class communities are, therefore, not available in the case of Berisso.

It would scarcely seem necessary at this juncture to argue that oral history can offer important access to areas of historical knowledge. The debate on objectivity and empirical validity with its explicit privileging of the written document can no longer be sustained on the old terms. The shifting in the terms of the debate can be traced in the difference between a book such as Paul Thompson's *The Voice of the Past,* with its essentially defensive posture concerning issues such as objectivity, the failings of memory and representativity, and a text such as *The Myths We Live By,* published a decade later and edited by Thompson and Raphael Samuel with its explicit celebration of the unique status of the knowledge generated by oral sources.[1]

Oral sources can also take us beyond the limits of existing empirical data. Although we do know a considerable amount about the implementation of rationalization schemes within the plants from sources such as company archives, how the workers felt about these changes is far more difficult to deduce from this sort of material. Doña María's account addresses the issue of how these schemes were experienced and handled by historical actors. Oral testimony speaks far more directly to this domain of working-class experience. The usefulness of oral testimony goes, of course, beyond the working environment. We have, for example, the casual mention in conversation that it would be unthinkable in the Berisso of the 1920s, 1930s, and 1940s for a man to go out socially on a Saturday night without packing his revolver. It was simply part of his dress — a normative accompaniment. This opens up a social and cultural universe largely beyond the realm of official statistics. Where such statistics do surface in sources such as newspapers and police and judicial archives they refer to basic indices of criminality; or perhaps more precisely to those occasions when violence occurred. The oral statement, however, when contextualized, speaks to a far more mundane, taken-for-granted level of experience. In a related vein, the use of perfect, Oxford-intonated BBC English by Don Rodolfo Caride when I started to ask him questions—an English acquired entirely on the job from his English bosses in the time and motion department of the Swift plant—bespoke a world of deference and paternalism, cultural power and symbolic violence.

In the case of Doña María's narrative it became increasingly clear to me as we talked that although her testimony was a rich potential source of empirical information, it was both limited in this sense and also involved something else besides. The limits were, of course, partly to do with the problem of memory, its limits, its failing, and its distortions. The issue of memory will certainly be a focal point of the chapters that follow. But what of the "something else" that I intuited as being involved in Doña María's narrative? One reason for the problems, the limits confronted in using this narrative primarily as a source of empirical knowledge, is that it involves a largely passive role for Doña María, as simply a repository of more or less coherent, more or less available, historical data. Yet it was clear to me before long that even in response to my most "factual," "information-seeking" questions Doña María was narrating, telling me a story about her life, reconstructing her past in a selective way that would both legitimize it to me and make sense of it to herself.

Contemporary oral history now rarely invokes the kind of claim to having privileged access to hitherto ignored historical facts and experience based on the practice of a sort of "naive realism." Influenced by trends in literary criticism that emphasize the importance of narrative and the construction of texts—and that have tended by extension to see historical reality as another text—oral historians are increasingly aware of the limits of oral testimony as a source for expanding our stock of historical facts about the recent past. The form of oral narrative is often taken now to be as significant as the content.

Increasingly, oral historians such as Luisa Passerini, Ronald Grele, and Alessandro Portelli have begun to challenge us to treat the subjective, textual quality of oral testimony as unique opportunities rather than the obstacles to historical objectivity and empirical rigor they had seemed to an earlier generation of practitioners.[2] As the editors of *The Myths We Live By* contend: "At the same time the individuality of each life story ceases to be an awkward impediment to generalization, and becomes instead a vital document of the construction of consciousness."[3] Portelli is equally forthright. At the start of one of his essays he offers both a concession and an affirmation: "The oral sources used in this essay are not always fully reliable in point of fact. Rather than being a weakness, this is, however, their strength: errors, inventions and myths lead us through and beyond facts to their meanings."[4] In particular, oral testimony enables us to approach the issue of agency and subjectivity in history.

Yet once more we must beware of falling back on the assumptions of a naive realism, of presupposing a mimetic quality in oral narratives as they express consciousness and feeling. For the issue of using oral narratives to gain access to the domain of consciousness, of "lived experience," is one of the issues complicated by an attention to oral testimony as narrative. If oral testimony is indeed a window onto the subjective in history—the cultural, social, and ideological universe of historical actors—then it must be said that the view it affords is not a transparent one that simply reflects thoughts, feelings as they really were/are. At the very least the image is bent, the glass of the window unclear.

Thus the relationship between personal narratives and history—as indeed between autobiography in general and history—is complex and problematic. Life stories are cultural constructs that draw on a public discourse structured by class and gender conventions. They also make use of a wide spectrum of possible roles, self-representations, and available narratives. As such, we have to learn to read these stories and the symbols and logic embedded in them if we are to attend to their deeper meaning and do justice to the complexity found in the lives and historical experiences of those who recount them.

We also need to be aware of the tension that exists between the notion of oral testimony as an empirical information-gathering tool and the notion of the oral interview as the production of a joint narrative produced by the interviewer and the interviewed. The text produced by this "conversational narrative" is not only structured by cultural conventions. It is also an essentially social construction, permeated by the interchange between the interviewer and her subject, and also permeated by other communal and national narratives. In addition, it has a profoundly ideological character.[5] If literary criticism has been instrumental in fostering a growing sensitivity of oral historians to the narrative qualities of the texts they study, we must also credit the influence of postmodernist anthropology for emphasizing the complex authority relations involved in the production of an oral text. The authorial shaping of ethnographic narratives and the attendant textual and rhetorical devices used to construct an apparently objective and authoritative account of another's life and society have now been firmly placed on the agenda, and oral historians ignore such warnings at their peril.[6]

The tension implicit in the production of this conversational text can indeed call into question the entire basis of the oral history project. The pitfalls attendant on this situation are partly epistemological in that they deeply affect the status of even the "hard" empirical evidence garnered from such interviews, signaling as they do the existence of subtexts and silences, evasions and tropes, used to filter, to resist, to deal with, and to confess. A too literal "realist" reading of the "evidence" produced in these narratives can be both blind and deaf to the nuance implied in such strategies. Partly, too, the pitfalls involve a more personal domain—they have to do with differences in expectations between the interviewer and interviewed, about the different status and prestige involved, the different allocations of cultural capital implied in interactions between young and old, formally educated and uneducated, foreign and native. Ultimately, too, the pitfalls speak to our ability, talent, willingness, and commitment to listen.

Many of the issues raised here are, as I have indicated, increasingly present in writings on oral history. Yet I was only dimly aware of most of them in 1987 when I began interviewing Doña María and others in Berisso. My awareness of the methodological and epistemological problems grew, as I confronted issues emerging from my own practice as an oral historian in Berisso. In this sense theory clearly followed practice, as I was forced to seek understanding of problems that were confronting me daily in my interactions with informants. But theory is not something that oral historians would seem to take to with much enthusiasm. Indeed, the directness of the genre, the apparently self-evident status of the communication and knowledge produced in oral history texts, has a powerfully doxic effect, compounding the traditional claims of orality to provide unmediated access to self-knowledge and knowledge of another. The best-known texts of the genre have largely eschewed conscious reflection on the conditions of their own production, a fact that both derives from, and helps sustain, the populist appeal of such works.[7]

Now, in the case of Latin America it is true that by the time I had embarked on my project in Berisso there was a growing body of work of potential relevance for oral historians. The field of *testimonio* studies was already booming. Centered primarily on the texts produced by Mexican and Central American women, these studies were to problematize fundamental issues of voice and agency, memory and silence, and the nature of subaltern cultural production.[8] Yet much of this critical production remained within the fields of literary criticism and romance studies, and to a lesser extent cultural anthropology. Despite a few prescient voices, very little of this had affected Latin Americanist historians. Whatever other borders were being crossed in these endeavors, the frontiers between disciplines still remained remarkably impermeable.[9] The announced era of blurred genres and joyous interdisciplinary miscegenation was to be largely confined to the safely ghettoized terrain of cultural studies.

A defining moment for me came halfway through my stay in Berisso in 1987. I am tempted to call it a sort of epiphany, though I am aware of the temptation to construct myths of origin, parables that help retroactively rationalize paths that ended up being followed. At the very least, however, I can truthfully say that the incident forcefully confronted me with the limits of a historian's commonsense pragmatism in dealing with, and understanding, certain crucial dilemmas with which I was faced. The incident occurred in the middle of winter and involved a long interview I did with a middle-aged Peronist militant. Doña María had mentioned him to me, as had other friends and contacts I had already made—

he was someone known for his militant past, he had been particularly active in the era known as the Peronist Resistance as a young,
firebrand leader in the Armour plant and a leading protagonist in
several crucial mass meetings of that era that had ended in gun-
fights and general mayhem. Although his family was of an impec-
cable Peronist lineage, there was also something, more alluded to
than explicitly spoken by my contacts and by Doña María, which
suggested that this was someone whose personal and family history
were beyond the normal. As I later learned, his father was famed
for stopping non-Peronists in the street and haranguing them, two
of his brothers had died in mysterious circumstances apparently related to their militancy, and he himself had been closely tied to a
Trotskyist group when he was active in the plants. After an initial
meeting over lunch he invited me to visit the following Saturday a
group of which he was a leading member called Centro de Adoctrinamiento Justicialista. Our lunchtime conversation had whetted
my appetite—he clearly had a lot to tell me about the Resistance
period and the internecine battles within Peronism in the post-1955
era, especially as they related to the meatpackers union. So I went.
The meeting was actually held over lunch on the site of a center
they were building from scratch with their own labor. Over a *bu-
seca*—a Genovese stew made of tripe—on a freezing day in the shell
of this building and in the presence of other associates of the center
he proceeded to give me a version of the history of the plants, his
role in it, and a general evaluation of the importance of Perón and
justicialism. It was a strange occasion, not least because I was freezing, eating something I didn't like, and because of the presence of
some Paraguayan laborers who were being paid to build the place.
During the meal some of them proceeded to get drunk, mostly at
the times when my host was being most eloquent about Perón—
this simply heightened an underlying tension that was really one
of status within the working class between the core group of affiliates and new migrants into Berisso who were still largely marginal
both geographically and socially within the community. After several hours of taping his monologue with the occasional Paraguayan
interruptions we parted with an agreement to meet the following
week at his house.

In reviewing later what had transpired I confirmed my initial impression that what I had got had been a particular story/narrative, a version of the past that had left out as much as it contained—it had been particularly evasive about the internal disputes. It seemed to me that the obvious reason had been the presence of an outsider and the desire not to wash dirty linen in public. At times indeed he had scarcely veiled his annoyance when I had pressed him for more details about disputes: he had said, "I don't know why you want to go back over that, I've already explained it." Yet he couldn't deny it altogether because he knew that I already had enough details—in fact, I had already interviewed one of the other protagonists. Also, he had to take into account the listening public. He was clearly the designated narrator of this group—by far its most articulate member, its intellectual core, guardian of its history, its official storyteller. And yet precisely because of his privileged status he was not free to invent, erase, elide at will. However much it may have seemed to me that I had listened to a monologue, what I had in fact witnessed was a dialogue between himself and his listeners/his public and, at a remove, with myself, the outsider. His story had to remain credible, and this credibility was rooted in several elements—among them notions of truth telling. As Henry Glassie asserts in his wonderful book *Passing the Time in Ballymenone,* both academic and local historians do much the same thing: "Whether they teach at Oxford or wheel turf in Ballymenone, historians get the facts as accurately as they can get them, but since the past has passed they cannot get all the facts, or get them all right."[10]

There was also some more profound referential pact between storyteller/local historian and the community and its needs, and this was something that went beyond my insight about his not wanting to wash dirty linen in public. The story he told me had to be based on the truth—but as in all effective storytelling, it also could be manipulated truth. Not at will, according to individual whim with arbitrary intent, but rather according to tacit, largely unspoken consensus between both audience and narrator about present needs, priorities, and imperatives. These were in turn arrived at through negotiation and concession with other alternative narratives within this community. As such, his annoyance with my desire to turn the

narrative back to the details of past divisions, to center his recollections on the internal fights and the sad chronicle of the decline of the meatpacking plants in Berisso, was rooted in a different appreciation of the uses of history and the stories in which it is
embodied. He wanted to use the story to draw wider conclusions
about the sources of community strength, about survival, about the
overcoming of differences, about the unifying power of Peronism
and the role of Perón in achieving that. My insistence on the aca-
demicist notion of "getting it right" of course threatened to open
old wounds, to expose the more unseemly underbelly of Peronist
unionism, but this was not the sole or even, I think, the main reason
for his evasions and omissions.

Much of what I have just said is the result of later reflection. At
the time I was convinced that with sufficient persistence I could
come up with the goods. As with any good ethnographer or oral
historian, effective questioning would track the beast of historical
objectivity, the facts, down to its layer. Evasion would be ultimately
useless. The informant could run, but faced with the array of devices
at my disposal—along with a basic assumption that I was smarter
than him—he could not ultimately hide. At the time I had not encountered postmodern anthropological speculations about the construction of ethnographic knowledge and authority. Later, as I re-
viewed the interview in the United States, I read James Clifford's
essay, "Power and Dialogue in Ethnography." There, I found the
following quote from Marcel Griault, drawn from his meditations
about the practice of ethnography in Africa:

> Active ethnography is the art of being a midwife and an examin-
> ing magistrate, by turns an affable comrade of the person put to
> cross-examination, a distant friend, a severe stranger, compassionate
> father, concerned patron, a trader paying for revelations one by one,
> a listener affecting distraction before the open gates of the most dan-
> gerous mysteries, an obliging friend showing lively interest for the
> most insipid family stories—the ethnographer parades across his face
> as pretty a collection of masks as that possessed by any museum.[11]

I was struck by how accurately this described what I had been
engaged with in Berisso. It would be nice to be able to report that

one of these masks had stood me in good stead in the interview at his home. In fact, the encounter, when it arrived, was both deeply disturbing and frustrating and also a humbling lesson in the pitfalls awaiting the overarrogant oral historian. When I attempted to take him back over the union story, he impatiently repeated the essence of his previous accounting. When I interrupted him to ask for clarification, he finally exploded: "You just want to get things from me, but you don't tell me anything about yourself, about what you think, about your ideas. What do you value? What do you think of Perón?" I was taken aback but sufficiently astute to realize that the fact-finding, inquisitorial mode that I had adopted was in danger of self-destructing. I had to try another tack if only to maintain any open channels of communication. I had to embark on the terrain that he wanted to explore—which I was slowly coming to realize was his principal interest in me and in our relationship. He was, in fact, challenging the entire premise of my activity, the power relationship I had taken for granted and which underlay my sense of myself as the author, the constructor, the editor of the historical knowledge that would come out of our encounter. He wanted some form of genuine dialogue and interchange, but also, more than that, he wanted this to be the basis of my listening to what he most wanted to say. And what he wanted to say certainly had to do with the larger-scale social history data I was bent on acquiring, but it was framed within a personal key and had to do with his place in that broader history, his sense of himself, the meaning of his life.

I would like to be able to say that with my slow coming to awareness of what was happening I was able to construct some new, more adequate "fable of rapport" and adopt a more appropriate mask. Unfortunately, the dialogue that followed was a fractured, deeply awkward encounter. He spoke of his life, of how he had attended college under Perón, how he had been involved in various drama groups, had written poetry, and of how all that had stopped with Perón's ouster, when access to education had been cut off and he had had to enter the plants. How he had been disoriented by Perón's overthrow, bitter about the changes in his life chances, hotheaded and hence drawn into non-Peronist left politics. How he had been blacklisted from the plants and during the 1960s had come to realize that he had been wrong, had been manipulated by the Trotskyists and had misjudged many of his former Peronist opponents. He had eventually sought reintegration into the movement, where he had become involved in something like cadre education, ending up in the early 1970s working for the Juventud Sindical Peronista—a union group closely tied with the Peronist right and José López Rega. He had also continued to be involved in drama and poetry as well as propagating official justicialist ideology. He had produced several pageants about Perón and Justicialism and their relationship with Christianity. At one stage he recited a long excerpt from his major prose poem on the theme.

By this time in the interview I realized that I had totally misjudged my informant and that I was very much out of my depth. The life story he was telling me was a complex story of disillusion, youthful error, and ultimately redemption all told in a tone of great emotionality. At many times he would seem on the verge of breaking down, his voice would crack and his eyes fill with tears as he spoke in Christian terms of forgiveness, love, and Perón and recite the Veinte Verdades (twenty truths) of Peronism.[12] Interwoven into this narrative were obviously elements of remorse and pain associated with the deaths of his brothers and the internecine warfare within Peronism in the 1960s and 1970s. It was clearly important for him to make me understand, to engage me in a discussion among equals about the intellectual underpinning of his life, about the moral choices he had made, about the Great Tradition (Peronism) that made sense of the Little Tradition (Berisso) in which he had lived out his life.[13]

The problem was that I was unable to adequately live up to my part of the implicit bargain being proposed here. Although I knew that my initial pretence of uncovering the sordid, if exciting, untold story of rank-and-file Peronism was no longer viable, I could not bring myself to enter fully into the new arrangement. I would like to be able to say that this was due to my refusal to embrace the bad faith involved in adopting a new mask. It wasn't. It was, I think now, a mixture of many things. In part, it was ideological wariness, especially as he spoke of his associations with the extreme right wing of Peronism. It was also due to intolerance and impatience on my part, a lack of sensitivity about his core beliefs—the Veinte Verdades and all they implied.

Something else also underlay my reluctance to engage with this man, and this was, I think, a profound sense of discomfort. It was in one sense a physical unease. The day was bitterly cold, the sort of winter cold that distinguishes Berisso from even La Plata, a scant eight miles away. It is a damp cold that comes straight off the estuary and is borne on the wind and which can penetrate you to the bone. His house was typical of many in Berisso constructed during the Peronist regime; it was made of concrete, with a cold slab floor and a single gas-fired space heater to give a sparse warmth. The interview started at dusk as the temperature was dropping. So I was cold, but this is hardly the entire explanation for my discomfort. I was used to Berisso's winter by this time; I had conducted other interviews in similar conditions. Indeed, Doña María's house was if anything colder. My physical discomfort was intensified by a sense of gloom that permeated the house and that had much to do with the presence of his wife, who was in the house but who played no part in the interview. There was a palpable tension between them; her body language, her gestures, and her glances spoke of resignation and resentment that I intuited had to do with the poverty of the household, evident in ancient furniture, the lack of paint on the walls, and the lack of food in the kitchen. I read in her presence an ironic comment on her husband's performance for the outsider. It was as if she were used to his claims and his emotions, as though she had resigned herself to the fact these would never translate into anything substantial in terms of some minimal comforts and basic hopes. Whether he was a Trotskyist or a Peronist, their lot would not change.

This sense of intruding on an intimate drama compounded what was an instinctive wariness on my part, a reluctance to empathize with the emotionalism with which he imbued his story and its telling. I felt like a voyeur and found the sensation deeply disturbing. He, of course, noticed my reserve, and the interview wound down. I have never returned to formally interview him. We meet on the street, exchange greetings, but my chance of access to whatever the deeper meanings of his story could be has gone, and with it even my chance of uncovering, through him, the key to the empirical information I had so craved at the start.

I am not sure that I learned any immediate lessons from the encounter I have just recounted. Its status as a morality tale has been largely constructed with hindsight. My interviews with Doña María continued, and although we had our good days and our bad days, nothing approaching this sort of breakdown ever occurred. My relationship with an elderly woman was, evidently, far more comfortable than that with a middle-aged man. I had established a degree of intimacy with her, I was welcomed by her family, and she had progressed from addressing me as "professor" to calling me Danielito. And yet the incident lingered in some semi-conscious way as something that I realized I would have to analyze sooner or later. When I did permit myself to think about it aloud—always in Buenos Aires, with friends, at a bar, never in Berisso—the simplest answer to the question why I had not been able to rescue the interviewer/interviewee relationship with him was to state the obvious: I had found his brand of religiously intense right-wing Peronism impossible to empathize with. But although this answer allowed me to bask in the genuine rapport that I had with Doña María, it could not hide the fact that the experience had raised issues that went beyond an extreme individual case of empathic failure between historian and informant. Beyond my distaste for his brand of politics were there not other, more general issues raised about the practice of oral history?

One that certainly occurred to me on later reflection had to do with the notion of truth telling, so powerfully raised by this incident. It is by now a commonplace of narratology that stories are not iconic renderings of actual sequences of events; all narration involves reconstituting events concerning a narrator's life or the history of the wider community.[14] And yet the criteria upon which such reconstituting takes place are scarcely arbitrary and are, it would seem, in the Western world overwhelmingly linked to requirements of truth and factuality. Although we can be open to other cultural possibilities, Henry Glassie's conclusions about the mandate to tell the truth among his Northern Irish local historians in Ballymenone would seem to hold in Berisso, too. After telling us that Oxford historians and their colleagues who wheel turf in Ballymenone do much the same thing, Glassie goes on to elaborate: "When they string facts into narratives, they will create something other than the factual past, if only by dint of omission, and the dynamics of presentation, but they do not do so to fool people but to help them by driving at a truth larger than that trapped in the factual scraps. . . . their joy is finding, holding, manipulating truth."[15] Whether the narrative was being performed in the Centro de Adoctrinamiento Justicialista or in Doña María's kitchen, my informants showed a similar respect for the truth.

And yet it seems that this is more complicated than Glassie would allow. For a start we must distinguish between the different levels of narration produced in the oral transcript. At one level, certainly, we could say that our subjects are able and willing to adopt the dominant narrative form of professional historical discourse, framing their narrative within the canons of expository narration.[16] In this sense they largely adopt a version of the formal political and historical discourse of their interviewers. The sources of such a discourse are multiple, ranging from formal school curricula to televised historical documentaries to historical narratives embedded in political traditions. Doña María would often move into such a mode, as she recounted crucial events in the history of Peronism or events that had happened in the union. Such a narrative was normally marked by a phrase such as "whether we like it or not, that's history and we can't ignore it."

On another level, we find that much of oral testimony consists of a far more informal conversational narrative, framed as personal experience stories, anecdotes, gossip. The two levels cannot be artificially separated. Indeed, the commonest way in which History is recalled is precisely in this minor key. As James Fentress and Chris Wickham argue: "No matter how keyed into historical culture one is, one's memories of major events—World War 2 for instance—can turn into simple exercises in day-to-day survival at home or at the front or sources of isolated anecdotes, whether terrifying, ter-

rible, amusing or life affirming."[17] Different types of memory—collective and individual—also correspond to these different levels. But
to these different levels of narration, and memory, we can apply different evaluative criteria concerning truth telling.

It is clearly important to try and verify the factual accuracy of
historical material found in oral interviews from other sources. Yet
I think that very often this, too, is largely an exercise in professional glorification on the part of the academic historian. We frequently know "the facts" better than our informants. And there is
a price to be paid for the aggressive interrogation of factual accuracy. As Glassie observes, "Dates alienate. They are a means to kill
the past and bury it in irrelevance."[18] Glassie's Northern Irish historians know this instinctively, though it is doubtful that their Oxford
colleagues would agree. Indeed, it is part of our role as historians,
our professional ideology, to enforce different criteria. My own pro-
pensity for aggressive intervention along these lines was evident
in the case I have just recounted. My search not just for dates but
for "historical information" in general led me to endanger the entire relationship. With Doña María, too, rereading the transcript
has brought home to me the frequency and insistence with which
I would interrupt her to insist on dating or on other forms of cate-
gorizing.

The damage done by such insistence can go much further than
burying the past in irrelevance. Ronald Grele has argued that there
is a fundamental tension in the oral history interview between narrative and analysis:

> If oral history is a conversational narrative this conversation often
> takes place in opposition to the power of the narrative. . . . while
> we destroy narrative as such the interviewed rapidly try to reestab-
> lish it. . . . the role of the interviewer is crucial but we fulfill it by
> adding details, forcing memory to its limits, destroying its very nar-
> rative capacity. We don't treat it like a story that keeps developing
> and that carries us along, rather we treat it like an object of analysis
> and deconstruction.[19]

If we add to this the fact that there are frequently great discrepan-
cies of cultural and social capital involved, too, in the social field

within which the interview is structured, then we can appreciate the very real potential for symbolic violence that could result from the insistence on the professional ideology of the historian.[20]

If the rigid application of criteria central to the professional ideology of historians has serious implications for the knowledge produced at this level of narrative discourse, its impact at the level of conversational discourse is even more problematical. Perhaps a comparison of oral history and autobiography can help us appreciate this issue. Philippe Lejeune in his analysis of autobiography as a genre emphasizes the importance for autobiography of what he calls the referential pact, the commitment on the part of the teller to "tell the truth, the whole truth and nothing but the truth" about her life. It is this that marks autobiography as a referential text exactly like scientific and historical discourse and that distinguishes it from fiction. The oath that underlies the autobiographer's pact is along the lines of "telling the truth as it appears to me, in as much as I can know it, making allowances for lapses of memory, errors, involuntary distortions etc."[21] Yet there is, according to Lejeune, a fundamental difference between the pact of the historian or journalist and that which underwrites autobiography: "In autobiography it is essential that the referential pact be *drawn up,* and that it be *kept;* but it is not necessary that the result be of the order of strict resemblance. The autobiographical pact can be, according to the criteria of the reader, badly kept without the referential value of the text disappearing (on the contrary)—this is not the case for historical and journalistic texts" (22–23). I would only add that on the contrary it *is* the case for oral history texts, or at least those predominantly framed within conversational narrative discourse. What test of verification could we possibly think of applying to the subjective experience recalled at this level? As Lejeune notes, "Autobiography tells us precisely, here is the advantage of its narrative, what it alone can tell us" (22). We are not talking about criteria of resemblance measured against an externally verifiable referent. The referential pact associated with the oral history text is likely to be, as with autobiography, premised on notions of fidelity to meaning rather than to criteria of strict accuracy associated with information.

We could perhaps also think of the distinction I am making in terms of the growing body of work on life story as a fundamental sociocultural practice focused on the narrative shaping of personal experience. In contrast to the more traditional model of life history "focused mainly on diachronic change within anthropology's traditional paradigm of naturalism or realism," life-story research "focuses on the cultural scripts and narrative devices individuals use to make sense of experience. [It] emphasizes the truth of the telling versus telling the truth."[22] Charlotte Linde, one of its foremost theorists, has defined the life story as consisting "of all the stories and associated discourse units, such as explanations and chronicles, and the connections between them, told by an individual in his/her lifetime."[23] This clearly directs us, once more, toward oral sources as narrative and the appropriate analytical procedures needed to interpret them. (This will be the central concern of chapter 2.)

Oral history texts are made up in varying degrees of both of these models, and each requires its own careful listening, the careful application of criteria of evaluation concerning truth and accuracy. Informants themselves are frequently aware of the distinction and the different expectations this generates are part of the, often implicit, bargaining that goes on within any interview situation. The abrupt interjection that transformed and ultimately unraveled my relationship in the cold house in Berisso was, I think, in large part occasioned by my informant's sense that I had failed to recognize such distinctions. He had told me the "true" history of Berisso, the union and his role in it in the public setting of the Centro de Adoctrinamiento Justicialista. Now, in his home, he expected that his life story would elicit another sort of attention and judgment on my part.

The issue of truth telling in oral testimony is, then, intimately related to the question of the nature of the relationship between the oral historian and her subject and the status of the knowledge produced by that relationship. Despite the rapport that existed between myself and Doña María, was the basic drive of what I was attempting to do with her all that different from what I had attempted to do, but failed, with my male informant? Despite the lesson that this parable told about the pitfalls awaiting the overly arrogant oral historian, the basic metaphor that informed my approach continued to be that of the detective uncovering secrets, breaking codes, tracking down beyond the grave the hidden meanings of Doña María's life. The following chapters stand as testimony to that enduring passion, which is in some fundamental way basic to the analytical function of historical discourse. It is simply what historians do. But what are the presuppositions of this approach and the strategy of representation associated with it?

In the first place it seems important to recognize what is going on when the oral historian produces a text that claims to speak about, and for, another. To bridge the gap between two radically heterogeneous fields of experience, between the historian and the other, between myself and Doña María, is to engage in what Alberto Moreiras has called prosopopeic representation. In an essay on testimonio autobiography Moreiras defines prosopopeia as "a mask through which one's own voice is projected onto another, where that other is always suffering from a certain inability to speak." As Moreiras goes on to argue, "The relational mediation is then always unequal and hierarchical, even at its most redemptive." [24] This would seem to be an unavoidable truth that no claims to empathic identification on the part of ethnographer or oral historian can fully offset. In recent times the figure of the "redemptive ethnographer" giving voice to the oppressed other in a process of reciprocal text production has appeared in various guises. Certainly, oral history's fundamental claim to distinguish itself by giving a voice to the voiceless, to those who do not enter the dominant narrative of history, shares this redemptive urge.

An implicit part of this trope is also the claim to a sort of "horizontal affinity" between the two sides engaged in the ethnographic relationship.[25] I personally find it hard to imagine such a claim of affinity between myself and Doña María. Clearly it could not have a gender basis. I could, perhaps, claim a class-based affinity. My parents were workers, both from mining communities. I grew up in a household permeated by a union and left-wing culture. I was frequently struck by parallels between Doña María and my mother. But I have spent my adult life moving ever further away from those roots, and the cultural alienation of social mobility has done its work. I admired Doña María and felt a deep affection and respect for her, but this falls far short of the sort of emotional fusion through which a self is apparently projected onto an alter ego. Whatever the innate attraction of the "passion to swim in the stream of their (the native's) experience" may be, this is, as Clifford Geertz warns us, ultimately an illusion.[26]

It may, of course, be a necessary and productive illusion, a powerful heuristic weapon. In an extraordinary scene from the documentary film *Number Our Days,* in which she speaks of her work among the elderly members of a Jewish cultural center in Venice, California, the anthropologist Barbara Myerhoff speaks of her move away from research on the Huichol Indians of Northern Mexico to the study of elderly Jews by explaining that "after all I will never be a Huichol Indian, but I will be a little old Jewish lady." It was very probably this conviction that enabled her to produce the profound ethnographic representations embodied in the book of the same title. At the very least this gesture may provide the basis for an effective "hermeneutics of solidarity," which is certainly preferable to the objectivizing appropriation of much traditional analysis. It may be, too, that there are reasons to question the overemphasis on the dire consequences of the hierarchical and unequal character of prosopopeic representation. Although we might agree that at a level of abstraction this is unavoidable, at the concrete level of the interview situation we may find countervailing tendencies.

One presupposition of the pathos of pessimism that informs much postmodernist ethnographic speculation concerning representation is the figure of the interviewee/informant as victim whose memory and identity are appropriated and exploited. I would suggest that this seriously underestimates the power of the interviewee to negotiate the conditions under which communication takes place in the interview situation. Let me give an example. Very early in our interviews Doña María and I had the following exchange:

DJ: How did the strike of ninety-six days come about?

DM: Because this woman, this one, that one all said to themselves. . . . Me, for instance, who taught me? The book of life, not the university, pardon me, professor, the university is the best that humanity has because there you learn and the shadows of the mind disappear and wisdom emerges but you know that the university of life is beautiful. When I put my children to bed at night many times with only a warm tea and a piece of bread and then cried and wet the pillow and my husband would say to me, this will get better, don't cry, that's where I learned. . . . pain taught me to free myself.

In the months that followed she frequently repeated this claim. We could interpret this in several ways. It is certainly a claim to establish footing, to equalize the gap in cultural status between a university professor and a meatpacking worker. The recent work on life-story construction has alerted us to the fact that there is generally an underlying mandate that life stories achieve coherence through a cooperative effort between teller and addressee.[27] We will elaborate on this theme in future chapters. However, here I want to stress the fact that I present particular problems for Doña María as the addressee of last resort in our relationship. In the first place, she had to make the assumption that I, as many outsiders were, would be critical if not hostile toward Perón and Peronism. Many of her stories had already been negotiated within Berisso with other addressees in mind. This fact is not necessarily a handicap. Indeed, it is precisely one of the preconditions of any possibility that the historian/interviewer can move from the individual to collective questions of agency and consciousness in later analysis.

Beyond this, the claim is also an assertion that there is a level of experience and knowledge to which I do not have access. And this is because I haven't lived it and had the experiences on which it has been based and because it is of a fundamentally different status. It comes from the heart, from the emotional core of a person, from the pain of life, which are radically different criteria from the book-learning criteria of the university professor. Without knowing or caring about it, Doña María is expressing the distinction between emic and etic, experience-near and experience-distant ways of knowing.[28] She is also, of course, telling me about the limits of empathy and prosopopeic representation, that there are things that I cannot understand or perhaps should not know. What would the most adequate response to such a claim be on the part of the oral historian? One possibility is that offered by Doris Sommer in an influential essay within testimonio criticism, in which she enjoined the reader/critic to respect the secret, to treat the claim as an ethically unpassable border that no form of interpretative representation should seek to cross. In her terms the reader should remain "incompetent" in the face of this "resistant text."[29]

Yet I do not think that Doña María is claiming an absolutely unbridgeable gap. Far from radically problematizing communication, we could interpret her claim as the first step in negotiating the conditions under which it might take place. Such conditions would ideally allow her to both posit her secret, the uniqueness of her suffering-based experience, and articulate her interpretation of her life and worldview. The possibility that the conditions for such an outcome can be negotiated in any interview situation is an uncertain one. Certainly, my experience in Berisso is a warning against overconfidence regarding this wager. And yet it might also offer a clue as to what might be needed. In my story of a failed encounter in a cold house the fundamental failure in my mind was my failure to listen, my refusal to submerge myself and my criteria in a gesture that would have signaled my willingness to engage my interlocutor on his own terms.

Although we might express this in semiotic terms I think that at root it is best framed as an ethical issue. Indeed, it is striking to note how some of the most profound meditations on this issue have been framed in these terms. Marc Kaminsky, the editor of Barbara Myerhoff's posthumously published collected essays, speaks of her concern for what she called the "pathos of the absent listener." Filling the void left by such absence was one of the fundamental roles of the ethnographer. In Myerhoff's own personal case Kaminsky assures us that listening was "a sacralization of a secular vocation" that was based on a unique "gift as a listener":

> Immersed in this full and unusually intense attentiveness, received by a listener who offered herself as a "partner in security" . . . ; met moreover by someone whose steadiness of attention by turns offered a supple, accepting, lucid, brilliant auditor, Myerhoff's interlocutors felt free to think and feel through dimensions of their experience that they had not owned or connected before. She was often present

at the saying out loud for the first time of something often lived with, subliminally. The interview felt emancipatory. The gathered material registered the sense of discovery.[30]

The tone of these observations is strikingly similar to remarks made by Pierre Bourdieu in his meditation on the interviewing practice drawn from the interviews collected in *La Misère du Monde*. Although he maintains that "there are limits to the procedures and subterfuges that we have been able to think up to reduce the distance" between interviewer and interviewed, Bourdieu claims in the end that any "true comprehension" must be based on "attentiveness to others and an openness toward them." This sort of attention would be the opposite of the "ritualized small talk" and "inattentive drowsiness" normal in social conversation. For Bourdieu the interview that arrives at true comprehension "can be considered a sort of spiritual exercise, aiming to attain, through forgetfulness of self, a true transformation of the view we take of others in the ordinary circumstances of life." He concludes that "the welcoming disposition, which leads one to share the problems of the respondent, the capacity to take her and understand her just as she is, in her distinctive necessity, is a sort of intellectual love."[31]

Fifty years earlier, in a text that struggled in a uniquely powerful way with the problems of representation and that has been strangely forgotten in the current speculations on the theme, James Agee spoke in a similar vein. Although the "nominal subject" of *Let Us Now Praise Famous Men* is "North American cotton tenantry as examined in the daily living of three representative white tenant families," Agee goes on to affirm: "Actually, the effort is to recognize the stature of a portion of unimagined existence, and to contrive techniques proper to its recording, communication, analysis and defence. More essentially, this is an independent inquiry into certain normal predicaments of human divinity."[32] Agee brought love, passion, guilt, anger, and an extraordinary ear for listening to his tortured effort to translate a "portion of unimagined existence" for his educated Northern audience.

The question of memory permeates the oral history project, though memory is mostly treated in oral history texts as a conundrum and

a problem whose noxious implications need to be 1
rarely seized on, interrogated as a unique resource, a
individual expression of the past in the present. In or
Alessandro Portelli comments that memory is inerac
up in an orality constantly seeking to counter the in
and unrepeatability inherent within it. Orality, thus, v
ory, but its practice is determined by the difficulty of remembering,
of holding the past in place and keeping access to it open. Telling
stories is one way — perhaps the most pervasive — through which we
"take up arms against the threat of time."[33] Recording those stories
and then transcribing them is, indeed, frequently justified in terms
of conserving memories and traditions that would otherwise fall
victim to the impermanence of orality. Although we may recognize the function of the oral interview in providing a space within
which individual and social memory can be retrieved, it is worth
considering the existence of other memory sites that call on other
processes of commemoration. Narrative may be the dominant mnemonic resource available to both individuals and communities, but
it is not the only one.

At the beginning of the 1980s a local photographer in Berisso,
Oscar Merlano, heard that the Armour plant, which had been closed
since 1969, was to be torn down. It was already common knowledge
that for years people had been raiding the building, walking off with
sinks, tiles, and many other things. Merlano decided to secretly enter
the building and record what was left in a series of photographic
images. At the time his motivation was simply to record something
that he felt needed to be preserved, something that he intuitively
felt to be important to the community, following a conservationist's
instincts. At the height of the military dictatorship there was little
hope that these photos might have any public role. After the return
of democracy to Argentina in 1983 he and a friend, Raúl Filgueira,
one of Berisso's best-known poets, put together a slide show with
soundtrack to commemorate the plant and its workers.

The show was titled "Requiem for a Frigorífico," and it was presented to the public in late 1984 in the meatpackers' union hall,
which was crowded with many former workers from the plants,
among them Doña María. The slides depicted the different sections

The abandoned
Armour plant
shortly before its
disappearance, Berisso,
1980. *Courtesy Oscar
Merlano.*

of the plant, much of which had begun to fall apart after more
than a decade of abandonment. The script of the soundtrack,* written by Filgueira, both drew on and helped construct a narrative
of an immigrant working-class community confronting the hard-
ship of industrial labor to build modest lives of decency and dignity
against powerful odds. I have spoken to many of the old-timers who
were present. All the testimony emphasizes the emotional impact
of the commemoration. Many were openly weeping; others seemed
dumbfounded, staring silently at the stark images. I have since seen
the show in the house of Merlano, accompanied by Raúl Filgueira,
in whose home I often stay when in Berisso. It is an event worth
considering for what it might tell us about memory and commemo-

*The script of "Requiem for a Frigorífico" was given to me by the author.
Translations are mine.

ration. In particular we may ask, why was the memory embodied
in the Armour commemoration such a profound emotional experience for those who had witnessed it?

To begin with, although the visual content of this commemoration was striking, we need to also be aware of the narrative framing of these images. Filgueira's script fulfills many functions. On
one level, he performs a task expected of the community's principal historian by laying out the basic chronicle of Berisso's past from
the foundation of the regional units of Quilmes, San Vicente, and
Magdalena in 1774 until Berisso's emergence as an autonomous municipality in 1957. As part of that chronicle he also includes a history
of the cattle-processing industry from the first salting plants established by Juan Berisso in 1871 to the building of the two frigoríficos
in the first decades of this century. All this is familiar for his audience, as is the story that he derives from the chronicle—Berisso's
construction as a community of immigrants: "Almost in unison
with your surprising appearance, a current of immigrants arrived
that filled the town with new musical sounds and virgin words,
a mixture of national and foreign languages, but which enabled
the inhabitants of your tower of Babel to understand themselves
after all was said and done." And these immigrants from all over the
globe will found, together with native Argentines, a community of
labor: "And these immigrants joined their desire for progress with
the spiritual need that is work, going together with the Argentine
born to the hiring office, sharing both courage and fear. Wagering
their future and that of their families on a yes or a no." This, as I have
said, is a familiar story drawing on deeply entrenched communal
and national narratives. Its images can be comfortably and nostalgically evoked. Filgueira does not, significantly, draw attention to
other narratives of social and political conflict, the fight for unionization, the emergence of Peronism. He could easily have done so.
He knew of them and had participated in them. However, as the
community's historian, he is, in Henry Glassie's words, "mediating
between life and death by selecting a few of the multitudinous facts
from the past and arranging them for other people to see and hear."
Glassie emphasizes the criteria on which such selection is based:
"Selection and arrangement are guided by the historians' reading

of society's needs: what should people know about the past so that they can live in the future?"[34]

But Raúl Filgueira is also a poet. Although he researches an infinity of topics about Berisso's past—its musicians, its soccer teams, its clubs—his preference is to write poetry. As a poet, he knows that he must do more than evoke nostalgia. He takes as his central theme memory and mourning. This is signaled clearly in the title of the commemoration: this is a requiem for a frigorífico, and a requiem is "a mass for the repose of the soul or souls of a dead person or persons."[35] It is also signaled by the dominant poetic device he uses to construct this requiem: the text is an extended apostrophe. Literally a turning away, a digression, to address a (usually) absent person or thing, apostrophe is also in Barbara Johnson's words, "a form of ventriloquism which enables the speaker to throw voice, life and human form onto the addressee . . . to call up, animate, the absent, the lost, the dead."[36] This device will involve the personification of the mute, the inanimate. The opening line of the script announces this explicitly: "Before we begin our dialogue, you and I . . ." The frigorífico will become a living person that breathes and suffers and ultimately is threatened with death. More than that, it will be rendered as an intimate friend, as the poet uses the familiar Argentine form of the second person singular, "vos": "How much time has passed, my solid and noisy little brother! How I still remember you with your heart of machinery and your piping for arteries."

The poet knows that this animation will provoke much pain. At the beginning he warns the frigorífico that the dialogue they will have will provoke "feelings, resentments, or melancholies" that "will burst forth uncontrollably, like blood through a broken artery." He knows where to locate the source of these emotions. The frigorífico is a metaphor for many things:

There I began to understand that, within your apparent indifference you generated in addition to proteins the solidarity between workmates. . . . you were not only a building with cold cement walls, no factory is just that because it contains implications and calories of the men who inhabit its walls.

After this he specifically enjoins the frigorífico to exercise its memory—"Do you remember when?"—and he proceeds to enumerate
the examples of solidarity called up by his reanimated friend: "The
fraternal gesture of the compañero who pats you on the back and
congratulates you when your daughter turns fifteen"; "an intersec-
tional soccer match or a drama group, brought together by those
who think that there should be more to life than sweat"; "the formation of new families through romances started on the production
line"; "a union protest to get a better standard of living." Filgueira is
calling on his audience to remember and relive the gamut of these
experiences.

Above all, he is invoking the ghosts of the dead, those who "despite the sick passion of some who would destroy you, still wander
your decrepit interior" as "shadows of those who resist abandoning you completely." This invocation struck a powerful chord with
his audience. Jaime Teixidó, a longtime communist militant in the
plants, told me as he recalled the Armour ceremony:

> I sat down once to write a leaflet calling for the nationalization of
> Swift. But I didn't just want to talk about the four walls, the ma-
> chinery . . . I was also thinking about all the people who died there.
> I began to make a list of the people I had known . . . because they
> don't only kill animals there, they killed people too, . . . Jesus . . . my
> sister died of TB at forty-eight, after working in the picada, I went
> through the list, so-and-so fell down the stairs, so-and-so hit in the
> head. . . . well, they should put up a plaque to all those people, it was
> a very cruel thing . . . and I was thinking of that as I watched.

Doña María, too, had intimate reasons to mourn the frigorífico's
dead. Her husband had died from injuries suffered in the plant.
For her, attending the commemoration brought out the ingratitude
toward the dead:

> That show was a tremendous thing, there wasn't a dry eye. . . . they
> tore the Armour down. . . . that shouldn't have happened to us, of
> course feelings don't count for anything, the spiritual side isn't there,
> because this was our second home, in there many men and women

who are no longer with us, have left their lives, they've been thirty years inside there working, but really working, leaving their last drop so that the companies could be multimillionaires. . . . it was a tremendous ingratitude to do that to those buildings.

Filgueira is drawing on a profoundly ambivalent emotional response. This is no elegiac reminiscence for a golden age. At the same time as the frigorífico is a site of solidarity in which memories of profound human relationships can be located, it is also the "monster that ate many people."

In the poem that ends the show the poet touches another chord, as one of the spectral figures who haunt its interior speaks of the approaching death of the frigorífico: "You seem a corpse that does not want to die," "advancing toward your own requiem, exhaling your last death rattle." But the apostrophized friend is not simply moribund, it is a fractured and wounded presence:

I look at your fractured skeleton,
with your bones exposed to the air
your severed tendons
symbols of a spasm of impotence
and that cross that tells us:
when a factory closes
many people die
many streets die
and peoples enter their death throes
on their way to underdevelopment.

The impact of all this was compounded by the fact that at the time of the ceremony the Armour site was already an empty space, abandoned to grass and wind with scarcely a brick remaining. The company had almost overnight finished the work that a decade of abandonment had begun. So the requiem is already an attempt to fix in memory, conjure up something that has been physically eradicated. The spatial coordinates of memory are crucial for both individual and social remembering; they provide the grid on which memories can be localized and mapped. As Paul Connerton, following

Maurice Halbwachs, has noted, "We conserve our memories by referring them to the material milieu that surrounds us. . . . It is to our
social spaces . . . to which we always have access . . . that we must
turn our attention if our memories are to reappear." [37] The mourning
associated with this event is, thus, complex. It was mourning for lost
loved ones, for lives wasted in the plants, for lives enjoyed, friend-
ships, solidarities, jokes, loves, and hates. But it was also mourning
for a physical and social space that was lost and with it, perhaps, the
possibility of recovering through memory the identities and experiences evoked by this mourning. The requiem ends up destabilizing
the very process of commemoration it sought to energize and animate, and the abandoned memory site itself becomes a source of
grief and mourning.

The photographic images reinforced this process of commemoration and mourning. The connection between photos and memory
has frequently been noted. As John Berger comments, "The camera
saves a set of appearances from the otherwise inevitable supersession
of further appearances." [38] Another name for this supersession is forgetting, and photography in some basic way resists this. Yet it does
so in its own special way, a way that intensifies mourning. Christian
Metz has noted that photography perpetuates memory, but it does
so by "suppressing from its appearance the primary marks of living-
ness while nevertheless conserving a convincing print of the object."
Metz calls this convincing print a "past presence." In this sense, he
claims that photos are similar to funerals and other rituals in that
they have the double function of remembering the dead but also
remembering that they are dead and that life continues. In this way,
according to Metz, photography points toward the healthy working
through of the feelings of grief and loss that constitute Freud's definition of mourning. [39] In a certain sense, then, attending the event
in the meatpackers' hall was akin to being present at a funeral wake,
or keeping a photo in memory of a loved one.

The mourning process associated with the remembering produced by these photos has both a collective and an individual register. As photos, the images taken by Merlano conform starkly to the
conventions associated with documentary photography. On their
own, published in a magazine, or exhibited in a gallery, separated

from the poet's commentary, they might convey a generic, time-less image of industrial decline as representative of Pittsburgh or São Paulo as of Berisso. They might provide information but no access to meaning and experience. Merlano's photos escaped that fate and acquired their power when contextualized within the arena in which they were shown and framed by the narrative that placed them in time and space. As such, they became powerful instigators of memory. Such memory clearly has a collective dimension. The closing of the packing houses, the destruction of the physical site of the Armour plant, was a wound in the fabric of memory in Berisso that had never been addressed in any public setting before. For a brief moment that night in the union hall, such a wound could be expressed and tended to in the unimpeded play of rememberance and commemoration.

The outlines of this social memory are present in Raúl Filgueira's narrative and inevitably frame the individual memories provoked by the commemoration ceremony. We could say that, in some way, the experiences and memories of the individual meatpack-ers acquired their meaning only insofar as they resonated within this broader social narrative. Yet having said this, we need also to recognize what one scholar has called "the tension between the personal moment of memory and the social moment of memory making/memorializing."[40] We ultimately experience our memories as peculiarly our own. The poet himself offers us an insight into the dialectic between personal and collective memory provoked by the photos. The images of the frigorífico, he tells us, brought to his mind the memory of his immigrant father coming out of the pack-ing house at midday to receive his lunch from his youngest son and to sit down and eat it on the grass at the side of the railroad lines that brought cattle to the plant:

My father while he chewed hurriedly looked deeply at me. Perhaps he wanted to tell me many things. Tell me of his Spain, of his vil-lage of El Ferrol, where his trade of fisherman allowed him to har-vest fishes; explain to me that when he came here he had to accept eating the fish that others caught. Perhaps he wanted to ask my for-giveness for the poor life that he could barely offer his family. But he neither said anything nor told me anything, possibly considering that I would not have understood him. It's a shame he didn't take the chance.

In this recollection, we can, perhaps, see the interplay of what Walter Benjamin called the "dual will to happiness." Certainly we can recognize the Proustian moment, the elegiac moment of retrieval of the past remembered with a profound nostalgia that gives the elderly poet access to his childhood. For Benjamin there is also what he called the hymnic moment, the moment when the significance of a remembered event or experience becomes clear for the first time in a moment of recognition that flashes up triggered by "images we never saw before remembering them." The poet probably had frequent access to his memories of his lunchtime meetings with his father, yet it was perhaps only now at the end of his life that, provoked by the stark images of an abandoned factory, he was able to recognize its profounder meanings, which resonated with his past and present life: the failure of father/son communication, the unconfessed shame of poverty, the yearning for another, different, better life.[41]

This recollection also speaks of the difficulty of accessing and translating such memories and confronts us with the limits of even the most sensitive hermeneutics of solidarity. The commemorative act in the meatpackers' hall that night expressed a vibrant, emotion-laden collective memory. But this collective memory must, too, have its quota of inaccessible and untranslatable personal memories. Stuart Hall has said that photos are marked by the multi-accented traces that history has left behind. The difficulty for interpretation, he says, is that "these are traces without an inventory," at least not one present within the frame of the photo. It is this inventory that can, in part, be provided by the "privileged" interpreter with elements at her disposal from outside the visual frame, such as the poet's narrative framing. But this inventory must have its limits, as it surely does in my case, as evidenced by my frequent recourse to the qualifiers "perhaps" and "potentially." There may well be meanings beyond the hermeneutic reach of even the most empathetic viewer or listener.

Indeed, in Benjamin's terms we might say that only if collective and individual, voluntary and involuntary, memory are brought together can even partial access occur. In his essay on Baudelaire, Benjamin offered some insight into the possible conditions under which this might happen: "[the mémoire involuntaire] is part of the inventory of the individual who is in many ways isolated. Where there is experience in the strict sense of the word, certain contents of the individual past combine with material of the collective past. The rituals with their ceremonies, their festivals . . . kept producing the amalgamation of these two elements of memory over and over again. They triggered recollection at certain times and remained handles of memory for a lifetime."[42]

For Benjamin, the idealized vehicle in the past who might act as bearer of this memory was the figure of the storyteller. The storyteller could translate individual memory and experience and offer it to the community: "It is not the object of the story to convey a happening per se, which is the purpose of information; rather, it embeds it in the life of the storyteller in order to pass it on as experience to those listening" (59). But Benjamin recognized that this was at best an insecure wager, citing Proust himself to the effect that "it was a matter of chance whether the problem could be solved at all." If Proust's eight volumes "conveys an idea of the efforts it took to restore the figure of the storyteller to the present generation" (59), it would seem to behoove the oral historian or ethnographer to approach the issue with appropriate modesty.[43]

In part, this modesty must be regarded as a reflection of the status of the memory recovered by the oral historian, which is a complex amalgam that partially corresponds, as we noted above, to the different sorts of narrative discourse generated by the interview situation. This memory combines different levels: an episodic, present-based memory attached to the quotidian and the mundane; a preformed memory centered on stereotypes that can reveal general views of the world; and, finally, "hymnic moments" of profound remembrance linked to life experience. Whether the oral historian can access, recognize, and then translate these is a matter of luck and some skill, though it is precisely these hoped-for, mainly illusory, epiphanies that keep us going. We could, of course, associate the ability to encourage this sort of profound remembering with the skill displayed by the "brilliant auditor" in the interview situation. It is interesting, in this regard, to note how Kaminsky's description of Myerhoff's interview practice parallels almost exactly Benjamin's account of the profound rememberance associated with involuntary memory: "[Her] interlocutors felt free to think and feel through dimensions of their experience that they had not owned or connected before."

Another reason for modesty on the part of the oral historian concerns the recognition of the difficulty of answering the question: under whose injunction does the recovery of memory take place? A pessimistic answer to this question argues that the memory embodied in the oral history text is a decontextualized, inadequate memory trace recollected for the historian's needs. It is a pure substitute, "of no use to he who remembers, even if it arouses nostalgia." The very act of writing/transcribing "shows that this act of memory is not a creative act."[44] And yet it would seem, once again, that this represents an oversimplification of the dynamics of the interview conversation.

The memory recovered in the oral history project is not the invention of the historian, though she certainly helps shape it and can perfectly well disrupt it. The issue of memory is not uninteresting for many respondents; indeed, it is often at the root of their desire to participate. For the elderly in particular, remembering can be both a moral and a psychic priority. On a cold, bright day in mid-June, six months after we started our interviews, Doña María and I took a bus down to the calle Nueva York, the street that led to the two packing houses. As we walked along the dock that ran along the two plants, we could see the empty shell of the Swift plant and we could survey the overgrown field that had been the site of the Armour plant. After a long silence Doña María spoke:

> You know this used to be like a city within a city. It was lit up twenty-four hours a day. I worked over there for many years, and my husband worked here. . . . but my grandson said to me the other day, "You know, abuela, grandfather gave his whole life working over there and now there isn't a brick left. When they pull Swift down there will be nothing to remind us of what you did in there." You

know he's right. . . . When I die my great-grandchildren will have no memory of our struggles and our lives.

I took it as both a statement of fact and of implicit desire. It was the nearest we ever got to discussing what she wanted out of our interviews.

No one has addressed the issue of the process of "re-membering" among the elderly as passionately as Barbara Myerhoff. Marc Kaminsky summarized the meaning of this notion for her: "Through 're-membering' the old people's rituals, storytelling and other cultural performances become forms for constituting a collective subject, a social individual in whom the ancestors live on renewed."[45] This powerful redemptive claim centers on the notion of "re-membering" as a practice of memory distinct from ordinary recollection and is embodied in cultural practices such as storytelling, which are vital to the psychological health of the elderly. The importance of re-membering lives is nowhere more explicitly stated than in the words of Shmuel, the taylor and central character of *Number Our Days*. In his last conversation with Myerhoff, Shmuel laments that his village and the Jewish culture of eastern Europe have all been erased by the Holocaust and other cruelties of history. That past and his loved ones exist now only in his stories—"all those people and all those places, I carry them around until my shoulders break." But even this burden does not suffice:

> Even with all that poverty and suffering it would be enough if the place remained, even old men like me, ending their days would find it enough. But when I come back from these stories and remember the way they lived is gone forever, wiped out like you would erase a line of writing, then it means another thing altogether for me to accept leaving this life. If my life goes now, it means nothing. But if my life goes, with my memories, and all that is lost, that is something else to bear.[46]

Now it may be the case that Myerhoff exaggerates her claim. Certainly, we need to be aware of the process of forgetting, which can be of as much interest to the oral historian as the culturally creative process of re-membering lives that Myerhoff celebrated. Indeed, any process of remembering is inevitably shaped by what is omitted, silenced, not evoked. More than that, it is also clear that for some old people the ethical imperative not to forget is more than offset by the pain associated with certain memories. One woman, who had worked in the Armour plant and attended the slide show, turned down my request to interview her about it. Her life in the plant had been "a very sad time," and she didn't want to be "forced to remember things that would cause me pain." She would later prove to be more than happy to talk about her participation in the social and cultural life of the Ukrainian ethnic association. The Armour commemoration had, in her case, simply provoked a memory that she did not wish to share, an experience she did not wish to transmit.[47]

In part Shmuel's legacy—the fate of his memories—depends on Myerhoff, his brilliant auditor and cocreator of his "re-membered" life. In a similar way the survival of Doña María's memories also depends on my good faith and skill as a listener. I suspect that all of us who undertake to record these sorts of extended life stories share, at some level, Myerhoff's contention that "such re-membered lives are moral documents and their function is salvific, inevitably implying, 'All this has not been for nothing.' "[48] Such a belief provides the ethical basis for the project we have embarked on. But there is also an element that inevitably escapes the dimension of the individual listener, and the efficacy and ethical content of the narrator/listener relationship. And that element has to do with the problematic status of modern memory.

In part we have already alluded to one source of this problematic status. We have spoken of the process of mourning for a past that is inevitably slipping away, as orality tries to stem the consequences of its own impermanence. It can do this by mobilizing the mnemonic resources available in the photographic image and the written narrative. Yet both of these imply a degree of distantiation. Orality presupposes a certain level of communal, social negotiation and control of meaning—though this certainly has its limits. The written document—the transcribed oral text—and the visual image will be ultimately controlled by others and escape the control of community interpretation. Beyond this, however, there lies the broader issue of the transmission of collective memory. As Andreas Huyssen notes, a central paradox of the postmodern West is that the society of "mnemonic convulsions" is also a society permeated by a "culture of amnesia."[49] Part of this culture of amnesia is precisely the crisis of collective transmission of social memory. We could express this by asking the question: what are the sites and social practices of re-membering that could carry out the social transmission of memory in the contemporary era? Both Benjamin and Myerhoff confronted this question, and both sought answers in the collective realm. Benjamin offers us the brief clue that individual and collective memory could be triggered through rituals, ceremonies, and festivals produced by society. For Myerhoff the ability to re-member could be fostered by providing the social space within which individuals could perform the cultural practices that give access to deep memory. Part of the crisis of contemporary memory in working-class communities is precisely the crisis of such social spaces that have fallen victim to the destructive power of de-industrialization, social dislocation, and simple irrelevance. In Berisso we might say that the fate of memory still hangs in the balance. It certainly still possesses resources that can underwrite social memory. We would, however, be foolish to ignore other tendencies. Even the vibrant memory of lives of labor centered on the *lieux de mémoire* of the packing house has a very tenuous purchase on contemporary memory, as the generations of packing-house workers rapidly dwindle in numbers.

2

"THE CASE OF MARÍA ROLDÁN AND THE SEÑORA WITH MONEY IS VERY CLEAR, IT'S A FABLE"

Stories, Anecdotes, and Other Performances in Doña María's Testimony

> A tale or anecdote, that is a replaying, is not merely any reporting of a past event. In the fullest sense, it is such a statement couched from the personal perspective of an actual or potential participant who is located so that some temporal, dramatic development of the reported event proceeds from that starting point. A replaying will therefore incidentally be something that listeners can empathetically insert themselves into, vicariously reexperiencing what took place. —Erving Goffman, *Forms of Talk*

When we speak of life stories, much depends on whether we mean *life* stories or life *stories*. We may insist that these stories are true — these people exist, and they relate events that actually happened — and, therefore, interviews allow us to glimpse the actual experience (life). Or we may work with the assumption that we are dealing with verbal artifacts (stories) shaped by the narrators' self-perception, by the encounter with the interviewer, and by the interviewer's perception and interpretation of them and their words. The impossible dream of attaining absolute "authenticity" and "lived experience" blinds us to the fact that we have at hand something which bears at least a formal relationship to the subject's experience. After all, the telling of one's life, is *part* of one's life. To paraphrase Walter Benjamin, the problem is not what is the relation *between* life and story; but rather what is the place of the story *within* the life. —Alessandro Portelli, *The Death of Luigi Trastulli: Form and Meaning in Oral History*

The transcription of Doña María's testimony comprises some six hundred pages of written text. It is a document that is by turns fascinating and complex, ambivalent and deeply moving, at times confusing and yet at others compellingly lucid. I have puzzled over this rich, multilayered text off and on for the better part of a decade. It continues to concern me, to haunt me in some ways; certainly, it continues to elude analytical closure. Other than my own obtuseness, what might account for the problematic status of this text? The move from an approach to oral testimony as a source of empirical information to one that recognizes Doña María's status as a narrator is an important one, but one that, nevertheless, leaves many questions unanswered. If this testimony is to be regarded as a story— or set of stories about a life—as the notion of "life story" would suggest, then we must also ask about how these stories have been constructed, the devices and conventions used, the way in which the narrative is to be read.

In part, the difficulty of undertaking such an operation lies in the complexity of the text's status as discourse. Although we may choose to focus analytically on the narrative/storytelling elements, it should be clear from the testimony presented in part 2 that there are other forms of discourse present. Doña María makes extensive use of description, argumentation, and exhortation during our interviews. There are many ways, too, in which the text defies established narrative conventions, especially those embodied in autobiography. This is most clearly seen in the violating of normal temporal sequencing. Within the first one hundred pages we move from Doña María's childhood to the crucial events of her adult life, centered on political and union activism in the 1940s, to meditations on the trajectory of Peronism, with a constant zig-zagging back and forth between childhood and events of her later years. This pattern will continue throughout the manuscript. In addition, the text is riddled with contradictions both of fact and of intention, with the narrator's point of view frequently fluctuating at crucial tension-filled moments of the plot. All of these factors pose clear problems of narrative coherence, so important for the construction of viable life stories.

And yet, of course, it would be meaningless to place the burden of responsibility for the difficulties in reading this narrative on Doña María. Its "resistant" qualities are not due to some narrative inadequacy on her part. Indeed, some of them are in large part due to my own framing of the interviews: the excessive length, the constant interruption of narrative flow with questions obsessed with establishing chronology or empirical detail, my encouragement of the long passages of argumentation, are all the result of priorities largely established by me. There have been many times over the last decade as I went back to the manuscript to reengage with it once more that I found myself amazed at my own deafness, my own lack of judgment, as I read myself cutting off a promising story or failing to encourage a tentatively offered line of response.

Then, too, why should I have expected the text that resulted from our collaboration to offer itself for any easy appropriation? For all the emphasis in recent scholarship on the cognitive importance of storytelling and narrative in giving order to the anarchy of un-mediated experience, it is also worth bearing in mind folklorist Richard Bauman's warning that "[narrative] may also be an instrument for obscuring, hedging, confusing, exploring, or questioning what went on, that is, for keeping the coherence or comprehensibility of narrated events open to question."[1] The interpretive problems this statement implies are compounded in life stories in which, despite the deeply ingrained appeal of a "metaphysics of presence," narrative functions precisely as a distancing, editing device, creating a self as other through the separation of narrator and protagonist.[2]

In this chapter I detail certain analytical approaches that I have followed and that have helped make this telling of a life story interpretable for this particular listener. What is involved analytically and methodologically in the reading of such a personal narrative as this? More particularly, how is the problem of coherence played out in Doña María's rendering of her life story? I have chosen to focus on a body of personal experience stories found throughout the text that bear much of the narrative burden of sense making on both an individual and a social-historical level. This sort of interpretation implies several analytical moves, by now well established in the literature dealing with oral narratives. First, the need to pay attention to what Bauman has defined as the "essential artfulness" of oral narratives, the creative constructedness of the text.[3] In a related fashion, the analysis takes seriously the specifically literary nature of the object produced in a dialogue and its attendant narrative organization.[4] Finally, the performative nature of oral narratives, the dialectic of narrated and narrative event, and the importance of performance on the production of narrative meaning in life stories will be analyzed.

Before analyzing specific personal experience stories we must examine what has been called "the key pattern of the narrative structure" of Doña María's testimony. Marie-Françoise Chanfrault-Duchet has defined this pattern as that "which reproduces throughout the narrative a recognizable matrix of behavior that imposes a coherence on the speaker's life experience, the coherence of the self."[5] The pattern reflects in fundamental ways the narrator's relationship with dominant social models. It also contains crucial value judgments that the narrator adopts in order to make sense of her life. Such patterns are embodied in, and mediated by, several possible narrative models and devices. Access to such models is generally assumed to come from the literary forms and genres found in the various expressions of popular culture and literature. More fundamentally, it has been argued that a repertoire of certain basic narrative forms is part and parcel of an individual's experience of the social world. In the words of Kenneth Gergen and Mary Gergen, "at a minimum socialization should equip a person to interpret life events as constancies, improvements or decrements. With a little additional training an individual should develop the capacity to envisage his or her life as tragedy, comedy-melodrama or romantic epic."[6]

The key pattern present in Doña María's testimony is that of the search for a better life, framed within the context not of a social mobility story but of a rejection of social injustice and a concomitant commitment to social and political activism. This key pattern, with its clear questioning of the dominant social arrangements, is narrated through several core community developments centered on the 1940s. The emergence of the union under Cipriano Reyes in the mid-1940s, the ninety-six-day strike of 1945, the foundation of the Partido Laborista in the same year, the events of 17 October, the election victory of Perón in February 1946, the role of Evita, the subsequent changes within the plants and the community, are the center of this story. They take on something of the aura of collective myths, stereotyped, predictable, and frequently repeated. We can name these mythic types—the Golden Age, the Exemplary Strike, the Leader of the Poor, the Revolutionary Upheaval, the Lost Paradise—whose archetypal status is attested to by their repeated presence in an array of working-class narratives.[7] Despite the fact that they account for only ten years in a long life, the whole life story revolves around these events. Once more this is a recognizable form of narrative organization. Alessandro Portelli came across it among workers in both Terni, Italy, and Harlan County, Kentucky; he compared it to "a wheel, with a circular rim and spokes branching out in all directions from one central core of meaning."[8]

The dominant narrative model that Doña María uses to express this "central core of meaning" is an epic one. Her absorption in these historical events, her insistent rendering of them as foundational moments in her life, leads her account to frequently assume the cadences and wording of epic. The rendering of the events of 17 October 1945 is particularly framed in this register. "It was like the taking of the Argentine Bastille. I never saw the French Revolution, but for me it was the taking of the Argentine Bastille." Frequently, throughout the narrative, the same analogy is made. The epic hero is, of course, Perón, who will redeem his people; he is a "tabla de salvación" who will bring material benefits and dignity. She emphasizes that "for us Perón was a God." The unique nature of the seventeenth is part of its epic characterization:

No, you can't imagine it , you have no idea Daniel, what the 17 October was like. . . . people don't realize that the Argentine people went
into the streets, all the people, even the sick, were in the street, the
people in the hospitals left their beds and went outside, the only ones
who didn't leave were the mad and the prisoners, you can't imagine
what the seventeenth was like, it was something so tremendous, the
shoes of the people flew into the air, shoes, hats, shirts, it was something tremendous, the person who experienced it knows, you could
see columns, columns that came from the north of Argentina, and
they kept on coming, Perón had already arrived, and they still kept
coming, this lasted all night. . . . it was something, I don't know, in
my whole life I never saw anything like it, it was the only time.

Its unique status also leads to its characterization as a crucial turning point, "un vuelco," which will divide the history of Doña María,
the Argentine people, and the people of Berisso, into a before and
after. Nothing will be the same again. The other crucial elements
of this epic tale are rendered in a similar fashion: the union and the
transformation of working conditions, the Partido Laborista and
the elections of 1946, Perón's government and the social and economic reforms associated with it. The values embodied in this tale
are suprahistorical and communal—respect, harmony, justice, and
happiness. The fundamental register of this narrative is collective
and class oriented. Life was hard, it has got better thanks to these
epic events, but the community must stick together and remain
vigilant.

An epic form implies the individual's identification with the community and its values, and leaves little room for the expression of
individual identity. This basic model is, therefore, complemented
by the presence of another narrative structure, that of romance,
through which a more specifically individual story of the self can be
narrated. Romance involves a quest for values in a degraded world,
whereby the individual's moral career is established through her
ability to overcome obstacles and difficulties. The vision of history
embodied in this model allows the subject to view "the possibility of
change through the notions of progress and individual challenge." [9]
Doña María's telling of her life story is in part framed by her sense

of her ability to go beyond her self, to meet challenges that lie outside the normal quotidian experience of a working woman, such
as those she encounters in the realm of union and political activism. A dominant motif in this story is the attaining of consciousness. Although Doña María defines herself as "having always been
a rebel," she also stresses that the experience of the union and the
Partido Laborista shaped this rebellion. Through this experience she
is able to place certain fundamental political and religious values at
the center of her life story.

I want to emphasize that there is no necessary contradiction between the social and the individual, between the narrative structures of epic and romance, in Doña María's life story. Indeed, a
clear parallel exists between her personal development and that of
the working class. Workers are educated by the experience of the
1940s and by the actions of militants like herself, who have themselves been transformed. On a more specifically communal level
there is a similar parallel between the story of Berisso's emergence
as a flourishing community of industry and labor in the 1940s and
1950s and Doña María's personal development. Social psycholo-
gist Kevin Murray has expressed the nexus between social development and individual identity by adapting the notion of the "social identity project" through which an honored place in the social
order is sought. Although we must beware of the insistently Euro-
centric focus of much of this sort of work and the stubborn ignor-
ing of specificities of class, Murray's formulation is still of interest
in understanding Doña María's text. The social identity project expressed through romance is, he suggests, based on an individual's
"history of success and failure in tests of hazard in which the con-
tempt of others is risked for the sake of their respect."[10] Respect is
a basic motif in Doña María's narrative, and respect is both a personal and a social value, expressed in private interactions and social
settings. The clear linkage of the two can be seen in the following
meditation on the value of respect in the plants:

> Respect, what is worth more than anything is respect, that a señor
> foreman comes and says to me, "Señora, I'm going to move that
> woman from that place." Do you know what that means? Me, a poor

little woman in that place, with some rights yes, from the union, but do you know what that represents that a *jefe* comes to me and tells me, "I'm going to move that woman, is that OK?" "Yes, that's all right." It means that there was a social evolution, that they understood it, that they had to respect it.

Respect is also a reciprocal value. "So we in the union used to say, well then we have to respect the bosses, because what happens if tomorrow they shut the frigoríficos?" Beyond this, Doña María repeatedly insists that she was respected within the union and respected more generally within the community and local Peronism, "I was not so much loved as respected."

We can, therefore, say that this key narrative pattern enables Doña María to impose a coherence on her life story, based on consistency of self-representation and continuity of her self-narrative over time. Such coherence and continuity is represented in her insistence that things have changed for the better, that what the union and Peronism accomplished has in some basic way endured. On a more personal level, continuity is expressed in her representation of herself as still a rebel, and through her continued identity as a Peronist.

At the same time, her life story is so complex, so resistant to facile interpretation because of the existence of another narrative pattern, which acts as a discordant backdrop and prevents her story from approximating the measured linear development of a typical biographical bildungsroman for which there are many models in working-class biography in Argentina and beyond. This narrative pattern is far darker and is centered on a series of disappointments and betrayals in her life. The first of these is Perón's replacing of the Partido Laborista with the Partido Único and later the Partido Peronista. This betrayal was soon followed by Reyes's arrest and imprisonment in 1948. Some years later Doña María's hope of continuing her career in politics is ended when she is replaced on the list of Peronist candidates for provincial deputy by a rich woman. Finally, after the overthrow of Perón in 1955 and Reyes's release from prison, she rejoins what she hopes will be a rejuvenated laborismo, only to have her hopes of a public career dashed again as she finds that the party has been bargained away by Reyes behind the backs of the members.

The narrative device employed for handling this far darker story might be more effectively compared to tragic irony, which revolves around "the contrast between an individual and her hopes, wishes, and actions on the one hand and the workings of a dark and unyielding power of fate on the other." [11] A resignation before the workings of fate is, indeed, a basic trope of Doña María's story. Her life, hopes, and desires are often represented as being under the control of fate, of destiny. This can have either a positive or negative connotation. Her ability to speak in public is simply something that is part of her destiny; she cannot explain it. In a more pessimistic vein, God's will is invoked to explain many of her disappointments. "God will know why," she says, when explaining why she was not successful in her ambitions to be a political actor on a broader stage. Then, too, as we will see, there are times when she attributes her disappointments to the burden of simply being poor and working class, a destiny that cannot be eluded and that necessarily limits her ambitions. Finally, there is an ironic tone implicit in looking back on the events of the past from the vantage point of the present, of commenting and interpreting from a position of wisdom attained through long experience of the frailties of humans and their schemes.

Clearly, the darker narrative threatens the cohesion of Doña María's life story. We could say that in part the discordant elements are in a formal sense subsumed, reconfigured under the dominant model of romantic epic. But this would be too neat a resolution. As the Gergens point out, "Life accounts are not merely reconstituted forms of art." [12] Although an individual's accounting for her own actions and the events of the community around her may tend to be framed within the narrative forms that the culture offers, there is no *necessary* mandate for life to imitate art in a directly mimetic fashion.

In fact, as we will see in the remainder of this chapter and in the following chapter, one of the richest interpretative veins that can be mined in studies of life stories lies in probing the relationship between key narrative patterns aimed at creating coherence and continuity and other elements that clarify, obscure, make more complex, or simply leave in the tension-laden coexistence of contradictory themes and ambivalent meanings in an account of a life. Indeed, the existence of such complexity should not surprise us and may again be rooted in certain deeply ingrained elements of the Western narrative tradition. It has been frequently observed, for example, that one necessary characteristic of Western plots is the presence of tension created when there is a disturbance in the normal flow of narrative events, a violation of the normative narrative pattern. The sources of such dramatic tension, which may sharply increase the rate of "decline of the narrative slope," can be multifold, ranging from individual physical danger to threats emerging from the institutional and social field. Another source of plot tension, and one that will be particularly important in the stories that bear the burden of this darker narrative, is what one scholar has called the "epistemological danger" that arises when an actor's view of the world is threatened by something uninterpretable.[13] The implications of these abstractly stated elements can be seen more clearly if we now turn our attention to analyzing the corpus of stories that form the core of Doña María's life story.

Story 1
Doña María and the Subprefecto

I see on this side of me a sailor and on that side another one, so of course I stopped working.

"What's up," I said.

They say, "Señora, you have to come with us, you must leave your knife and stone, put them away and come with us."

"But on whose orders have you come to take me?"

It was the naval subprefecture, because that area was under their control.

I said to him, "But what is the reason?"

"I don't know, the subprefect will tell you what the reason is." And the foreman comes up and says, "Señora, go with these men," and I say, "If a guard, a woman, doesn't come with me I have no reason to go with these two men. Where are they taking me?"

"To the subprefecture, señora," said one.

I say to him, "That's exactly why a woman from the company has to come with me, I am not going with you two."

It was logical. So they said to a forewoman who was there, who was very bad, "Go with the señora." She took off her overall and gave it to the foreman, took off the hat, half tidied her hair and came with me. They took me to the subprefecture, and they wanted to come inside where I went to take off my overall and change, to my locker, because each one of us had our locker and padlock, our things, so I said, "No sir, you stay here outside, the forewoman can look after me because I am not going to escape, señor, since I know that I am already in the grip of the oligarchy, the shameless ones who have many dollars, so I give myself up, but you cannot come in here, I am not going to change in front of you, no sir, so I'll go with my overall."

He started off and went down the stairs, but it was only logical, I was a young woman, and even if I had been old, what business did that one have watching me change? I changed, came down, and they took me.

The subprefect says to me, "Sit down."

I said to him, "Good afternoon, señor," because, "sit down," and he hadn't even introduced himself.

"What are you?"

"Argentine." He didn't say what he meant by "what."

"I am asking you, what party do you belong to?"

It was when we were just starting to work for the Labor Party.

"Ah, señor, since you said to me what are you, and I was born here in Argentina, I told you Argentine. I am a laborista. I have a laborista membership card, Cipriano Reyes at the head, we are struggling for a greater Labor Party, the workers of Berisso, and I think the whole Argentine people, anything else, any other information?"

"Yes, señora. Why are you a laborista?"

"Ay, señor, you are asking me too much, just like if I were to ask you why you are the subprefect. I am a laborista, you know why, because we have created the Sindicato de la Carne, and we now want to express ourselves purely through a workers' party, to deal with all the ingratitudes we the workers, not just the meatworkers, are facing in the whole Argentine Republic, so señor, the information I can give you is that, yes, I am a laborista."

"And since when has laborismo existed in Argentina?"

"Oh, about two months," I said to him. "The English Labor Party for a lot longer, but Argentine laborismo, two months: perhaps we Argentine citizens don't have a right to form a party, if the law allows it; that is all señor subprefecto, you can do with me what you wish because you have me here like a little pig from India, but what I have here and here is mine, señor, not yours. Anything else?"

"Yes, look, señora, I am going to give you some advice. They have told me that you are an intelligent woman, why don't you get involved in school cooperatives, in something else, not in politics and unions, this you should leave for men."

I say to him, "No, señor, I am going to say something else. Will you allow me, señor subprefecto? In my home there isn't a cent, there's no money, do you have money to give me? If so give me it, but don't give me advice, at this stage of my life, with three children to keep and with our poverty I don't accept advice from anybody."

As he kept quiet, I said to him again, "Anything else?" Where does he get off coming to give me advice, when I was banging pots together so that the neighbors would think that my kids were eating, because I didn't have anything to give them to eat. And I'm supposed to listen to a buffoon with spurs.

DJ: But things were that bad at home? Why didn't they have food?

DM: But there were moments, I am speaking of difficult moments when my son got ill, when we spent everything on him, when we were calling doctors, every doctor that came charged us, there were moments when we lacked for things, that was true, I told him the truth.

So he says to me: "Very well, señora, you are not going to be able to return to work."

"Perfect, if that's what you say, that's the way it will be."

"You are going to stay in your house for ten days, and the police will be posted at your door. You won't be able to go to work because your section follows you, and when you make a sign with your hand the women stop work." I used to go like this (she raises her hand) and they used to all stop, all of them.

DJ: How did you get to that point?

DM: I don't know. God knows the answer.

Story 2
The Turkey Section and La Intrusa

Sometimes I laugh at myself because I see myself so small and yet I was so tough; they are things that you do once in a lifetime and you never do them again, that opportunity that the force of destiny gives you—as the great musicians say. The order came down from the union to strike my section, my women, I was the delegate, we had to say enough is enough! we won't work anymore. But I thought, what about the women working in the turkey plucking, who don't have a delegate? They didn't have a steward, and at that time they exported a lot of turkey, there were a lot of women working. They used to put the turkey half alive into an enormous iron pot with boiling water and then they would take it out and pluck it.

So I upped and went there, and when I went in the foreman said to me, "You are an intruder."

I say to him, "I accept that, yes, I am an intruder, but let's get going girls, outside, the packing plant is at a standstill."

I hadn't finished saying this when they were all outside.

"He doesn't even let us go to the bathroom, that SOB," they say, "we couldn't go on for wanting to pee."

He didn't let them go to the bathroom, for fear that they would leave work. That same man—these things that life offers us, sometimes it seems impossible that they could happen—one day I am going to speak in Mar del Plata, a political act of Peronism, and we're all prepared there with a fancy stage, bouquets of flowers, lights everywhere, flags, photos of Perón, photos of Evita, Cipriano Reyes was there, he can tell you, and there's a man setting up the electrics on the stage, and I look at him and he looks at me—this must be more than thirty-five years ago, yes, more—and he says to me, "You are María Roldán."

"Exactly right, and you are the man who called me an intruder."

"How strange life is," he said.

"You know what the difference is? They didn't throw me out for being a thief; I left the plant for my own reasons, and you they threw out for thieving, because you stole two typewriters. See what an enormous difference, I am an honorable worker and you are a thief," I said it to him slowly, because it was a public meeting, there were a lot of people. The man stood still, not knowing whether to fix the electrics or what.

He says, "Señora, let's not remember old times."

"But I remember when they threw me out like a dog, you said, 'Get yourself out of here, intruder,' but I was defending what I had promised to do in the union, and if I had to do it again, I would. So you are involved in politics?"

"Yes, Señora, now I live in Mar del Plata."

"Well, may God go with you. I wanted to make you remember, that's all, so that you won't do that again in your life, all you had to do was say, 'Señora, please retire from here,' you didn't have to insult me or touch me, because you shouldn't touch a woman, not even the police can touch a woman."

Because he had pushed me. He was fixing my microphone so that I could speak, later he didn't show up, he sent another.

These two stories are representative of a corpus of personal experience narratives found throughout Doña María's life story. They can be defined in genre terms as being anecdotes. In general, anecdotes are "short, entertaining accounts of some happening, usually personal or biographical."[14] More specifically, a recent study of anecdotal form has noted several characteristic features: a focus on a single episode or scene and a tendency to limit action to two principal actors. As a corollary, anecdotes tend to be heavily dialogic in construction, often culminating in a punch line in the form of a striking, especially reportable, statement rendered in direct discourse.[15] Doña María's anecdotes also belong to a category of tale widespread in a variety of working-class cultures: authority stories that detail the interaction between the narrator and someone of greater social standing and power.

In formal terms the two stories quoted above show many of the characteristics of anecdote. The tale about the subprefect primarily involves the extensive reporting of direct dialogue between Doña María and the official, whereas in the story of the turkey section her verbal interactions with the foreman, rendered in direct quotation, clearly form the core of the narrative. Indeed, the evaluative sections of narrative—those sections by which the speaker conveys the point of the story—are essentially composed of dialogue in both cases.[16] In both cases, too, the coda of the tales—the moral underscoring of the point of the narrative that summarizes and winds up the story—is rendered in the form of a punch line. In "La Intrusa" there are, in fact, two such punch lines: "I am an honorable worker and you are a thief," and "You didn't have to insult me or touch me, because you shouldn't touch a woman, not even the police can touch a woman." The story about the subprefect also reaches its effective climax in a punch line that has the status of indirect speech: "And I'm supposed to listen to a buffoon with spurs."

In another, less elaborated version of this story related later in our interviews Doña María offered a different coda. After returning to work from house arrest she confronts the foreman from her section:

> I went back to my section, to my table, to the same little place. So the foreman who had turned me over to the sailors comes up and says, "How are you, señora?"
>
> "Entregador," I said, "you are an entregador, you have a wife and daughters, some day they are going to hand over your wife and daughters."
>
> "Well, I'm only fulfilling my mission, like you."
>
> "Yes, the mission of a pimp."

The multiple repetitions involved in the use of forms of the verb "entregar," the parallelism found in the penultimate and last line centered on the word "mission," all contribute to the sense of closure achieved in the ironic, cutting punch line, "Yes, the mission of a pimp." This ending certainly corresponds closely to the formal punch line orientation of the stories found in Richard Bauman's classic study of West Texas anecdotes.[17]

Yet, beyond this, what are the deeper meanings of these anecdotes? How do the formal characteristics of the tales relate to these meanings? First, we should not take their apparently casual, relatively brief format at face value. Anecdotes are essentially monadic in nature. Literary critic Frank Lentricchia has argued, for example, that anecdotes are "a concentrated representation of the idealized story that a culture would like to tell about itself."[18] Scholars of the life-story form have followed this general line of analysis. Anecdotes represent the relationship of the individual to a dominant social model and attitudes. They express in a synthesized form, on a local scale, the transgression or acceptance of hegemonic values. At the same time, we could also say that anecdotes have a very individual register. They dramatically fashion what Marie-Françoise Chanfrault-Duchet has called "foundational myths of the self," certain "primal scenes" central to the narrator's "process of individuation."[19] On this level, they can be said to play an important evaluative function in the overall life story as a demonstration of the kind of person the speaker claims to be. Anecdotes are, then, in some fundamental way morality tales with both a social and individual register: they are about proper and improper behavior, responsible and irresponsible actions, about the way the world is and the way it ought to be.

The playing out of these morality tales is complex and nuanced. In stories 1 and 2 we can clearly see the elaboration of a common foundational myth of the self centered on Doña María's presentation of herself as a rebel, *la impulsiva,* someone always ready to stand up to authorities, to defend her own and her compañeras' rights. If we look more closely, we can also see that the issue of morality is placed at the center of these tales. The unusually long orientation section of story 1 is almost entirely dedicated to addressing the issue of proper behavior between the sexes in the plants, and in particular that between male figures of authority and women workers. At great lengths Doña María demonstrates her own insistence on propriety and respect from the sailors and the foreman. The broader context within which this moral claim resonates is clearly that of the dubious legitimacy accorded to female factory labor, and certainly union and political activism, within the dominant culture. Indeed, the subprefecto specifically embodies this standard moral version in his advice to Doña María. In this context we can interpret the presence of the detailed demonstration of her own respectability as an index of the tensions existing in both working-class and elite culture around the issue of female presence in the public sphere.

In the later version of the same tale, the new coda adds a far harsher moral contrast. Doña María contrasts her own behavior with that of the foreman who is an "entregador" and a "pimp." The weight of this contrast, as we have suggested, is underlined by its framing as a punch line. In story 2 we find a similar contrast present in the punch lines. Doña María is "an honorable worker" and the foreman is a "thief," who it turns out has violated an even more important ethical norm—he has touched her and insulted her, and "not even the police can touch a woman." Again, comparison with another, less developed version of this story is instructive. In this version the chief criticism of the foreman's behavior is directed at his refusal to let the women go to the bathroom. Doña María says to him: "Criminal, imbecile. Would you do that to your own mother, to your sister, to your wife? Why couldn't these women go to the bathroom? Degenerate." Now this is harsh criticism to be sure, but it lacks the contrastive evaluation with Doña María's own behavior, which gives a greater moral freighting to the later version.

I want to now extend this analysis by looking at three other tales that fall within this category of anecdotal authority stories.

Story 3
The Useless One

Once I stopped in front of a boss, when trade unionism had already taken root in us and we could defend ourselves, a boss says to a woman: "Señora, you are useless."

So I say, when I saw that she didn't answer him: "This woman has a husband, she is a señora and a mother of a family, with what right do you call her useless?"

"Well, she doesn't know how to work," he says to me.

"Have the decency, señor jefe, to call her aside in your office and explain to her what is happening, but don't insult her in front of everybody, remember that you were born of a woman, not of a plant, or weren't you born of a woman?" I said to him. The impulsive one they used to call me.

DJ: La impulsiva?

DM: The impulsive one, because I shouted in their faces, where does he get off saying in front of all her workmates, you are useless? The woman stayed there like a person who had killed another, like a condemned person.

I said: "Raise your head up dear, we know we are among Fiends here, you are not useless; it's just that you only arrived a few days ago and haven't adapted yet, you'll soon get to work like us."

But this was when we already had use of the word, we had a union that defended us, so we knew we weren't going to end up on the street just for anything, because they would have grabbed me by the hair and thrown me out ten thousand times a day because as a delegate I assumed the responsibility of defending my compañeras.

Story 4
Doña María and the Vote for Women

I remember that I went with Professor Vechioli to speak with Perón, and Perón was guarded by a bodyguard, a black man, a colored man. Cipriano Reyes, Colonel Perón, and Alfredo Mercante up on stage. And we are in the seats. So, Colonel Perón said, "I was wanting to know what is the reason for the visit of these ladies"; he knew why we were there. They had designated me to speak.

So I said to him: "Look, Colonel, we wanted to know you better, to hear you close up, because the night that you arrived from Martín García and were a prisoner, forgive me for reminding you of unpleasant things, there was such a mass of people that we could scarcely hear your voice, now we can hear you well. We also want to ask you a great favor, I would go so far as to say for something that is an obligation of all the world's governments."

"Of course, señora, speak. Who are you?"

"My name is María Roldán, I am from Berisso, I work in a frigo-rífico."

"Well, what is it you want to say?"

"I want to tell you that we, Professor Vechioli, and the poet who came with us, the Fontana girl, and Señora Roldán, who is speaking now, are very grateful that you have received us. We come to ask that you approve civic rights for women, we want to vote. Because I have felt very hurt many times, when my husband would come back on election day and say to me, "The people has voted." And I used to say to him, "The people didn't vote, half the people voted, be-cause a woman is a citizen, too, because if tomorrow the four horse-men of the Apocalypse—poverty, suffering, pestilence, ruin, hunger, misery—are knocking at the gates of the fatherland, she will also have to be an unvanquished soldier defending her children, her coun-try. She is a part of the people, and if the people have every right in the world to elect their government, we cannot allow any longer, Colonel Perón, that alcoholics vote, that the insane vote, even the dead vote—he started to laugh—because you know that the dead have voted, Colonel, when the conservatives ran things the dead would vote; monks also vote, with all the respect that they deserve, I said to him, and we have to listen to our husbands, brothers, uncles tell us that the people voted. And aren't we the people, Colonel?" And I looked at him a while, I stood by his side; they had made me go up there to talk.

DJ: What did he say, did he agree?

DM: He asked Reyes whether I was a *doctora*. And Reyes let out a belly laugh, nooo, she's a meatpacker, he says.

Story 5
Doña María and the Visit of Francisco Manrique

Well, I've had in my house, not here but in the other house, Fran-cisco Manrique. He came here with two ladies who were deputies, I was younger at that time, they were the first elections in which he had taken part.

"Señora Roldán," he says, "we have thought of you, and spoken a lot about you and we would like to have you in our party if you don't mind leaving Peronism, we would give you a place at the top of the list, you would have a car and a chauffeur at your disposition, to take care of you, etc." And we spoke about many things.

So I said to him: "Look, Don Francisco, I cannot leave my children anything because I don't have anything, but I leave them something that is worth a lot, it has an immense value. What I leave my children is honor and decency. I on the seventeenth of October 1945, driven on by this little heart I have here, asked Perón in the Plaza de Mayo, because things were very bad in my home and in the homes of many workers that I knew, because Berisso was a *paño de lágrimas,* because they had killed some of our compañeros with bullets, because fathers of families had to go fishing to find something to eat, because I have seen them bury a compañera in her factory overall because we didn't have money to buy her a shroud—because of this I wrote the poem—because I have suffered and wept much since my youth, so Don Francisco Manrique listen to me well, that is mine, that which I have here and I have here, is mine, and nobody can buy it from me. You can offer me all you want, I thank you for remembering this little person, but I am still a woman of the justicialist movement."

"But, don't you see"—he said—"that it is being perverted, that everything is turning upside down, that there are men in Peronism who don't belong."

"I see many things, but I also see that Perón did not tell them to be that way, and these are the bad children who disobey an old father, but the day when this other stage of younger people react, Peronism will perhaps be stronger than the Radicals. Look Don Francisco, I thank you very much for your visit, but don't count on me."

These stories reproduce the characteristic features of this genre of tales, which we noted in our analysis of the first two stories. They are, for example, intended to embody a moral story that speaks both to Doña María's projection of herself and to wider issues of social morality. Story 3, "The Useless One," repeats the basic foundational myth of the self present in the first two stories. She is "la impulsiva," who confronts authority and shouts in its face, defends her compañeras, and runs the risk of being thrown out of the plant "ten thousand times a day" for her impulsiveness. There are also interesting additional elements present in this tale that take us beyond a straightforward "confrontation with authority" narrative.

Clearly, the self-presentation conveyed in this tale is that of a rebel, a heretic. What we also see, however, is the figure of a heretic with a strong maternal character. She is not just defending workers, she is defending other women, and the dominant gesture is one of maternal protection. If there is a mythic archetype structuring this projection of the self, it might be what Chanfrault-Duchet defines as that of the Foster Mother, one of a range of "social symbolic images of Mother and of Woman" incorporated into collective social myths.[20] This protective, maternal tone is present as well in story 2, as Doña María with a simple "Let's go, girls" overturns a situation where her girls had not even been allowed to go to the bathroom. The model for such a protectress of women would obviously be Evita.

There is also another archetype present in this anecdote, this time one with a more biblical provenance. This is not simply a tale about insisting on the dignity of a woman worker in the face of power relationships that consistently deny that dignity. The second part of the story, while it elaborates on the basic message of the first part, also adds a crucial narrative image that comes not so much from the secular repertoire of the socialist-anarchist tradition but rather from popular religious imagery. Doña María's actions invoke a Christlike gesture of defense of the defenseless, a personal intervention to redeem a suffering fellow creature. The scene of the woman standing with bowed head, "like a condemned person," voiceless and desolate before she receives Doña María's injunction to raise her head up, powerfully reproduces a fundamental image of Christian iconography.

Once more we should be alert here to the interlining of individual narrative projection and the broader social universe that the anecdote calls on. The Christian imagery of this anecdote, together with the maternal tone we have commented on, can be regarded as forms of self-representation that in Luisa Passerini's words "are taken to reveal cultural attitudes, visions of the world and interpretations of history."[21] In fact, Doña María is explicit about this broader context; she frames the story by saying that it takes place "when trade unionism had already taken root in us," and defining her personal actions as part of her responsibilities as a delegate. What these self-representations allow us to do is to interrogate both the psychic and cultural framework within which union organization and activism occurred in this era.

Stories 4 and 5 represent a variation of the authority tale. Here there is no confrontation with authority. Instead, Doña María is shown respect by those with greater social and cultural status. The self-representation is not that of the confrontational rebel but rather that of someone who has earned the respect of her superiors and is treated as an equal by them. Although the confrontational action is missing, these stories still demonstrate Doña María's willingness to insist on the hard truths of her life and experience in her interactions with these authority figures. She is unyielding in telling these truths, and these stories exhibit the same concern for the projection of a morally whole sense of self that we encountered in the other stories. They have a fundamental moral element. In story 5, in particular, she establishes the emotional basis of her political identity as a Peronist, based on a listing of the sufferings of herself and other workers in Berisso. This suffering is implicitly contrasted with the privileged status of her interlocutor, Don Francisco Manrique. Doña María's moral standing is also established by her explicit rejection of the material benefits that Manrique offers in exchange for her reneging on her political identity. The temptations that she resists are not simply material. Manrique, like the devil on the mountaintop, also tries to make her doubt her beliefs, "Don't you see, that it is being perverted, that everything is turning upside down?" Yet this temptation, too, she is able to resist.

These last three stories also share the other fundamental characteristic of anecdotes: they are heavily dialogic in construction and focused on conversational interactions between the narrator as protagonist and her principal interlocutor, rendered in the form of direct discourse. Indeed, the presence of directly reported speech is the principal characteristic of all the stories in Doña María's life

story. In fact, the first authority tale in this corpus, that of Doña
María and the subprefect, establishes the prototype with its elaborate reporting of the direct dialogue between her and the subprefect,
in which she consistently takes and keeps the initiative in the dialogue. How are we to interpret this dominant pattern? In part, the
explanation might be sought in what some scholars have claimed
are the different discourse strategies employed by men and women.
Women, it is claimed, among other distinguishing characteristics,
directly report their own and other's speech much more than do
men.[22] The primary factor underlying this difference has generally
been attributed to the different definitions of the self that develop
in men and women, as the process of socialization and individuation
proceed from childhood.[23]

I also want to suggest, however, another explanatory factor,
rooted in the gendered nature of the experience underlying these
authority tales. Given the realities of the plants, and the power
relations existing in the community, Doña María's confrontations
with authorities do not have the option of expressing themselves
in terms of direct actions or physical retributions against unjust superiors. Hence her confrontations with authorities are far more ver-
bally constructed, with dialogue playing a far more crucial role. It
is instructive to contrast Doña María's stories with those of male
workers recounting conflicts with authorities. A typical male telling
of such a tale is that of Alejandro Chible. He describes an incident
that occurred shortly after he entered the frigoríficos at the age of
eighteen in the mid-1940s. He orients the story by explaining that a
foreman had fired him for smoking at work. The foundational myth
of the self present in this telling is equally clear from the first lines:
"I was a young tough. . . . I was born to be tough, to work. Tough to
my very bones." Yet the point of the anecdote is not his own toughness, which he admits was naive, but rather that of the shop steward,
who was a "monster . . . with many years in the plants, who had
suffered many blows."

So he says to me, "Where are you going, kid?"
   "The foreman told me to go home, that they're firing me because
I came in with a cigarette."

"No, you're not going anywhere, stay here with your clothes and boots on, you're not going anywhere."

So he goes and says to the foreman, "Rosas, what's happening with this kid?"

"Nothing, I threw him out because he was smoking."

And Putero, the delegate, says, "Stop fucking about, you don't have any kids," so he takes this huge knife and bangs it on the corner of the table and stops the section. The foreman wasn't going to mess with this guy.

Although the reported speech plays a part in this narrative, it is not the essential evaluative component that demonstrates the point of the story. It does not embody the complex verbal questioning of authority that we find in the subprefect story, with its formal politeness covering an ironic, cutting tone. The climax of Chible's story is an action, not an utterance. Alessandro Portelli describes a similar emphasis on physical confrontation and action in his interviews with male workers in Terni.[24]

Now, clearly, on one level we might say that the different status of direct discourse in Doña María's stories is a reflection of the gendered class reality within the plants. Working women, even delegates, did not adopt the same aggressively physical responses as men in their dealings with authorities. But we must also beware of taking the self-representations too literally. Luisa Passerini, for example, specifically addresses the rebel stereotype in working women's presentations of the self in Turin. She notes that

> the rebel stereotype . . . does not primarily aim to describe facts and actual behavior, but serves a markedly allegorical purpose, which changes continually through contact with different life experiences. It is a means of expressing problems of identity in the context of a social order oppressive of women, but also of transmitting awareness of oppression and sense of otherness, and hence of directing oneself to current and future changes.[25]

We should also note that the dialogue that Doña María is quoting is constructed as she tells this tale many years later. As many studies of the use of direct discourse in conversational narrative have pointed out, this construction does not involve the exact reproduction of the spoken words. Oral narrators use constructed speech as a resource toward a larger goal; rarely are the exact words accurately recalled.[26] In a crucial way these anecdotes involve stereotypes that call on complex forms of self-representation. The use of stereotypes does not mean that the speech can simply be invented; the authenticity of the words placed in the other's mouth by the narrator must be maintained. But it does imply that its function is other than that of simple direct reportage. This accounts, too, for the formulaic nature of the speech involved in authority stories. Authority figures "speak with public voices" intended to convey the authoritative version of truth, of dominant social values, of received wisdom. The figure of the subprefect in story 1 is a classic example. Indeed, the conventionalized nature of his utterances is so marked that we find the words he uses in this story attributed to other authority figures in other tales. And at times, too, Doña María's own responses also take on a conventionalized form that can be repeated in other tales recounting her confrontations with authority.[27]

It is clear, then, that the status of these anecdotes as historical documents is problematic. The problem of documentary veracity is not, of course, limited to women's authority tales. It is very possible, too, that many men do not behave in anything like as aggressive a manner toward authority as their stories would have us believe. Conversely, some women may in fact have acted far more aggressively than their stories indicate. They would not, however, have necessarily felt empowered to express this directly, given the norms governing the parameters of working women's public activity. In fact, for example, it may well be the case that Doña María's confrontations with authorities in the plants had a more aggressive side, in terms of her participation in picketing and other forms of direct union action, than that which she chooses to recount in these anecdotes. This possibility points to another important interpretative variable. These stories, like all anecdotes, are framed within a broader public discourse, and much of their form and content is shaped by the exigencies and pressures generated by the expectations and norms of Doña María's particular discursive community. (This issue is addressed in more detail in the following chapter.)

Doña María's prowess in verbal exchanges with authority figures is, then, the dominant feature of these stories. Her sense of herself, her self-representation, is intimately connected to her ability in these tales to assert her worth, her meriting of respect owing to her verbal and linguistic skills. In this sense, these stories are about the accruing of symbolic, cultural capital. This capital does not finally depend on the specific actions recounted, or even necessarily the moral outcome of the tale. Rather, it is embodied in the linguistic interaction itself. The predominance of direct dialogue in these tales is in this sense a statement about the importance of language itself. A similar understanding is present in Erving Goffman's notion of "footing," the process by which a projected self is presented through the management of a speech interaction.[28] Doña María's management of dialogue in these anecdotes—the footing she thereby manipulates—allows her to establish that despite her "little self," her powerlessness in traditional terms, she is able to confront power within the plants or be treated with respect by powerful men outside them.

The dialogue she recounts with Francisco Manrique in story 5 is an example of this. As we have noted, the story carries a clear moral message. Doña María is concerned to create and to demonstrate "an image of the whole self as worthy of authority."[29] This image, indeed, may be taken to be the goal of most life stories, and in this sense the anecdote—like the others—is concerned with projecting and maintaining on a microlevel the overarching coherence present in the macronarrative that Doña María tells. She tells Don Francisco that she has nothing to leave her children in material terms; the only things she can bequeath them are "honor and decency," which have "immense value." What she also bequeaths them are her words, the discourse through which this claim to "honor and decency" is articulated, the speech act by which a working-class woman puts Francisco Manrique in his place. This claim she owes to language, which is in part a gift from God, which defies her powers of explanation. In part, too, on a social level, it is a gift that comes from the union and the social and political changes of the 1940s. Doña María defines the entire time frame of the anecdotes as being the era "cuando ya teníamos la palabra" [when we already had the word].

Wherever the gift may ultimately come from, its power is undeniable; in this sense, these anecdotes may be said to be, like Bauman's West Texas stories, ultimately "about the transformative capacity of speech."[30]

A final feature of these anecdotes is worth noting. They are strongly performative in character. Performed stories involve the speaker acting out a story as if to give the audience the opportunity to experience the event and her evaluation of it. This performance frequently involves the dramatized recounting of an event that is almost literally reenacted as a play with scenery and role distribution. Social linguists like Erving Goffman have claimed that the performative aspect of narrative goes beyond the function of increasing the authenticity and vividness of the story told. He argues that

> what talkers undertake to do is not to provide information to a recipient but to present dramas to an audience. Indeed, it seems that we spend most of our time not engaged in giving information but in giving shows. . . . the point is that ordinarily when an individual says something, he is not saying it as a bald statement of fact on his own behalf. He is recounting. He is running through a strip of already determined events for the engagement of his listeners.[31]

Several features distinguish performed stories. The principal feature, once more, is direct speech. The narrator, in playing the roles of the participants in the drama, invokes the words of others to heighten the sense of authenticity. Other features include the use of asides, repetition, and kinesic markers such as physical gesture. A common syntactical feature is the presence of the continuous historical present verb tense to increase narrative vividness and highlight particular exchanges.[32]

Doña María's stories embody many of these features. It is precisely the performative aspect of narration that is most affected by the transcription process. The move from the spoken word to the printed text has the effect of flattening out and minimizing many of these features. In fact, many of the stories were told by Doña María while she was standing up beside her kitchen table, making full use of a range of gestures, punctuating her narrative with body language for added emphasis, adopting different voice tones for different roles. Some traces of these performances survive in the transcribed texts. In story 1 the gesture of touching her heart and her head that accompany her words to the subprefect that "what I have here and here is mine, not yours" are clearly implied in the text. She makes an almost identical gesture when she tells Manrique "that which I have here and I have here is mine." Some of the anecdotes are very explicitly framed as dramatic performances, where through asides Doña María specifically provides stage directions and settings. The most explicit example of this comes in story 4. As part of the orientation section of the narrative she sets the scene: "Cipriano Reyes, Colonel Perón, and Alfredo Mercante up on stage. And we are in seats." At the end of the story she recaps the position of the principal figures, herself and Perón: "And I looked at him a while, I stood by his side, they had made me go up there to talk."

As we have indicated, one principal function of performance narratives is to heighten the vividness of the story and hence enhance the authenticity of the events being narrated. The replaying of the events will therefore in Goffman's words "be something that listeners can emphatically insert themselves into, vicariously reexperiencing what took place."[33] Beyond the theatrical nature of these performances, which are said to enhance empathetic identification on the part of the addressee, I wish to also suggest that they are in important ways cultural performances. Such performances may have varied functions. Barbara Myerhoff argued that cultural performance among the elderly and marginalized is rooted in a crisis of invisibility. Cultural performances, which for Myerhoff could include storytelling, public rituals, murals, protest marches, are, among other things, "opportunities for appearing," which, she notes, "is an indispensable ingredient of being itself, for unless we exist in the eyes of others, we may come to doubt even our own existence."[34] For Doña María, marginalized by both her age and to an extent by her personal history within the community, these performances are in part an affirmation of presence, whether recounted to me in her kitchen in 1987 or in gatherings over the years within local Peronism. Yet these enacted stories are not simply about affirming visibility. They could also be seen as performing "rites of status elevation" whereby Doña María's status within the social hierarchy ascended. This status elevation was attained symbolically in various ways. In part, it was through the display and mobilization of linguistic cultural capital, now heightened by the overt display of her oratorical and performative skills. Partly, too, it emerges from the performance of her own self-definition as a morally worthy individual who was demonstrably accorded respect and equality by her social and cultural superiors. Myerhoff, after noting that self-definition can be attained through performance, notes that "this is tantamount to being what one claims to be."[35]

We can see this clearly, for example, in the story of Doña María's lecturing of Perón on the vote for women. Beyond the basic narrative claim to have given Perón such a lecture, and the status acquired by the rhetorical performance of the lecture, the stage directives appended at the end symbolically reinforce these claims. At the end she looks Perón in the eye, standing by his side. In this way she symbolically reverses the spatial distance between Perón and herself; she has moved from being seated below to a position of equality where she is standing by his side. The weight of this claim is attenuated somewhat by the ironic belly laugh that accompanies Reyes's clarification "nooo, she's a meatpacker." Nevertheless, such a clarification was only necessary because Perón had asked Reyes whether she was a doctora. If these performances can be viewed as embodying claims of status elevation, it is also true that they can represent the puncturing of officially claimed status. To some degree this reversal is effected in all the authority conflict stories, though nowhere more subtly and effectively than in the almost carnivalesque inversion of status and deflation of pretensions displayed in the rendering of the subprefect as "a buffoon with spurs."

The fundamental task of the tales that we have been examining is the sustaining of the key pattern of Doña María's life story. They embody her fundamental sense of her life through the use of specific narrative models. In particular, these anecdotes tell of the acquiring of an honored place in society through the display of moral rectitude and the affirmation of the basic values of caring, solidarity, respect. These form part of what we have defined as a key model that utilizes the narrative structure of romantic epic, whereby challenges are met and overcome and during which an honorable life story is fashioned. The social context within which this story resonates embodies a basic questioning of dominant social arrangements and an affirmation of an alternative.

At the level of the anecdotes the key pattern of the life story is expressed through the elaboration of certain self-representational stereotypes. These foundational myths of the self, of which the rebel woman is the most prominent, function as stability narratives that provide a basic sense of continuity over time to the broader life story. As Charlotte Linde notes, the ability to create and sustain a sense of historical continuity of the self is a fundamental achievement of the normal personality and a fundamental goal of the telling of a life story.[36] The authority anecdotes analyzed above are a key means of carrying out this narrative function. We should also note that they enable Doña María to express not only a certain psychological and emotional consistency throughout her life but also a politically consistent identity. In another version of story 5, for example, after she tells Manrique that "I am still a woman of the justicialist movement" she adds "I am enclosed in my own convictions, in what my parents passed on to me, of being of a single piece and a single truth." In a similar vein, in a story not included above, she tells former president Arturo Frondizi, "I must be by definition Peronist, we the humble ones report to that great military figure, Juan Perón." Although on the level of personal and political identity these stories reflect a basic stability, on the social and political level this stability is allied to a progressive narrative. Things have improved in terms of living conditions in the factory and the community. Thus, to repeat, we can say that these tales sustain and complement the overarching narrative model; they do not challenge the basic underpinning of the life story.

I wish now to look at what I defined earlier as the darker narrative pattern that acts as a backdrop to this key model. To do this I will analyze two further stories, "The Great Disillusionment" and "The Visit to Magdalena and the Arrest of Cipriano Reyes." Both stories are far more extensive than the authority tales, with considerable expository elaboration deriving from the narrative core. The thrust of my argument will be that these stories can be understood most profitably if they are analyzed as narrative devices through which Doña María both expresses and staves off what we might call, following Alisdair MacIntyre, an "epistemological crisis" that emerges when interpretive support systems are called into question and threaten the coherence of a life story.[37] This crisis was rooted in the split between Cipriano Reyes and Perón, the suppression of the Partido Laborista, and the impact of all this on Doña María's ambitions within local and national politics. As such, it expressed a complex concatenation of factors both personal and public, ideological and moral, local and national.

The two stories were recounted toward the end of our interviews. I have kept the original order in which they were recounted.

Story 6
The Great Disillusionment

DJ: And you never felt deceived, tricked with some aspect of Peronism? Some aspect of politics?

DM: I felt let down once when I was going to be a provincial deputy and a woman appeared, a woman with a lot of money, a fancy car, some fine coats, and they removed me from the list and put her on it because she paid for a whole election campaign, María Roldán had nothing but her speeches. It was for this that they gave me the land in Punta Lara. Two men who thought a lot of me gave it to me, and I couldn't say no, no I don't want it, because it wasn't they who had done me any wrong, the one who was at fault was Evita.

DJ: I don't understand, how was this?

DM: If a person is going to go because in an assembly they voted for her, and another appears and goes because they haven't yet made up the lists, who is to blame? The one who is in charge of the whole thing. There were other cases like it, a woman who was going to be deputy for Tucumán, too, they took the post from her and put a man in her place, that woman was outside crying like a baby.

DJ: And how did you react to this?

DM: I reacted pretty badly, I retired a little, I couldn't believe that something like that was going to happen to me. I was studying the national labor laws, I was spending all my time in La Plata, in Buenos Aires, I was living in San Martín in my sister's house, so that I could be nearer to all of that. I had practically abandoned my family and work. I had asked for special permission, which they had given me. But that's what happened. Betrayal was lurking on all sides. Women with two or three houses, and by that I say everything, I have only one house, I live here. . . .

Because we should really ask Juana Larrauli, she's old now like me, and many others who were deputies and senators, what did they leave for posterity, what did they leave for young people, what did they do while they were legislators? Change their fine gowns, go to receptions, travel to Mar del Plata, go to see the pope and come back. This doesn't help the Argentine people, the one who helped the downtrodden was Evita directly, let's not fool ourselves. I never saw a photo in any awful magazine or newspaper where Juanita Larrauli is visiting a hut, curing a wound. Which is to say that we women workers of Berisso and the noble sort because I consider myself to be noble but there were many other women here in Berisso who were worth their weight in gold, we who gave the best years of our lives, who knew how to bear a long strike, to stop an injustice, all those things, we were all used, we were used to raise Perón up ever higher, and he deserved it. But the bunch of people up there with him arrived first because they were the adulators who were day and night at Evita's side, hanging on her collar. Do you understand me now? It's very easy to understand. I complained about what happened to many people, but you have to understand that there came a moment when Perón didn't send more money, money was lacking for political propaganda, many thousands of pesos were needed and whoever could provide them was God, and whoever had capacity and talent like the orators, and we were many not just me, were thrown to the wind, dispersed looking for funds. . . . Those who controlled the thing were bad, they were enemies of the really capable because politics is very dirty, when someone distinguishes themselves, I have had so many bunches of flowers in my life when I've spoken in public that I feel really happy when I remember it, poor people, who at most got together a peso from each one to buy the flowers. But on the other hand, they might have thought that Señora Roldán would become a candidate because she spoke that way, but I never got there for this or that reason, because God wouldn't have wanted it, he knows why. There is so much jealousy, evil in politics. I can tell you a story, I was once going to speak for the Partido Laborista on Radio Belgrano. There was a man called Gómez whose nickname was Churrinche, but a man of that type, no? He went to the party and said, be careful of Roldán because she's not going to go to Radio Belgrano to speak—because he could see that the signal for Radio Belgrano didn't reach there—I think that she's going to speak for the Radicals. I got back that night with my husband and we go to the laborista local, and I see all these strange expressions looking at me.

"Good evening, how's things, where are you coming from?"

"From Buenos Aires," my husband told them, "from Radio Belgrano, my wife went to speak on Radio Belgrano," my husband said, ah, they said, because so-and-so came and said that she had gone to speak for the Radicals, because the Radicals had come to speak to me.

DJ: The question I would ask then is if you didn't think that it would be better to have a different Peronism, a more working-class Peronism?

DM: That's what we wanted, but unfortunately it was becoming more bourgeois, and the case of María Roldán and the señora with money is very clear, it's a fable, perhaps in a century there might be four, the person who comes with money passes to the chamber and goes to legislate. What? if she never lacked for food for her children, if she always lived with two or three servants, if that woman had goods, rents, a car, a palace, if she had everything, can she tell of what I can tell, can she speak of the miseries that I experienced with my kids in the frigorífico, or in my childhood? So, was it becoming bourgeois, or not? Because they installed in the legislature a woman with money and not a working woman from Berisso? There you have the why. Because she brought with her dollars, and Señora Roldán had nothing but reasons, rights acquired with the nobility and capacity that was hers as a poor working woman. That's why Peronism became bourgeois.

This was not an easy story for Doña María to recount. She had referred to the incident very briefly in one of our early interviews, in response to a question about whether she thought that Perón and Evita had their faults. Her answer began by affirming that she had not received anything from Perón. She went on: "Once I was going to be a national deputy, and a woman with a lot of money came along, put the money on top of a desk, and Señora Roldán wasn't a deputy. It doesn't matter, but I am Señora de Roldán, and she is a poor woman who everybody had handled, because she had three homes; many things happened that I can't say or let you record, because I don't feel like talking about it, and even less about a woman. If I can, I cover up a woman's faults with my skirt." The heritage she has left her children can be measured, she insists, in memories and the respect of others, not in political posts.

The answer to a question about the possible faults of Perón and Evita is, therefore, turned into a somewhat elliptical morality tale that turns on Doña María's evaluation of herself as a morally upright, incorruptible person who has gained nothing from her public activity. She establishes this persona in contrast to a rich woman, of dubious sexual virtue—she had been "handled by everybody"—whose sole advantage is the possession of money. The relationship of this morality tale to the question of Perón and Evita's faults is left unspoken.

The story was no easier for her to tell several months later. Indeed, the essential narrative is told in the first ten lines in which she recounts the basic elements of the first telling. She adds, however, a crucial final evaluation: "The one who was at fault was Evita." Pushed to develop this evaluation by my questions, spurred on perhaps by a need to finally confront a difficult theme, she embarks on a long expository discourse whose basic elements she will insistently return to during several interviews spread out over many weeks. In formal terms this story is a hybrid, containing elements of both personal experience and expository narrative. This tale is not in the same genre as the anecdotes analyzed above; it lacks the predominant presence of reported speech and the attention to the punch line embedded in the dialogue. The weight of the expository sections is due, we may suggest, to the need Doña María feels to deal with the problematic elements of her life story raised in the short narrative core of this tale. This is a tale about failure and disappointment, the stunting of a career that might have taken a working woman beyond her life in a poor meatpacking community, and the allocating of responsibility for that failure. It is problematic because it runs against the grain of the progressive narrative that informs the basic pattern of Doña María's life story. My own interjection after the core narrative, "I don't understand, how was this?" confirmed its questionable status. Indeed, Charlotte Linde has suggested that explanations are used as a discursive device in life stories precisely "to establish the truth of propositions about which the speakers themselves are uncomfortable, or to defend propositions whose validity they feel their addressee has in some way challenged. . . . explanation is a remedy that we employ once things begin to go wrong in some way." [38]

Although Evita is initially blamed for what happened, and the criticism is later extended to Perón, the bulk of the story absolves them from responsibility for the wrongs that are detailed. This absolution is accomplished in several ways. Blame is primarily attached to the hangers-on who surrounded them: "The adulators who were day and night at Evita's side, hanging on her collar." The merits of Perón and Evita are not questioned: Perón deserved his stature, and "the one who helped the downtrodden was Evita directly." Politics is also assigned much of the blame. It is a space dominated by jealous mediocrities who were "enemies of the really capable." The secondary narrative about Radio Belgrano is told precisely to make this point. Finally, a pragmatic explanation is offered for what happened. Money for election campaigns had become tight, and whoever could "provide [money] was God."

In an important sense this story is held together by establishing its primary meaning on an abstract political level. Alessandro Portelli, in his extraordinary analysis of the story of the death of

Luigi Trastulli, observes that most narrators try to achieve coherence by choosing to place the events of their story within a particular mnemonic "mode." Portelli identifies three basic modes: the political, which is the sphere of governments, parties, unions and elections, and ideology; the collective, which addresses the life of the community, the neighborhood, and the workplace and such events as strikes and natural disasters; the personal, which deals with private and family life and personal involvement in the other two levels. Portelli argues that one way in which problematic events are handled, made to cohere in memory and narrative, is to shift them from one mode to another. An event such as the death of Luigi Trastulli, which would be properly located in the collective mode, may be shifted in memory to one of the other two, to avoid the pain and the blow to the coherence of the community's own story.[39]

The story of "The Great Disillusionment" belongs in a basic sense to a very personal domain of memory and experience. It is about disillusionment and betrayal, the frustrating of desire and achievement. Yet it is clear that this story is very painful to tell on that level. The very brevity of the actual narrative is testimony to that. In part, it is also difficult to tell, because it is about personal ambition, a difficult theme to address for a working-class woman whose ambitions had extended beyond the home and family. Finally, it involves a personal betrayal by someone on whom Doña María modeled her public career and ambitions—Evita Perón. If she is to tell this story, then, Doña María must place it in another mode—that of the political. At this level she is able to fashion its essential meaning as a political fable—she even calls it a *fábula*—which speaks to the political degeneration of Peronism. Peronism has become "aburguesado," and the story of her great disillusionment is presented as a metonym of that larger process. Her own personal ambitions are minimized; she is simply one of the "noble sort," one of the "many women in Berisso who were worth their weight in gold" and who sacrificed so much in the struggle that had elevated Perón.

The coherence achieved by this maneuver is, however, tentative and fragile. Partly this is because of the inherent implausibility of some of the explanations. To explain the fact that she was replaced by a rich woman in terms of the need for campaign money strains credulity. Peronism in 1950, with its near monopoly on the state and the political process, scarcely needed the money of rich women to finance its campaigns. More importantly, it would seem that the depth of the emotion the event tapped into precluded any stable closure. In subsequent interviews over the next few weeks she returned to the theme many times, and despite her attempts to maintain the story within the parameters of a general political fable, the personal pain of the episode frequently takes over the telling:

> I'm going as deputy, a woman with a lot of money shows up, I don't know anything about it, I'm a woman who is struggling for her family's welfare, of course, we all want to be better off in life, but I carried within my soul from the time I was very little the desire to struggle for the weakest, because that's what my father taught me, because that's what the university of life taught me, what doesn't appear in books but that beats in your heart. On the other hand there is lying, there is betrayal. There is the person who destroys her soul shouting and saying things and there is the one who is there behind the scenes saying, "Let her speak, after all I'll end up on the list of candidates, because I'll put up the money."

This is the last time in her life story that she addresses the event, and we can see how fragile the resolution of the issues raised by the telling of the story remains. She is still concerned about the issue of personal ambition. She feels it necessary to justify her "desire to be better off in life" in terms of her character as a person who has always wanted to defend the weak. She here returns to the safety of her fundamental stability narrative, her projection of her self as someone with a consistent identity based on core values inherited from her father and confirmed by the "university of life." Yet the reward that this assertion of moral consistency merits, the confirmation of a valued status in the wider national community, is thwarted by cynical betrayal. The language used to portray this betrayal is not that of abstract political ideology. Rather, it is a language that speaks in an emotional, deeply personal register of pain, about carrying things within the soul, things that "strike your heart" and that lead you to "destroy your soul giving voice."

Story 7
The Visit to Magdalena and the Arrest of Cipriano Reyes

There were different thoughts here about Reyes's arrest. There were those who said that there was some reason for him being a prisoner, they didn't arrest him for nothing, because in a meeting of theirs they put microphones in the house and he didn't know, and they took the recordings to Perón, and we didn't participate in those meetings, and God illuminated me in such a way, in the town of Magdalena, well I believe strongly in God, perhaps that was why. I'm not Catholic, I don't go to church, I don't throw myself on my knees, I don't light candles, I don't say good day, father, to a priest, because for me he is a man dressed in black. But I firmly believe in God. My husband says to me—there was a block of land that I lost, that came to me through my mother, because when she was small her mother and father died. In Argentina, my Spanish grandparents and Luis Monteverde, brought up the three children, Ramón my uncle, Andrea my aunt, and my mother, Natalia. So my mother always said that she had lost her parents very young and that Luis Monteverde had brought her up, and I know that he has left us some property in Magdalena, a block of land in front of the train station, with a house. But my sister and I were young women with our children and husbands, and I said to my husband, "When are we going to see that property in Magdalena? That my mother says is there, just ask in the municipality in her name."

My husband used to say, "But daughter of God, the people from Magdalena escape to La Plata because they are dying of hunger there."

Did you know that on that piece of land there is now a military housing complex, with tall houses? Well, this story of the block of land of my mother is relevant for the following reason. The day that they arrested Reyes and that they went through the streets of Berisso with an effigy of him, with a rope here shouting, to the gallows, to the gallows, that very day my husband said to me bright and early— it was one of those hot days that starts out a little chilly, "Let's go to Magdalena, what do you think?"

I said, "Finally, you've thought about it."

"Let's go," he said, "we'll lunch there and come back in the late afternoon."

That was the day they took Reyes off, when there was a meeting that was so dangerous that if I was there I would have bought seven years like them. . . . Reyes was arrested in his house, they took him to the capital, to the prison of Las Heras, incommunicado, because there were microphones, a person who had entered the house like a great friend took away the microphones, the recordings, and talked of everything, and if not, why did they get seven years?

Well, we arrived in Magdalena and went to the town hall; "Look," the mayor tells us, "I'm very surprised that living in Berisso, three hours away from here that you never came, you've lost it because you wanted to lose it."

And I said to him, "I used to say to my husband that, but he said that in Magdalena there was much poverty, that it wasn't worth paying the taxes."

"But," he says, "Señora, in thirty years you didn't pay a single day's taxes. You've lost any claim to the property, the municipality auctioned it off. Broke it into lots." Can you imagine a block of lots? I would be very rich. It doesn't matter, but let's get back to the facts of what happened to me that day. So at midday we were feeling hungry and we were walking about, and there is a beautiful plaza in Magdalena, and there was a lad, a soldier seated on a bench taking the sun with his cap in his hand, and my husband asks him, "Did you eat?"

"No."

"Come and lunch with us, because I remember when I was a soldier being hungry, let's go and eat."

"Well," the kid says, "if you insist."

So we went in a hotel on the plaza and we ate, and my husband had the habit when he paid the bill of folding it and putting it here in his jacket, to look at it later, in the house, whatever, one of those habits. Look at the way life is. That night they came looking for me as well, and they took me off. Well, we were finishing eating, he paid the owner, and a man comes in and says, "There's a terrible revolt, they've taken Reyes away, they are going to kill him."

Another man comes in, "In Berisso there's a real mess."

"What's happening," asks my husband, "I'm with my wife, we're from Berisso."

"You won't be able to get there, they've stopped all the trains, everything's stopped."

"Ay, ay," we said, and we went out into the street, and he put the bill, here. One of those unconscious things. That bill saved me from being taken away. Well, if I was in Magdalena I couldn't be there, obviously. Well, a man with a truck took us as far as the roundabout, the other side of La Plata there's a roundabout, with a big flower bed that divides one barrio from another.

The man says, "Look, señor, I don't want problems," like saying you've gone to Magdalena to escape, something like that, "I'll leave you here."

My husband says, "Thank you, from here to Berisso we'll get there, even if we have to walk, because the kids will be afraid."

You could hear all the noise, the fireworks going off. Reyes wanted to kill Perón. . . . how were we not going to believe it if the federal police arrive here with the commissar general of the Argentine police force to detain a man planning a rising with some military figures to overthrow the government of Perón, how are the people not going to believe this, I myself believed it.

I said, "Viejo, what's happening with Reyes? What does he want to do?" He said to me, "You, be quiet, you stay quiet, you stay in the house while I make some calls, tomorrow I won't go to work, I'll stay with you."

At 3:30 in the morning they turned up, knocking, ringing the bell. So my husband says, "Who is it?"

"Does Fernandez live here?" I think they asked, and my husband said, "No, this is the Roldán's, I am Roldán."

"You are the husband of María Roldán?"

"Yes, sir, I am," he said from inside.

"Well, we've come to detain the señora."

I had gone to bed more or less dressed, with no nightdress. So I lifted the edge of a curtain in the dining room, and my word, there was a gang of men, a military thing outside, with lights that were going, tu, tu, tu. Ah, I was afraid that the kids would be shocked.

I said to them through the window, I did that so that they would listen to me, "Do you have a judge's order?"

"Yes, we have a judge's order."

"Let me see it." He put it like this up against the glass and shone a lantern on it. It said why, etc., I read it carefully. It said, detained, federal police.

There they would explain everything to me. Reyes was already there, Estapiche was there, Giovanelli, another who died, Sedan, who died a short time ago, was there. There was something like a dozen, more, maybe four dozen. They were rounding up anybody.

So I opened up, when I saw the judge's order, the seal of the judge, my husband opened up, and eight people came in, and there was one, a big black man, with a hat down to here, I looked at him a little, I didn't say anything to my husband, who had to go to work in a few hours, let him at least sleep for some time.

And I say, "Look, señor, if you find anything in this house, I will be very grateful because you have entered a home that is a temple."

And he said to the other man, "She's bad, this *gallega*."

They were all dressed in civilian clothes, none was police, and I knew they were police.

"Look, señor, excuse me, once more, I'm not gallega, my mother yes, but if I were gallega, if you had studied a little our history you would know that Spain is our mother country, so why offend the Galicians. Let's leave Spain out of it. Why are you here?"

"To detain you, señora, do you have a problem with that?"

"Absolutely not. If you are going to check out the house, do so, don't leave anything unturned. There is nothing hidden here."

"Señora," he says, "there is a communication from the federal police saying that you have had meetings in this house."

In that house I used to have a large room, but I never had big meetings. Sometimes meetings with four or five women. I was a delegate, they would come to ask me something, and I would meet with them.

"Here there were more than thirty or forty people at night, bla, bla, bla."

I said, "Well, look, señor, let's not discuss it here. You take me and I'll discuss it with Señor Comisario Marsillac, when I'm in the Federal Capital. I'll answer whatever he asks, but here no, because I have two children, and I want quiet in my home, this is a home, not a police station."

"That's fine, señora." They went through everything, even a tank of rainwater that we had for when there was a scarcity of water in Berisso. They poked around in it with a stick. I said to them, and my husband, too, "You don't seem to realize señores, that if there were machine guns there, if there were weapons, we wouldn't throw them in the water and soak them, wet gunpowder is useless. You are wasting time." They opened the closets, checked through the knives and forks, the books, my daughter had a tray, with artificial flowers, and they started to mess it up, and my daughter said, "One moment please, the one who's involved in the union is my mother, so don't touch my school things, I'll never forget it, be careful touching my flowers because it took me hours to put them in."

Well, I took something warmer, all my documents, and my husband says, "Wait a minute, vieja."

"The señora cannot waste anymore time," one of them says, and my husband says, "I married her, not you, my wife has to listen to me before leaving, I'm going to speak."

"Take this," he says, and goes to the wardrobe, gets out the jacket and takes out the bill, from the place in Magdalena, where we had lunch, the bill has a symbol with three telephones on it. So I took it.

They took me to the San Miguel asylum, and kept me there three days. They took me in a car. The only thing I asked God was that they not kill me, that I had children to raise. A woman like me, a laborista almost got us sent to the gallows, hijo querido. Three days of coming and going, a little sleep, a tea, a little potatoes with oil that seemed like grease, and back to the interrogation.

And finally the police chief says to me, "Señora, I'm going to give you some advice, you are an intelligent woman, capable, impulsive, and you love the working class very much, you love children very much I would imagine, why don't you put yourself to work in the schools, in the cooperatives, in things like that, not in the union, in unions there are a lot of weapons, a lot of upheaval, funny business."

"There is much justice, which is not the same thing," I said, "thanks to the union we are eating a bit more bread, thanks to the union the bosses respect us, thanks to the union our kids go to school with full stomachs, in white overalls and new shoes, thanks to the union we have many things, even mutual clinics for when we get sick, and I'm going to tell you something, Señor Marsillac, forgive me saying this, instead of giving me advice, in my house we need money, if you have money why don't you give me some instead of advice, because, you know, at this stage of my life, with all I've been through, advice is what I don't need."

He pushed a button, take her away. Inside again. They kept me three days. They wanted a declaration that said, yes sir, I'll leave everything, for what was all this struggle, look what happened to me. So anyway, I opened my pocketbook, they let me have it because they had already checked it. Where were you yesterday? Here sir. He pushed another button. A huge guy appeared, tall, with a body like one of those who eat a kilo of meat at a sitting, these negros who are on horseback, the cavalry.

"Do you know the señora?"

The man says, "I don't have the honor."

"I don't know you either," I say.

"This señor official has been about Berisso, he has been observing your house with other police, and he says that last night there was a meeting in your house, no, that yesterday there was a meeting in your house," in the afternoon when I was in Magdalena, "and there were more than thirty people in your house, what did they talk about in that meeting, señora? Tell the truth."

I said, "It's quite simple—I wasn't there, the children stayed with a neighbor, the oldest was going to play football. Here, señor, someone has lied."

The one who stood there behind me, "In the señora's house there was a meeting," he said with the face of one who is accused, he was accusing himself.

I said to him, "Look, señor official, I don't know who you are, if you need another stripe here, if your salary can't feed your family, go and wash dishes at night, as many other policemen do, but don't lie, because I was in Magdalena, and if you don't believe me, look at this, and if you still don't believe me you have a phone here, señor comisario general, speak with those numbers on the bill and ask if the Roldáns didn't have lunch there with a lad, a soldier, who had been in the square and came to eat with us. I'll tell you even more. In the afternoon we visited the church and all the town of Magdalena, and a man brought us back in a truck to the beginning of La Plata, because if not we would have had to walk. So see how you've lied. A man can be anything but not a liar."

The other one pushed a button, take her away — because there was always someone behind me, inside again, two hours later they'd bring you back again and so on.

At last, they said to me, "Señora, the declarations you have made have had a rebellious and angry tone."

"And how do you think I'm going to feel, señor comisario, if the only thing I've done is sometimes abandon my family to defend the rights of my compañeras to a piece of bread, and you drag me here like a criminal, like a whore, like a good-for-nothing from the street. You don't come looking for a lady like myself at three in the morning with eight men, you come at midday, because I'm a lady like your señora. That's why I get mad, señor, because there was no delicacy. And I'll tell you something else, when I was going to the police wagon I dropped a bottle of aspirin, and when I bent down to pick it up one of these henchmen gave me a kick; you don't do that to a woman, tell your people to be more disciplined, because you don't strike the people, because there'll come a day when the people strike you. So if you want I'll go, if not I'll stay, whatever you wish."

In front of such disgraceful behavior what was I going to do? Stay at home and cry? No, it wasn't the time for crying, it was the moment to make them understand that the potatoes were burning and someone had to save them from the fire, and we did that, because until the plants closed — the other day I met a woman who had received her indemnification from Armour, she received the envelope. These are all conquests that still exist.

They brought me back to Berisso in a huge car, black, I seemed like the queen of Java. When I left, I went in a truck, the sort with cells that they use for all the good-for-nothings, the prisoners who rob and kill.

One of them said to me, "Forgive us, señora, we are acting as our chief orders us."

"Yes," I said, "you were born to strike the people, my husband has to go to work tomorrow in the frigorífico with a knife that is the only weapon that we have, truth and work, but don't be so keen to strike the people, things are going to change, because you are also poor. I know policemen who go around asking for a kilo of meat on credit, a liter of milk for their kids, and I know wives of policemen who go to wash floors and clothes. Do you know what harm you have done to the women of Berisso giving me a kick like that, that kick doesn't hurt me anymore, that kick is a kick of the devil, of satan. But do you know how bad that is, when you could pick me up with your finger and throw me wherever you want, why give me a kick."

"They are things that happen, señora, we had not had any sleep for three days."

"That's not my fault, señor, but if your wife merits respect, so do I. When you pick up a woman, even a good-for-nothing from the street, you should never lay a hand on her."

That's how I carried myself.

This story was told toward the end of our interview sessions in 1987. It came in response to a growing attempt on my part to understand the nature of Doña María's relationship with Cipriano Reyes and the Partido Laborista. I knew, of course, that Reyes had been a key figure in her life. I had been originally introduced to her by Reyes. He, in turn, figured prominently in the narrative of her early years of union militancy and political activity. My interest in this aspect of her life story was initially due to a simple desire to acquire a better understanding of the impact of the split between Reyes and Perón in the community that had been the base from which Reyes's national career had been launched. And yet the few times that I had specifically tried to probe this issue, Doña María's response had been vague and confusing. Part of that confusion was centered on chronology and labels. She consistently referred to herself as a lifelong Peronist and in the early part of her narrative would refer with some bitterness to the fact that Reyes was responsible for the disappearance of the Partido Laborista. Yet I also realized that she had in fact maintained her contact with Reyes while he was in prison and had joined him when he had relaunched the Partido Laborista after the fall of Perón in 1955. A newspaper cutting that she showed me—one of the very few documents that she had—reported a speech she had made on behalf of laborismo during the midterm elections of 1960. Her decision to finally address the issue in depth, after many months of interviews, may have been related to the fact that she had recently told the story of her great disillusionment and that in her mind, for reasons that will become clear, the two themes were related. It may also have been due to an increased sense on her part of my trustworthiness as a sympathetic listener.

There are several features worthy of note about this story. First, it is indeed a story that she tells. Her response to my insistent queries for clarification is not to offer a chronicle of her relationship to Reyes or of what had happened to laborismo. Nor did she offer an exposition. Instead, she tells a story about herself and an event that happened to her. Indeed, she falls back on the genre with which she is most familiar—the personal experience anecdote framed as an authority tale with strong performative features.

We should note, too, that this is an extraordinarily complex and sophisticated piece of narration. Formally speaking, it involves several features beyond the use of directly reported speech: the embedding of several secondary narratives and the frequent use of metanarrational statements to establish the relevance of these to the central narrative. She also uses asides to maintain a parallel commentary on the arrest of Reyes and others and their possible guilt in the affair, using these as a counterpoint to her own claim of innocence and her bettering of the authorities involved in the case. I am not, however, primarily interested in analyzing the formal elements behind this sophisticated narrative. Rather, I want to ask what this sophistication might tell us. It is instructive to contrast this story with that of "The Great Disillusionment." The latter is a far less accomplished narrative that struggles to contain the experiences and emotions that it frames. "The Visit to Magdalena" is far better formed as a story, even though it, too, deals with painful and traumatic issues, in large part because it had been rehearsed and performed much more frequently. Here the importance of contextualizing narrative performance becomes evident.

In an important sense narratives are social constructions framed by the active negotiation of meaning between actors within social and discursive communities. In a basic sense the narrating of stories within a life story usually follows the injunction that a speaker's account must not directly challenge the core elements of an addressee's own life story. It is, of course, far easier for analysts to enunciate this principle than for storytellers to follow it. Yet, as Kenneth Gergen and Mary Gergen note, the cooperative negotiation of meaning "is especially invited under circumstances in which the individual is asked to justify behavior, that is when one has acted disagreeably with regard to the common frame of understanding."[40] Such negotiation can be publicly achieved through the sorts of cultural performances that Barbara Myerhoff speaks of, and through other social interactions within the family and community. It can also, however, be achieved through the implicit, anticipatory negotiation of which the Gergens speak. They argue that "people try to avoid the threat of direct negotiation by taking prior account of the public intelligibility of their actions. They select in advance actions that can be justified in terms of a publicly acceptable narrative" (269).

Within Berisso, among her own generation in particular, Doña María was known as a laborista. She herself told me that even in the mid-1980s she was often reminded by people in "Peronist meetings" about "how laborista you were, María." The exact import of this observation is difficult to assess. She does not elaborate on it, though the clear implication is that it was something that called for some sort of justificatory response on her part. The status of Reyes and laborismo within the collective memory of Berisso was a complex issue. As a public figure, Reyes has been almost completely erased from this memory. In private, many of those who remember the struggles of the mid-1940s, particularly those who had been union activists between 1943 and 1946, pay him his due as an important figure in the community's past. Publicly, however, there is no such recognition. Reyes was not invited to, nor was he mentioned in, any of the public events surrounding the fiftieth anniversary celebrations of 17 October 1945 in Berisso. His own actions and statements had compounded this silencing. In 1983 he had openly called for a vote for Raúl Alfonsín, the Radical Party candidate, in the elections that ended the military regime. In 1987, at the time I was interviewing Doña María, he published a book of memoirs titled *The Farce of Peronism*. In earlier years the issue of Reyes and laborismo had been still more difficult for Doña María to negotiate. He was registered in the collective memory of Berisso, and in the broader narrative of national Peronism, as one who had fallen out with Perón and plotted to assassinate him. After 1955, as Peronism entered a protracted period of union and political opposition to a series of anti-Peronist regimes, the Partido Laborista was one of many parties seeking to benefit from the political proscription of Peronism. Reyes was elected to the constitutional convention of 1957 that drew up the charter that replaced the Peronist constitution of 1949.

We can begin now to appreciate the context within which this story was shaped. Its basic function is evidently to establish Doña María's innocence of any involvement in a plot against Perón. At the same time, in the asides that comment on Reyes's arrest she voices uncritically the vox populi on the case: "Reyes wanted to kill Perón. . . . how were we not going to believe it if the federal police arrive here with the commissar general of the Argentine police force to detain a man planning a rising with some military figures to overthrow the government of Perón, how are the people not going to believe this, I myself believed it." Her own distance from Reyes in this matter is clear. "Viejo, what's happening with Reyes? What does he want to do?" she asks her husband when they get back to Berisso. Symbolically, her presence in Magdalena is intended to underline this distance. Geographical separation from the events would seem to metaphorically imply political distance. Her desire to establish her innocence in this affair also accounts for the volume of detail included in this tale, detail that goes beyond the immediate needs of the story. Extrathematic detail very often has an evaluative function, helping establish the narrator's credibility and the authenticity of the story with an audience who can be expected to verify the detail offered.[41] Finally, Doña María invokes God's authority. "God illuminated me in such a way in the town of Magdalena," she says.

She was saved by God, and the clear implication is that she would not have been saved if she had not been innocent.

We may also note that, beyond the affirmation of her own innocence and the asserting of the community's vision of Reyes's guilt, the narrative strategy that she adopts also serves her needs in "the cooperative construction of meaning" of these events. By telling this story as a personal experience anecdote she is able to rekey it, establishing its fundamental meaning on a personal level centered on her arrest and ill treatment by the police. The coda of the story establishes her victory in a battle of wits with the authorities. She arrives back in Berisso "like the queen of Java" in a big black car. This theme was guaranteed to evoke a shared, sympathetic response from her audience. Thus the personal level of meaning is also played out within a communal mode. Her comment to the policeman at the end of the story, "Do you know what harm you have done to the women of Berisso giving me a kick like that?" explicitly frames the story at this level. Shortly after she had finished the story, I asked her how she had been received by her compañeras on her return:

> The way of speaking of the poor, of the people, of the *chusma* [the lowest ones]. "What did they say to you, those good-for-nothing cops? What did they do to you, María? Did they hit you? That is the way in which the people react, and it comes from the heart; it's a virgin question, because the woman with a cup of tea playing canasta doesn't speak like that, but here inside she has the devil, the woman who speaks like that it's because she defends another woman who has done well by her, because it is the people who haven't got culture but who have in their chest a heart, that's the way they received me back."

The story's meaning is thus established at a community level as an affirmation of solidarity among working women.

Once more we can see the shifting of mnemonic modes at work in the recalling of important events. This time Doña María explicitly avoids placing this story at the level at which it would present most problems for her—the political. By establishing its meaning

within the other two modes she is able to evade the thorny problem of confronting the larger, political context behind this story.
Reyes's arrest and that of the other laboristas was the culmination
of a process that Perón had begun two years earlier with his call to
subsume laborismo within a new state-controlled party. It represented Perón's clear determination to not tolerate the existence of
an autonomous working-class party. Reyes's immunity as a deputy
had been the only thing that had prevented his arrest before 1948.
Within Berisso this process had already been played out in the union
and in the streets. By late 1946 those trade unionists loyal to Reyes
had already been forced out of the leadership by their erstwhile
compañeros and former fellow laboristas. Shots had been fired in
the streets, as rivals broke up each other's meetings. The laboristas
had held their own, separate celebration of the first anniversary of
17 October in La Plata. Yet none of this political context appears in
Doña María's story of the arrests of 1948. Indeed, it is difficult to see
how it could have appeared and still functioned successfully as an
acceptable narrative within the community.

Over the years, then, Doña María had managed to successfully
negotiate the meaning of Reyes's arrest and her own escape through
the manipulation of levels that effectively silenced important elements of this story and enabled her to frame the story as a personal
experience anecdote. Although understanding the social negotiation of meaning is important in analyzing the form and content
of particular narratives, we must also realize that narratives are also
at bottom intensely personal documents. The wider life story must
succeed not only in terms of meeting certain social criteria but also
in terms ultimately of cohering for the narrator herself. The process of achieving personal coherence, of staving off epistemological
crisis, is nearly always far more complex than analysis of a single
story would indicate. Indeed, the very success of a story such as that
of "The Visit to Magdalena" in formal narrative terms in asserting
its version, with its silences and evasions and manipulations, tends
to preempt a recognition and analysis of the wider process. In this
particular case, access to the complete text of the life story offers
us insight into this process. The theme of Reyes, Perón, and laborismo continued to haunt much of the latter part of her life story

in what might be called an extended expository coda to "The Visit to Magdalena."

Much of this coda consists in elaborating on the theme of her own distance from the events. She also puts much of the blame on Reyes for what happened and, again, minimizes Perón's role. She does this partly by directly ascribing the crisis to Reyes's ambition, "He wanted to be more than Perón, and that couldn't be." At times, too, it is described as a standoff between two headstrong men that didn't involve her. Perhaps most interestingly, we find a frequently repeated pattern of shifting the historical sequence in a particular fashion. This pattern appears at first glance to be due to problems of memory on her part. Indeed, much of my confusion during the interviews when we spoke of this theme was due to this pattern, which I ascribed to personal problems of recollection. With hindsight I now think that this was a symptomatic form of misrecollection that served her needs in terms of life story coherence but was at variance with my needs as a historian for empirical clarity. Portelli in his essay on Luigi Trastulli observes that in addition to shifting events and their meanings from one "mode" to another, memory does its healing work by means of "horizontal chronological shifts." In the case of Luigi Trastulli's death this meant that it was "misremembered," enabling it to be placed within a communal mode in accord with the community's sense of dignity and self-respect.

Something of this sort happens in Doña María's recounting of the events surrounding the Perón-Reyes split and the fate of laborismo. In 1947, for example, Reyes survived an assassination attempt, which was widely assumed to have had official backing and signaled a final breakdown in the relations between laborismo and the Peronist movement. Doña María in fact places this event in the period before 1946 and claims that it was part of the anti-Perón inspired campaign designed to buy off or eliminate union leaders like Reyes. By reallocating it temporally she is able to establish its meaning as part of the union struggle against the bosses. Concomitantly, she is able to evade the issue of Perón's responsibility.

The most common example of this pattern of confusing temporal markers involves the issue of the disappearance of the Partido Laborista. There are two historical moments in this drama. One refers to when Perón declares in 1946 the disappearance of all the pro-Perón parties under the umbrella of a new centralized state-sponsored party. The other happens in 1960 when Reyes, behind the backs of the members, abandons the party that had been relaunched in 1955. Doña María asserts many times that nobody outside the circle of a few leaders knew what had gone on. They simply woke up one day and found the party and its locals closed. Doña María consistently conflates these two moments, telescoping the two stages. At one moment in an interview shortly after the telling of the Magdalena story, when she has returned to the theme of how difficult it was for the laborista militants in 1946 to accept Perón's dictate, she adds, "but in the end we knew who was right, the party was sold, it was handed over, there was funny business." Or again, after stating that Peronism was suffocating laborismo, she adds, "But it was suffocated because there was betrayal, if it had been handled right it would still exist, but something happened, something that we'll never know, but there was betrayal by the principal leaders, behind closed doors." Once again, the chronological shift permits her to minimize Perón's role in the fate of laborismo.

These mnemonic mechanisms raise the broader issue of how painful memories are handled in life stories. In the Magdalena story and its extended coda we are dealing with memory traces, the remains that are left within individual and collective memory many years later. The Partido Laborista was in historical terms a failure, a road not taken. In the Berisso of the 1980s it lacked any physical, spatial embodiment that could have served as a site of commemoration. From the point of view of working-class militants it is extremely difficult to talk of failure, of miscalculation, of historical moments that were not seized. This was especially the case within a community in which the dominant alternative that had won that historical race was so powerfully present. We have already examined some of the narrative ways in which Doña María handled this problem, dealt with her own epistemological crisis. But underlying these narrative strategies there were a set of painful personal choices. In the end, I suspect, she made the decision to opt for the assurance and comfort of redefining her life story within the dominant community mode, and that implied minimizing her role as a laborista. Whereas

Reyes had left Berisso immediately after his election as a deputy in 1946, Doña María lived out her life within the community, pursuing her ambitions within the terms which that community offered. In this way she was able to negotiate the pain of historical defeat and maintain a sense of consistent identity and dignity. As Alessandro Portelli notes when speaking of communist militants in Italy, "If the past is to justify the present, a life of struggle can found self-esteem and personal identity only if these struggles are described as a success. . . . the need to defend one's own dignity and historical presence is often at the root of a 'consensus' version of history."[42] This commitment to the consensus view implied as a corollary the presence of an overarching progressive narrative as a framework for her life story, her ability to identify her own life trajectory with that of Peronism. As Peronism had succeeded, so in some final sense had her life.

The alternative would have been difficult to sustain. As Portelli goes on to note of his dissident Italian communist militants, "The discourse of negation is burdened by the fear of disapproval and isolation" (113). All narratives to some extent try to attain consensus. In a fundamental way stories are told to socialize, to achieve consensus. Victor Turner argued, for example, that social dramas—the dramatic structure that social actions follow and that underlies a culture's socially sanctioned plots—reach their conclusion in a phase of reintegration. For Turner this phase was characterized by "a process of converting particular values and ends into a system of shared consensual meaning."[43] And yet the discourse of negation is also difficult to finally suppress. Turner himself notes that the achievement of such consensus is always provisional. The tension that accompanies this negotiation can result in narrative terms in the assertion of an alternative historical and personal truth. This "uchronic imagination"—the term is Portelli's—can have a dual purpose. It can be one way that memory's healing urge goes to work, through the expression of a utopian wish-fulfillment in which historical reality is made to correspond more closely to desire and aspiration. This can be a mechanism for dealing with painful and unpalatable truths that can threaten a sense of individual worth and dignity. Such utopian statements are frequently figured by the creation of mythical categories. In Doña María's narrative the union appears in this way as the ultimate mythical land of harmony, where respect is always granted, where her definition as a laborista has no costs, where finally the civilizing, educational process undertaken can be equated with the work of Jesus. At the same time, such representations can also be powerful assertions of what ought to be, of the social world in idealized terms that carries within it a critique of the world as it is.

The suppression of the Partido Laborista was in a profound sense a traumatic experience for Doña María and other laborista activists in Berisso. Doña María recalled that "there were grown men crying, who couldn't believe Perón could do such a thing." Most found some new form of accommodation. For some it was the simple changing of a formal label. For others like Doña María it was a more complex, tenuous arrangement. For many it meant abandoning political activity for good. In 1995 I interviewed an old laborista in Berisso who recalled that era. He had, he told me, spent the Perón era as director of popular libraries in Berisso, a quiet retreat very different from his activism prior to 1948, but a position from which he could "continue to serve the people." After 1955 he had resumed political activism within a revived local Peronism. He considered himself, as did Doña María, a "lifelong Peronist," and yet when I asked him what had gone wrong in 1946, he simply shook his head and, with tears in his eyes, said "that should never have happened."[44] The trauma was rooted, too, in the realization that they had not had the support of the rank and file. Despite the sacrifices, the activism of the preceding years, the rank-and-file response to Perón's order to abandon laborismo was overwhelming. Alfredo Panelli, the secretary for all laborista union groupings in 1946, told me that those groupings, including the one in Berisso, voted massively to abandon the Partido Laborista and enter the new Partido Único de la Revolución Nacional.

For Doña María the trauma was also given a very personal note by what happened to her in 1950. The story of her great disillusionment is intimately linked to the visit to Magdalena. Although she tells the story to prove her innocence and her credentials as a Peronist, the fact was that she continued to be viewed with suspicion within Peronism. Her continued identification as someone whose loyalty was suspect was, I think, the real reason for her removal from the list of candidates rather than Peronism's need of the money of rich people. Again, her recognition of this possibility comes only at the very end of her life story, which contains traces of the trauma of these events, a trauma that is both expressed and contained in this complex narrative. Yet such containment is a precarious achievement. The existence of other elements is also evident. Most notably, they express themselves at moments in the text when Doña María's deepest feelings conflict with the various containment strategies. There exists a space between the coherence schemas of any life story and the actual narrating of that life. This is a space where emotion, loss, and mourning are inescapably present, and where, for this very reason, final coherence is elusive. In the extended coda to "The Visit to Magdalena, at the very end of her narrative, Doña María expresses words of doubt, sorrow, and anger:

> I kept on with laborismo after 1955 because I couldn't believe that Perón could simply erase laborismo, I couldn't believe it, for me it was something that simply should not have happened, because I went up and down the country many times shouting long live the Partido Laborista, long live Juan Perón. I knew many people who had sold their house, many had separated from their spouses, many sold tickets to raise money to pay for a wall poster, I said to myself, how can they just erase all this just like that? . . . when he did that I cried a lot because it was something that was ours, from our sacrifice . . . years of putting our lives at risk and of seeing many dead comrades, not just months, years, so my husband said to me, "Struggles are like that, at times they fill you with flowers, at others with thorns," and that's the way it was. A woman of my caliber, this isn't to boast, but of my caliber there were many in the country, women of the packing plants especially, hard workers, capable of doing great good and of struggling for their workmates, women who should have made it as deputies, as senators, as mayors, very capable women, but they never got that chance.

Such ultimately indigestible feelings are the source of the deep dilemma at the root of what we have called the tragic irony of the darker side of Doña María's life story. It is a source of irreconcilable narrative elements that must simply remain in tense coexistence within the story. She is at one and the same time in her telling one who "had always been a woman of the Peronist movement" and also someone who could never finally reconcile herself to what history, and Perón, had wrought:

> If a party in which I was a militant, which took a man to the presidency, for which I spoke on 17 October, for which I risked my life, and I see that, I say, he's not going to ignore us, erase our existence, and yet he did just that, did Perón, I adore Perón and I believe that a better government than his Argentina never had, but I can't fail to recognize that there were things that happened that shouldn't have happened.

3

"TALES TOLD

OUT ON THE BORDERLANDS"

Reading Doña María's Story for Gender

The processes of working class autobiography, of people's history and of the working class novel cannot show a proper and valid culture existing in its own right, underneath the official forms, waiting for revelation. Accounts of working class life are told by tension and ambiguity, out on the borderlands. — Carolyn Steedman, *Landscape for a Good Woman*

Oral history has long assumed a privileged place within the practice of women's history. The use of oral testimony to retrieve the historical experience of women marginalized from the master narratives of history has become a standard part of the analytical repertoire available to feminist historians. At its most basic level, the use of such testimony has served to inscribe a broad range of women's voices within the construction of what Joan Scott has called "herstory." The range of female actors present within historical narrative has been greatly expanded during the last three decades, particularly in the case of working women doubly marginalized by both their gender and class status. However, the claims for oral history have frequently reached beyond its use in expanding the range of historical agents. Many feminist scholars have argued that oral history is a uniquely feminist methodology that undercuts the normal hierarchical relationship between scholar and informant.[1]

And yet in some paradoxical way the more that women have been written into the historical narrative the more problematic has the enterprise of recovering hidden voices, of rescuing female subjectivity, come to appear. This paradox is in part due to a recognition on the part of those who use oral sources of the difficulty in assuming that such testimony offers unmediated access to subjective historical experience. In part, too, the problematization of the use of oral testimony is one aspect of a broader reaction on the part of historians of women to the realization that no matter how far the inscription of women into historical narratives has proceeded, the lived experience of women cannot ultimately be represented except in terms of the dominant male discourse. As Julia Swindells and Lisa Jardine summarize this position, as it emerged in debates within British social history in the 1980s, "These feminist historians wanted to argue that there was no evidence of women's lived experience in a form available to the historian, even if she *is* a feminist historian."[2] Beyond a critique of the practice of British social history and its privileged texts this position could lead in two directions. For the feminist historians referred to by Swindells and Jardine psychoanalysis would lead into the female unconscious, the conflictual site of women's subjectivity and agency. Alternatively, some scholars were drawn to a more explicitly poststructuralist position. Joan Scott would, for example, argue that "experience" as an analytical category was itself problematic, leading to a nostalgic search for authenticity and hindering analysis of the discourses that produce difference and the experience of difference.[3] In a parallel fashion we can see a similar gesture of problematization on the part of those scholars associated with the Subaltern Studies group. Modifying her by now famous question, "Can the subaltern speak?" Gayatri Chakravorty Spivak would go on to affirm that "there is no space from which the subaltern sexed subject can speak."[4] Gyan Prakash, another member of the group, has summarized the import of Spivak's position in the following terms:

"It is impossible to retrieve the woman's voice when she was not given a subject-position from which to speak. This argument runs counter to the historiographical convention of retrieval to recover the histories of the traditionally ignored—women, workers, peasants and minorities. Spivak's point, however, is not that such retrievals should not be undertaken but that the very project of recovery depends on the historical erasure of the subaltern voice."[5]

In this chapter I want to maintain this problematizing gesture as a sort of epistemological warning against the too-easy reading off of a subaltern woman's voice from the transcript of an oral testimony. Although it is clear that there is a prima facie difference in status between contemporary oral testimony of working women and the fractured texts of nineteenth-century Indian subalterns, I wish to argue that uncovering a gendered voice in such transcripts is still a complex practice fraught with difficulty. In particular, we must bear in mind the injunction taken from textual criticism that "one has to read for gender. . . . it will seldom read for itself."[6] The issue of "reading" returns us, once more, to the condition of the oral history transcript as a text and the practice of textual interpretation. If the central injunction of chapter 1 was the importance of listening, the central focus of this chapter is the need to read. I want to suggest what a "symptomatic" reading for gender of a text such as Doña María's might involve.

At first glance gender is scarcely a promising theme to isolate from the narrative, particularly if one is interested in reclaiming through such personal testimony an authentic, repressed woman's voice and, thus, uncovering something approaching a counterdiscourse. The central events and experiences of Doña María's life are recounted principally in class terms. The dominant events are clustered around her role in the formation of the union in the meatpacking plants, her actions as a shop steward, the 17 October demonstration in favor of Perón, her role in the election campaign of 1946 with the Partido Laborista, her later activism within the local Justicialist Party in Berisso. Although she is clearly aware of the exploitation of women in the plants, this recognition is placed within the overall context of the crucial and basic changes made in the quality of workers' lives— male and female—by the emergence of the union and Perón.

Doña María also emphasizes the respect and equality of treatment she received from male union leaders in the plants:

On the contrary, I was accepted to such an extent that shop stewards
came to ask me questions to clear up problems. For example: María,
what do you think, there is a worker who did such and such, what
should I do, shall I take action, because he arrived late and every time
he comes he gets mad; now leave it alone, at work you don't argue,
later outside tell him to come to the union and we'll all talk about
it for a while. . . . No, I got on fine, they liked me a lot, I have no
complaints.

In a similar vein, Doña María paints a picture of an ideal marriage,
based on mutual respect and understanding between husband and
wife. At different times throughout the narrative she emphasizes
both her acceptance of the role of the good wife, as traditionally defined in Argentine society, and her husband's support of her activi-
ties outside the home. Describing her early life in a tenement house
containing many families before she went to work, she stresses that
she never had problems of lack of respect from the men despite the
forced intimacy of the situation:

> I always say that the woman who knows her place never lacks for
> respect. Nothing strange ever happened to me, but then it never hap-
> pened because I never went around being cute, joking around with
> the men in the patio; I waited for my husband, gave him his food,
> cleaned, stayed with my children.

Her account of the initiation of her activism in the union is framed
in a similar tone:

> Reyes came to see me in my section, the picada, "I come on behalf of
> your husband, he is already in agreement, and if you want to be the
> delegate for this section, because you have the qualities, your hus-
> band says it is fine. . . ." I said to him, "If you have spoken to my
> husband and he has said yes, then I'll also say yes."

Once she is launched on a career beyond the home, she is careful
to emphasize that she was able to do it with his support: "He sup-
ported me in everything I did, if I hadn't had him as a husband I
wouldn't have done what I did."

If one form of self-representation used by Doña María to construct her narrative is that of the "good wife," that of the "good mother" also figures prominently. This self-representation is often expressed in terms of the importance of providing good welfare and love for children as a basic social priority, and the ultimate rationale for political and union struggles—"to give a piece of bread to our children"; "I often had to listen to my children go to bed crying because they were hungry." In Doña María's narrative we also find this notion generalized into a guiding principle that should be used to define the role of women in society. At one stage of her testimony she took out an old newspaper clipping of a speech she had made that was directed specifically at rallying women to the Partido Laborista. The speech started with an affirmation of a basic principle:

> The home is the place where the great national principles are nourished. . . . the home is the very image of the nation, the stronghold of the fatherland, where mothers sing to their children of the hope of a better world, in the home the invincible force is the woman, it is the woman who with her silent sacrifice entrusts the blood of her blood, her children, for the defense of national sovereignty. She is the people confronted with any state that persecutes, terrorizes, and kills.

In line with this general affirmation of the role of mothering and nurturance Doña María also expresses opposition to both divorce and abortion within her narrative.

This construction of a self seems relatively unproblematic: in some ways it is the prototypical Peronist woman's life script, conforming to the dominant representation of women found in Peronist discourse and formally articulated in Peronist ideology. Yet we should be cautious about accepting it at face value. The very logic of the narrative argues against it; other elements and themes Doña María uses to create her story speak of a more complex, ambivalent process of self-identification and story construction. The typical elements of a working-class woman's biography are juxtaposed and overlain with other images, roles, and themes that give Doña María's story a different "twist."

In Doña María's life story we have clear indications early on that her story will contain unconventional elements. Speaking of her childhood, she says:

> I gave my family quite a few worries because I had the rebelliousness that my father had, for me to stay shut up with a needle, sewing and hemming and things like that, was a waste of time, I thought that you had to go beyond that and do other things.

> I was very predisposed to curiosity as a kid, to know what was going on here and there, where there was a political meeting, for example, there I would be, listening.

> Once some friends and I stopped by a button factory in San Martín, listen to this, and we said to the girls working there, "Why are you working for free? Why don't you rebel one day and not come in? Or why don't you have a sit-down strike inside?" . . . We poked our noses in because we felt the pain, the pain of exploitation that was imposed on other girls. Because my father protected me, gave me clothes and food and a place to live, but these others girls, no, they had to go out to give food to an invalid mother, a widowed mother or a father who had lost his wife.

The image of herself as irreverent, as disposed to rebel, forms a crucial part of the emerging plot in Doña María's narrative. Her refusal to turn a blind eye to suffering and injustice, her rebellious temperament lead her into a series of actions and situations after 1944 that form the core of the plot of her story. Yet these crucial elements of her story are made possible by events beyond her control. The emergence of Peronism, the consequent mobilization of the organized working class, with its greater access to the public sphere, all provide the context for her divergence from the accepted story line of a working-class woman. The emergence of Perón will provide the stage on which this individual woman will make her decision to break with her traditional domestic role. In her telling of this story two things are made clear. First, the prior establishment of her image of adolescent curiosity and rebellion enables her in a sense to stress the continuity and rationale of her decision in the mid-1940s, after more than ten years of apparently quiescent domestic bliss, to enter the workforce and adopt a role of union and political militancy. Second, she phrases her explanation of her crucial decision to start work in solidly material terms. She, like many other women in Berisso, went into the meatpacking plants for basic economic reasons. In her case, above all, her husband's salary could not cover the medical bills for her second son, who caught polio. Although she had no illusions about the nature of work in the plants, she thought it better than entering domestic service and cleaning up the "mess of others."

Her activism in the public sphere beyond the family, in both the union and in politics, during the following decade forms the central theme in her life story. The events cover a span of only a decade in a long life, yet they have a disproportionate weight in her narrative. Although the issue of her role beyond the confines of the family is encountered in many forms in her testimony, it is most crucially expressed in a series of anecdotes that recall confrontations with authorities. These personal experience stories, analyzed in depth in chapter 2, serve to confirm her agency in the public sphere.

If the plot that Doña María constructs establishes her heretical status as a rare bird, *una mujer atrevida* (a bold woman), whose life history clearly breaks with the conventional script of women's biography, how are we to read the far more conventional themes and more standard forms of self-representation mentioned at the beginning? Is one set of images true and the other false? Does one set merely reflect a formal conformity to established conventions of working women and their lives while the other represents the authentic woman, the repressed voice normally hidden from history? I think that by looking more closely at the factors in play here we can start to appreciate what is at stake in oral history, particularly as it relates to issues of gendered consciousness and ideological process.

We should start by recognizing the complexity underlying the textual representation of any gendered subjectivity of working women. James Fentress and Chris Wickham have commented that in general "many current discussions of working-class cultures . . . fail to do justice to the kaleidoscope of difference." The factors they list as making up this "kaleidoscope of difference" within working-class culture are daunting in their range: workplace, family and geo-graphical community, religious and ethnic identity, political activ-ism, and the cultures of clubhouse and bar.[7] Luisa Passerini has given us a similar listing of the factors involved in what she calls the "exca-vation of oral traditions" underlying the construction of life stories: "On the one hand, we can imagine church-sermons and religious education classes in the oratory, and on the other political speeches, branch discussions, political party training schools, and even les-sons in prison."[8] As Passerini notes, the impact of such unstructured oral traditions has largely gone uninvestigated. At the very least, however, I suggest that the range of these traditions implies that the category of gender emerges in the life-story text profoundly overdetermined by other, often contradictory, cultural elements and ideologically inflected meanings.

An attempt to itemize the elements that helped produce Doña María's story as a gendered one would need to start, for example, by taking account of the impact of Peronist ideology. Many of the representations of gender present in her narrative are clearly taken from, and reflected in, Peronist discourse as it addressed women. During the crucial decade from 1945 to 1955 Peronism, through its political and cultural institutions, both mobilized and legitimized women as actors within a newly enlarged public sphere. At the same time it attempted to redefine appropriate forms of behavior, ap-propriate divisions between public and private. Although the tradi-tional subordination of women to men was denounced, many of the traditional virtues associated with women were reaffirmed within a reworked ideology of domesticity. By the early 1950s, at the height of Evita Perón's influence, women's work outside the home was expressly condemned, and women's political activity was sharply distinguished from that of men. Politics was considered to be an inherently masculine preserve for which women were ill-adapted. Women's political activity was taken to derive from their unique virtues as mothers, wives, guardians of the hearth. They were intrin-sically unselfish, capable of self-sacrifice and communal in nature, not the greedy individualists symbolized by men in politics. Their nurturing role at home was taken, by extension, to be a metaphor for their unique role as guardians of the nation.[9]

Echoes of this ideology are clearly present in Doña María's life story. Indeed, sometimes they are drawn directly from political speeches expressing this formal rhetoric. Much of the official rhetoric was reinforced by cultural stereotypes embodied in popular cultural images. Meatpacking had a particular niche in both popular culture and the official rhetoric of the Perón era. Many novels were written, for example, in a style that might be referred to as "Peronist realism." Although the fundamental political message of the narrative was to glorify and sentimentalize the struggle of workers and contrast their conditions of life before and after Perón, they were also strongly gendered texts that established, largely by omission and silence, powerful images of gender relationships and hierarchies in the meatpacking plants and communities. A detailed analysis of the representation of women in these texts is presented in the next chapter. Suffice it to say that women are noted by their absence from the main narratives. They appear either as long-suffering mothers or hard-pressed housewives. They are simply absent from the main theme of consciousness-raising and union organizing. The images conveyed in this literature are of an overwhelmingly masculine universe.

This is true not simply because of the characters and the formal structuring of the story line but also because of the presence of what Beatrix Campbell, referring to George Orwell's descriptions of physical labor in *The Road to Wigan Pier,* has recently called the "cult of the masculine."[10] The physical nature of meatpacking labor is a prominent feature of the genre of popular literature to which we are referring. Muscles ripple, sweat pours, and men are driven to superhuman feats of physical endeavor in images that act as a sort of corollary to the male camaraderie and intimacy celebrated in the text.

The point I wish to suggest by referring to both official Peronist ideology as it addressed women and the set of roles and images, particularly in meatpacking, presented in popular cultural texts is not that they were absorbed and then found direct representation in Doña María's narrative. Rather, I am interested in emphasizing that they are certainly one part of the repertoire of roles, conventions, and forms of self-representation that had influenced Doña María in

her life and that she drew on when reflecting on her life, selecting among her experiences, constructing her life story. Bearing this
in mind also helps us understand the tension and sense of dissonance occasioned among women who had entered the workforce.
This tension was particularly strongly felt by those who had adopted
an active role on the public stage of factory and political party, as
they were confronted by a discourse that seemed to challenge the
legitimacy of the decisions they had taken in their lives.

The tension between official ideological forms and locally focused, culturally constructed forms of self-representation can reso-
nate within a life-story text in different ways. The power of such a
tension can often be more easily noted from outside the life story
through related cultural references. In the case of Doña María's
public activism, for example, the sense of tension was highlighted
through the testimony of another woman I interviewed. Irma Pintos was younger than Doña María; her father had formed part of the
leadership group surrounding Reyes in 1945. When I interviewed
her in 1992, some three years after Doña María's death, she recalled:

> But women didn't go on the street, later María Roldán a little . . .
> but my father didn't allow us. . . . I was already seventeen then, I
> had received my aviator's license, but still nothing, we had to stay
> in the house, the woman who wanted to go there, to the union, to
> the street was not, how shall I say, well looked upon, in reality it was
> nearly all men, the few women who got involved were seen as being
> contaminated.[11]

This testimony needs to be contextualized within the local cultural
setting. Although I have no reason to doubt that she was recalling accurately a common local response of the 1940s and 1950s to
female activism, Irma Pintos is also reflecting certain internal dif-
ferentiations within the working-class community of Berisso in the
1940s. She came from a family that had entered a more "respectable"
location in Berisso's sociocultural landscape. This location was very
subtly constituted. It certainly was not a story of embourgeoise-
ment. Her father, Hipólito, had sided with Perón against Reyes and
left the frigorífico to pursue a career within local Peronism. This
choice enabled him to display a certain status that was reflected in

the ostentatious embrace of old values. He insisted that his daughters stay at home, and Irma even had to abandon her career as an aviator. His daughters were invited to dances on certain occasions organized by what passed for the more respectable members of the community—doctors, lawyers, factory foremen, shopkeepers.

Irma Pintos's testimony points to the psychic and social cost of Doña María's life course in a more direct way than does Doña María's own story. Although we can notice the formal juxtaposition of officializing strategies and an individual's life story in the older woman's testimony, this remains at an abstract level. The weight of local values within a vernacular culture permeated by notions of respectability comes across clearly in Irma's comments. The shaping power of these conventions on Doña María's testimony in 1987 is, of course, a complex question. The evaluative judgment—the local wisdom—passed by Irma Pintos had modified since the heyday of Doña María's activism. The harshness of judgments about women and the public sphere had modified in the intervening years. Doña María is, in 1987, reflecting on her life from within the accumulated remains of her memories, the complex, layered mosaic of contemporary attitudes and old coercions and repressions. It is this that makes it difficult to specify which of the possible variables may be dominant in shaping the perception and memory as it was offered to me. Certainly, however, it was not simply "the view from the present" that shaped her remembering. Any view from the present is already profoundly imbricated with influences from the past. The weight of such influences is undeniable. Irma Pintos's words still have a shocking quality. In particular, the almost casual cruelty of the word "contaminada" [contaminated]. It caught me unaware when she said it, and it continues to work on me. Its implication is clear; it connotes sexual disease and impurity. In this sense it can be read as a direct descendant of the medically inflected discourse about women and factory labor, women and the public sphere prevalent in Argentina since the early twentieth century.[12]

The tension and sense of dissonance reflected throughout Doña María's narrative is crucial to understanding many of its contradictions as far as gender relationships are concerned and the difficulties involved in reading it for gender. Although life-story narratives have a tendency to seek coherence and subsume contradiction, this is, as we saw in chapter 2, rarely fully achieved. At times tension and contradiction are starkly presented in competing narrative accounts within the life story. We may take an apparently trivial, but nevertheless suggestive, example from Doña María's life story. In the transcript of her testimony there are two versions of how she acquired her own house. The first version, told early in our interviews, is really not much more than a passing reference to explain her move from the tenement rooms she and her husband had first occupied when they moved to Berisso: "We rented here and there, until one good day my husband says, 'Look, querida, I am going to buy a lot, it's going to be here, and we are going to put a house on it, near the avenue, you and the kids are going to be comfortable.'"

The second version was told much later and involved a narrative of considerable complexity. Doña María framed the story in the following terms at the very beginning:

> Well, it's a story that is a little homely, a nice little story and also a little tough in the sense that my husband, because rents were so cheap, used to say that there was no need to sacrifice ourselves to buy a lot and build a house, that we might not be able to feed the kids, but I, without asking my husband's permission—I've always been a little authoritarian—had taken the initiative.

The story is simple enough, and common enough, too, in Berisso. Doña María heard of a real estate man in La Plata who was offering lots at low monthly payment rates. Without telling her husband, she went to La Plata and bought a lot in a barrio of Berisso called Villa San Carlos, about a mile from the packing houses. The monthly payment would be nine pesos. At the time there was no house on the plot. Eventually, she told her husband of the land:

> One day I say to my husband, "You know, querido, that I bought a lot." "What, what's the matter with you, where did you buy it?" I say, "Look, I went to Tilh's house, the auctioneer, and I bought a lot." My husband got a little angry with me; "here's the payment book." "And what will we give the kids to eat, with what will we buy shoes

for them?" Well, to make a long story short, he got angry and made an issue of it with me. "Look," I say to him, "don't get angry, at least we have some land, someday God will help us to put some bricks on it, but at least we have the plot." He started to laugh: "Well," he says, "we'll have to think about putting aside nine pesos every month." "Don't worry," I say, "I'll find a way to save all that I can."

The next stage of the story involves what Doña María herself calls the intervention of Providence. One day, as she was entering the bank to pay the monthly quota on the plot of land, she encountered a contractor she had known for some time, Distasio. When she explained what she was doing at the bank, and elaborated on her frustration about ever having the money to build a house on the land, Distasio told her that as luck would have it he was going to build a new house for someone, but first they needed to sell the old house and remove it from the land. The owners only wanted $200 for the house. He suggested that this was an ideal solution for Doña María; all she would have to do was to pay for the moving of the house to her plot of land. Doña María showed great interest and told Distasio to call when the time was ready:

> So one day a message arrives for my husband, my husband says, "Why is Distasio calling me?" so I told him the story. "Ay, María, you're going to get us in more trouble"; I say to him, "No, querido, wait and see what he says." The two of us went to the phone. Distasio says, "I spoke with your señora at the bank, and I have a house that's going for $200, it has two bedrooms, made of wood and corrugated tin, like the ones you see all over." . . . That's the way I got my house.

In fact, as she makes clear, it was more complicated than that. Her husband at first told Distasio they could not afford it. After Distasio replied that he would buy the house and they could pay him on a monthly basis, Doña María and Distasio conspire to persuade her husband to accept the deal.

> That's how I got my house, Daniel, in that way. Everybody did what María Roldán and her husband did, but it was me who gave the push to my husband and said this is what we have to do, and chau [ciao]. Look. I'll take the train and go to my sister and ask for money, be-

cause my sister was married to a jeweller, the two are dead now, they had a lot of money, but my husband was one of those proud men who used to say that a couple when they get married and have kids have to rely on their own forces, not go begging from their relatives, . . . people were buying their houses, but the difference was that I went to buy the lot behind my husband's back, don't forget that. I knew my husband really well, I knew that afterward he would say that I was right, and thanks to you we have a roof over our heads, but on his own he wouldn't go because he was afraid that there would be no food for the kids. We were two characters, on his own he wouldn't take the decision and I would.

Doña María recognized from the beginning that this was a difficult story to tell: it was a little tough on her husband, she warns. The coda to the story returns to this point and attempts to shape how we are to evaluate the meaning. A first version of the evaluation is offered in which her husband's reticence is attributed to the fact that he was a proud man who didn't want to borrow money. The second version is framed in a less favorable way for her husband. Doña María went behind his back, she connived with Distasio, she knew that in the end he would agree that she was right, but that on his own he simply did not have the character to take the decision.

The fact that she offers two moral readings of this narrative indicates the tension she still felt in telling this tale. We need have no doubt that this is, factually, the authentic version of how she acquired her first house. The detail offered and the richness of the narrative in contrast to the formulaic nature of the original account point to the veracity of this version. We might be tempted to explain the second version in terms of the emergence of an account that challenged traditional gender roles in working-class families. Doña María felt authorized to offer a story that more adequately fit the reality of her experience, that offered a far more appropriate vehicle for expressing her agency than that afforded by the conventionalized story of the male-dominated working-class household. Certainly, the lack of fit between conventionalized cultural forms and gendered experience has been noted by several recent studies of female personal narration. Faye Ginsburg, for example, referring to the life stories of pro- and antiabortion women activists in the United States, speaks of "the dissonance between their experience of changes in their own biographies and the available cultural models for marking them."[13]

The lack of fit between conventions and experience may be part of an explanation, but I still want to emphasize the tension present in the life-story narrative. Not only does Doña María offer competing evaluations within the story of her house but the second, authentic version is never reconciled with the earlier version; it simply remains as a competing account. Anthropologist Michael Herzfeld tries to analyze this sort of tension with his concept of "disemia." Disemia consists in the "contest between ambiguity and order" in social life in which order and the formalism of official discourse are subverted by social experience framed in a register of localized usage and intimate context. Herzfeld argues that the contest revolves around the "collective self-display" generated by conventionalized official ideology and the self-knowledge acquired in intimate social settings.[14]

It is this intimate context that alerts us to the difficulty and costs involved in any contest involving officialized gender roles and their subversion. The stereotyped categories available to mark women involved in such subversion are clear: "the woman on top," "the woman wearing the pants," "the nag," "the harridan." Doña María might choose to risk the attribution of such stereotypes for herself. There was, however, a corollary to the masculinization of the woman authoring her own life story; the feminization of the male. She was aware that within the norms of Berisso's vernacular culture real men did not allow their wives to speak in public or go around buying houses behind their backs. The frequent deferential gestures toward her husband in her narrative speak to her awareness of this vox populi. There had been rumor while her husband had been alive, and the popular commentary lived on. Irma Pintos voiced her own version of this: "I can still see them now, she striding along and her little husband running along at her side." Irma knew, as we have seen, how to wound with words. The demasculinized characterization of her husband implied by the word "maridito" should warn us of the cost involved for Doña María in assuming an appropriately gendered narrative.

This analysis of available cultural models and the role of official ideological discourse concerning gender points us toward an examination of the limiting, defining—in a word, structuring—role of the available cultural vehicles, interpretative devices, available to Doña María. The recent "blurring of the genres" has induced an increased sensitivity among historians—perhaps most intensively among oral historians—to the importance of narrative as an ordering, sense-making device at both a collective and individual level. As David Carr argues: "At the individual level, people make sense of their lives through the stories that are available to them, and they attempt to fit their lives into the available stories. People live by stories."[15] At a more general level, communities, too, adopt narratives that inculcate and confirm their integrity and coherence over time. These communal stories are created and accepted by the participants in a constant process of negotiation between different versions. This process indicates the essentially practical function of this sort of narrative counting, serving to draw the community together and enabling it to formulate action in the present and future based on a common understanding of the past. The "collective memory" thus formulated is constructed on the basis of various devices: public myths, founding stories, crucial transforming events, evil and good characters, the division of the past into the time before and after a "golden age."[16]

In Berisso, as we suggested in chapter 1, there were several master narratives within whose parameters Doña María could potentially frame her story. I am here referring to local, community narratives rather than those produced at a national institutional and ideological level. These local stories overlap and intersect at many points but can be distinguished.

At a most general level, if Berissenses have a "story they tell themselves about themselves," it is that of the immigrant. This story has official legitimation, since Berisso was officially designated "The Capital of the Immigrant" by government decree in 1978. It is symbolically enacted and played out every September on the Day of the

Immigrant, when the different ethnic associations parade through the center of the city in their traditional costumes and later perform dances and other cultural events. Woven into this story, indeed the crucial core of it, is a morality tale about the hardness of life, the dedication of Berisso's founding generation and the virtues of hard work as a vehicle for bestowing a better life on one's children. It also speaks of the beneficence of the host country and its embrace of the poor of all countries. As such, Berisso's story is emblematic of Argentina's history—the city's official history is titled *Berisso: un reflejo de la evolución argentina*. This theme forms a dominant part of the history produced by Berisso's native historians.

A related story—though one with a more polemical, divisive, class-based character—is that centered on the emergence of the unions in the meatpacking plants and the role of Berisso in the founding and later history of the Peronist movement. This narrative centers on several epic themes: the repression of the strike of 1917; the toughness of working in the plants; the appearance of Perón; the great strike of ninety-six days in 1945; Berisso's role in the events of October 1945; the changes in work conditions brought about by the union; the golden era of 1945–55; the long and bitter decline of the meatpacking industry; Berisso's fall from its former glory; Berisso's keeping faith with Peronism, living up to the legacy implied in its claim to be "la cuna del peronismo" [the cradle of Peronism].

Many elements of these communal stories are to be found in Doña María's life story. She uses them to shape her story, to express her sense of some of its meaning. The point I wish to make is that although on one level they are adequate vehicles, like all narratives they also attempt to impose their own "closure," using "strategies of containment." Women are either marginalized or allotted certain stereotypical roles. The communal story of the strike of 1945, for example, leaves little room for Doña María to express the extent of her role or that of other women in the strike. Although there is a formal recognition of the support of the women workers for the strike, the crucial "heroic" figures are male in all the versions of this story. Cipriano Reyes with typewriter and clandestine press holed-up in the "monte," controlling and directing the strike; his male lieutenants running the gauntlet of police repression, taking on the strikebreakers, trying to deal with the government. There is little room in Doña María's account for an expression of a more active role in the strike. And yet we can ask, What are the interpretative alternatives here? Is it possible for the oral historian through a recuperative hermeneutic act to pry open the discursive closure and containment that structure this life-story account?

In the case of the strike of ninety-six days we have some elements with which to potentially challenge the silencing power that the dominant community discourse exerted on Doña María's narrative. When Doña María speaks of active picketing, of tarring and feathering, she attributes this activity to "some muchachos." Community rumor may offer another version. After her death I was offered the following testimony by a man who had been a neighbor of Doña María in his childhood:

> I lived near her on calle 21. I remember a number of people telling me that during the strikes of 1945 she went around the barrio enforcing the strikes. I think even my mother told me of this, she used to go around the stores with a pistol in her handbag together with some other women saying that they were the "pistoleras de Reyes" and they would close them with her pistol if they didn't close of their own will.

There is other evidence, too, that some women activists at this time did undergo some training in the use of weapons. Inés Marini told me that her husband had taught her how to use a pistol as defense against the attacks that often occurred at this time.

It is clear, however, that no simple act of textual recuperation is possible. There are profound difficulties associated within any such analytical attempt. In the first place, my access to the "silenced story" of the strike comes from a third party. This party also told me that his mother "was terrified of Doña María": "You know that women like María Roldán intimidated many of the older European women who were by custom far more timid. My mother was a traditional Arab woman, and she was both impressed and terrified by María Roldán and others like her." This account is, then, structured by a notion of Doña María as a figure beyond the range of normative immigrant and working-class images of womanhood. In its own way it may be as overdetermined by formalized gender conventions as the communal narrative it apparently questions. In this case, does this third-party testimony enable us to challenge the silencing of a working woman's "true agency" by a repressive discourse that does not allow its bearer to express the "true" scope of her subjectivity, even from the relatively more "enlightened" moment of the 1980s?

It may be that there is simply no way to definitively answer this question. Analytically, an attempt to address the question returns us to the theoretical questioning of the convention of retrieving women's voices with which we opened this chapter. Gyan Prakash offers us the remedy of recognizing "the aporetic condition of the subaltern's silence," of seizing on "a discourse's silences and aporetic moments."[17] But in practice how do we interpret silence? On the larger scale the recognition of the importance of lacunae, of contradiction, of silence has become part of the analytical apparatus of oral historians. Thus Luisa Passerini has creatively questioned the silence that informs the testimony of workers who lived the Mussolini era on the subject of fascism.[18] Through creative analysis she is able to "rearticulate the pregnant silence" imposed by fascism on working-class testimony. We can certainly take inspiration from this sort of analysis and try to apply it to an individual life story. The story of Doña María's strike activism points, however, to the limits of eliciting subtexts and hidden voices from narrative silences. Rather than uncovering repressed female voices, such silences may point toward other interpretative possibilities. In the case of the "pistoleras de Reyes," for example, may we not be faced with an embodiment of a male fantasy provoked by women who break through the conventional molds and are thereby codified in terms of the aggressive virtues normally associated with men?

A similar closure is present, I think, if we look at the representation of work in her narrative. Factory life, work in the meatpacking plants, is an important part of the union story, and it is very much a masculine story. Stories of the plant abound in tales of the physical nature of the labor, the appalling work conditions, the latent violence, the presence of a sheer mass of men subject to an inhuman work system. This male universe had its roots in the very structure of the workforce and work process with its strongly gendered hierarchy. Men dominated the higher-skilled and higher-paid positions. The crucial figures found in packing-house folklore are men drawn from all-male sections such as the killing floor and the stevedore gangs. Anecdotes told by male packing-house workers of their time in the plants make frequent reference to this folklore and certain mythical figures. Women, on the other hand, confined to inferior positions within the work process, rarely figure in the lore of the plants. The killing floor was the source of the most recounted stories, with the matambrero—a sort of meatpacking equivalent of the "great hewer" of mining legend—as the key mythical figure. A close second in status was the leader of the stevedore gangs, who could fill the hold of a ship with carcasses with no room to spare and in record time. These tales are elaborated by male storytellers around themes of physical endurance, skill, work conditions, confrontations with foremen, jokes.

As a narrative, then, the story of the meatpacking plant leaves women only a marginal space within which to express themselves. Indeed, to the extent that women are represented in the folklore of the plant, it tends to be as the polar opposite of the public myth of woman as mother, nurturer, pure and homebound—that is, as the morally weak woman corrupted by the dominant male ambience. Once more I wish to emphasize that this story is not unusable for Doña María, but rather that it is inherently limiting and that these limits have to do with the dissonance between the parameters found in such stories and their representative figures and the meaning and richness of an individual life that seeks to burst the parameters and violate the stereotypes.

The ambivalence and tension resulting from this dissonance are evident in Doña María's handling of the theme of gender and work in her life story. It is evident that the workplace, the frigorífico, has both a positive and negative value in her story. In general, of course, it is portrayed as the locus of a work system that sucks people in— Doña María frequently uses the Spanish verb "chupar" with its connotation of literally sucking in liquid—and uses them before spitting them out. She refers to the plants using various metaphorical terms—"ese infierno negro" [that black hell], "ese monstruo" [that monster]—and emphasizes the human cost for those who had to go into them, including her husband, whose health was destroyed by the work he had to perform.

Within this general evaluation, the plant is portrayed at several stages of her narrative as a potentially hostile environment for women workers in a tone at times apparently in tune with the masculine universe portrayed in the fictional representation of the meatpacking world to which we have already referred:

> I think that all the women who went to work in the frigorífico felt the same . . . because it's a place, well, it's like a monster when you go in there, in that darkness and dampness, in that situation of lines of men with knives in hand. I don't think that that was very nice, you felt bad, but necessity obliged you to get used to it.

Yet despite the recognition in her narrative of a virulently masculine shop-floor culture related to the brutality of the work systems and the celebration of physical prowess that was an intrinsic part of that, Doña María's story does not simply draw the moral explicit in the reworked ideology of domesticity propagated by Peronism. She recognizes the special problems that entry into this world involved for women, both in terms of the world inside the plants and in terms of the role of women as mothers. Commenting on how her children had to stay inside and help prepare the food when she was at work, she says: "Only someone who has worked outside the home, the mother of the family who has worked outside knows what it is like." At other times, too, she laments the sacrifices she had to make in fulfilling her role as a mother owing to her union and political work.

Nevertheless, the conflict between work and nurturance is juxtaposed with a more positive evaluation. In a basic sense, entry into the meatpacking plant is the fundamental step that makes the plot of Doña María's story possible, for all the sacrifices it implies—and to the end of her story there are times when one is never sure that she thought the sacrifices were worth the price—it is this that gives her the right to demand a little more from life, to break with some of the conventions of a working-class woman's biography, to be true to her image of herself as a rebel formed in adolescence. This story is very far from being, as Doña María tells it, an affirmation of work outside the home as a liberating experience. Working at the plant is always in her story first and foremost a material necessity, and it is always ultimately defined by her vision of this work—for both men and women—as simply awful:

> Blood on the floor, bits of grease. . . . you're continually in contact with the blood of the animal, with the fat, with the nerves, with the bones, and it's a continual contact with something that is cold, the meat is always cold, in addition there was also the frozen meat, do you know what it is like to try and cut frozen meat with a knife?

But work and its pain are mediated by perhaps the crucial institution in Doña María's story, the union. The union does not simply function to mitigate the conditions of work in general; more specifically, it is seen implicitly as a means of lessening the vulnerable position of women in the plants and limiting masculine power and authority over women.

In addition, at various stages of her narrative Doña María refers to how entry into the workplace brought about changes in the performing of domestic labor in the household. She emphasizes that her husband helped out with the domestic chores, and she generalizes to establish a general point that women who work are entitled to expect equality in the division of household labor. Once again, the way this principle is framed in the narrative demonstrates the ambivalence and tension she feels over this issue, for she couples it with a reaffirmation of the traditional domestic role of women: "Woman has been born to be in the home with her children, to raise her children, to take care of the house, clean it."

The themes of matrimony and abortion similarly reflect the tension and dissonance that accompany the issue of gender in Doña María's narrative. Again, one consistent role she adopts for herself, one of the most persistent forms of self-representation that she projects, is that of the good mother, that of the good wife. Through these self-images she expresses ideas about marriage and abortion that apparently reflect official Peronism's (though it of course was not the only influence here) hostility to divorce, birth control, and abortion. Yet close attention to how she handles these themes shows that the formal enunciation of these principles is mediated by a rich subtext that relates them to the stern realities of working-class women's lives and the painful choices of everyday existence in a community like Berisso.

In the case of abortion, for example, after a brief comment that she is against it "because of my religion," she goes on to describe without any censure the common practice of illegal abortion among the women of Berisso. She describes the desperation of women who could not afford to have children, and she states quite clearly that it was routine in the meatpacking plants for the women to take up a collection on payday to help a compañera pay for an abortion. In the case of both abortion and divorce an attention to the context in which Doña María places her criticisms shows that the influence of the dominant ideology is mediated, relativized, and ultimately minimized by her own sympathy and understanding of the limited options open to women in the real world.

Moreover, her testimony indicates that her opposition is not primarily an ethical one. Her constant concern when she talks of divorce and separation is expressed in terms of the children, which at one level is consistent within her story with her stated concern for the future and care of children in modern society. Beyond that though we may suggest that it is also a way of talking about the vulnerability of women in Argentine society. Separating male sexuality from child rearing and marriage through either divorce or abortion would seem to worsen the burden that women already bear in this area. When speaking of her own compañeras in the picada section who had abortions, she refers to a typical case in which "the man abandons them with a child in their bellies." The reality of women's unequal status and power in a society with profoundly hierarchical gender relations makes the adoption and valorization of elements of an ideology of nurturing and domesticity a rational option.

The role of Evita Perón must be taken into account in any reading of Doña María's testimony for gender. Evita functions in various ways in Doña María's life-story text. On one level, Evita represents the embodiment of female virtues and appropriate roles. Above all, she is the dutiful wife whose sense of self is constituted through the power of her husband. She is the shade to his sun. Her actions for her people are in the last instance authorized by Perón. At times in Doña María's testimony the formal gender ideology of Peronism appears as an almost literal transcription from Evita's official autobiography "La Razón de Mi Vida." There is also, however, something far more complex at play in Doña María's representation of Evita. In part, the presentation of Evita as a new semantic figure who can furnish a public model serves as a narrative reference point for Doña María's story of her own political and social activism. This female semantic figure does not finally depend on a written textual embodiment for its power to convoke. Whatever the influence of "La Razón de Mi Vida" as a text, Evita's influence was fundamentally performative. Her life story, whose praxis and intimate experience was given public narrative expression in anecdotal form, was taken as exemplary, as "equipment for living" in Kenneth Burke's sense of the term.[19]

This exemplary, performative status was rooted in a recognition and valorization of her impoverished childhood origins. The abjection of her childhood leads to her condition of "protectress of the grasitas, of the negritos, of the filthy ones."

> The life of Evita, well, you can see from the beginning that it was very sad, from the moment she was born, because she wasn't born in wedlock, from her childhood she was very unfortunate, so she had to turn out good, she was a woman of the barrio, arrabalera, her mother took in numbers, she was from that sort of people, what's the point of denying it?

It is the experience born of this suffering that underlies and legitimates Evita's political practice and provides a model for Doña María's own activism. Ultimately, this experience undergirds a religiously inflected politics articulated in terms of feeling and emotion rather than formal ideological tenets. We can find an analogy of this position within formal Peronist ideology. "La Razón de Mi Vida" is full of references to "feeling" as the ultimate explanation for Peronism's uniqueness. We can recall also Doña María's insistence that she had been driven since childhood by feeling in her soul that she had to defend the poor, and that her own suffering gave her a capacity that professional politicians did not have. It is this ethic of decency and feeling toward the other that underpins Doña María's notion of politics:

> For example, if I'm at the table in the voting hall telling them where they have to vote and a woman arrives all dirty, with her belly out to here, with three or four children, black and abandoned, I say to her, señora, take a seat, where do you live; I speak to her as I would someone who just got out of a car dressed in furs, because for me it is a human being like any other, I have that advantage of having the sensibility to treat my fellow human beings the same, whether they have one aspect or the other, for me they are human beings, that is very important. . . . to love the people is to love everybody, it's to love a kid covered in snot, it's to love a drunk and help him cross the street so he doesn't get hit by a car, it is to love, that is what Evita did, that is politics.

The impact of this ethically based politics can be measured in terms of concrete measures to help the poor, which Evita accomplished during her short life and which Doña María on a local scale within Berisso tried to emulate.

The anecdotes that embody this exemplary practice can be read at various levels, in both class and gender terms. Some of these stories recounted by Doña María have already been recorded in part 2 of this book. They form part of a body of tales told about Evita in communities like Berisso. In my experience they are almost exclusively narrated by women. I wish to analyze one of them in particular:

> DJ: The fact that she had all that fine clothing, she had a lot of money. Did this bother the poor?

> DM: It didn't bother them because it was money that had been given to her, that she had a way of taking it from the rich and giving it to the poor, and that requires a special value and a tremendous capacity to be able to give it to the poor and take it from the rich, and I'm going to say why, professor. I worked for many years at the race track, and one day some elderly rich people came in, with gold chains in full view, those cars that you don't know which side the engine is on, a blond woman, a thoroughbred dog and I don't know what else. And a blindman says:

"Brother, will you give me something, I'm blind."

And they walked around him. And another man comes up, in an old coat and with cloth shoes, who is going to put money on some nag whose name he's been given. And he gives him one hundred pesos. So I stood there and watched. I thought this will come in useful for the tribuna [speaking platform].

It's very important: he who has, doesn't give; he who doesn't have, gives.

So the fact that she had those fancy trinkets, that she had fine clothes, any woman nowadays if she can she puts it on a little, why not the wife of a president? All those jewels were gifts, gifts given her by the oligarchy so they could control her, because she had the nation in her hands, though it's hard to believe.

Once again a populist-inflected class reading is perhaps most apparent. The story functions as a "popular-democratic interpellation" expressive of the "people/power bloc" contradiction, in which the rich are shown to be morally and ethically inferior to the poor. They fail a fundamental test of Christian virtue. The story has the form of a parable that contrasts Evita's ability to take from the rich and give to the poor with the unwillingness of the rich to practice simple Christian kindness. The model for this story is clearly the biblical parable about the difficulty of the rich passing into the kingdom of heaven. In Doña María's version Evita is able to use her guile and her power to take from the rich and give to the poor.

This is a complex web of ideological articulations. It is in some ways a reproduction of dominant ideological notions of female nurturing that reflects the determining influence of formal notions of the role of women in politics. Unlike men in politics, women do not speak of politics in terms of power but rather in terms of service, of nurturing, of selflessness. I commented on something similar in chapter 2, with regard to Doña María's speaking of her union activism, which was often coded in terms of her maternal role as protectress and guide. At the same time we know that Doña María was quite capable of discussing Peronism in terms of more formal ideological, conceptual forms. Here, though, we have a popular cultural expression, articulated in an idiom of popular religiosity. This

popular form frames what could also be read as a class antagonism—
especially if we bear in mind Doña María's earlier definition of politics in terms of compassion and sensitivity for the other. The roots
of such a religiously inflected popular subculture are difficult to be
precise about at this stage. Once again, we could take its textual
embodiment in this anecdotal form as a direct reflection of the influence of Peronist state discourse. On the other hand, it is likely
that Peronist discourse was also, in fact, appropriating an existing
popular religious subculture (which perhaps most particularly inter-
pellated women), which spoke of rich and poor, political rights and
obligations within the terms of a sort of popular moral economy. In
this case, what may be figured in such stories are traces of popular
discourse that are being directly incorporated into state rhetoric (or
at least that part of it dedicated to the construction of the figure of
Evita). I would suggest that this incorporation is an example of the
process described by Ernesto Laclau whereby "popular democratic
interpellations ceased to be a subculture and became incorporated
into national political life. The *sermo humilis* took possession of the
language of power."[20] The presence of such a language in the testimony of Doña María would seem to indicate that this sermo humilis
remained a powerful component of popular political discourse long
after its exile from the formal language of power.

There is, however, another possible reading of this story that
would give us access to a subtext involving the construction of gender identity. In many of the stories told about Evita by working
women she functions as a sort of empty signifier available for appropriation and use by working women. At times Evita as empty
signifier serves to confirm formal ideological tenets about gender,
on other occasions she can help frame experiences at variance with
official discourse about women. In the case of this anecdote, she
functions as a vehicle through which a desire for material things can
be expressed as well as resentment at their denial. Carolyn Steedman
has suggested that such desire, and the envy that it generates, often
deeply conflicts with the official interpretative devices a culture
offers working women. Steedman is drawing on her own mother's
working-class experience of living a life in the endless streets of
South London, but her analysis of the "politics of envy" resonates

in Doña María's story, too. Such a politics, Steedman notes, violates the iconography of working-class motherhood dominant in the culture. In a similar vein, Doña María finds it difficult to express her desire for the things of the world or her ambition for a career beyond the factory in her life story. Her references to her political and social militance are often framed by the disclaimer, "we didn't want their chimneys or their dollars." Yet it seems clear that Peronism as a social movement both created and mobilized the desire for consumer goods, and the trope of envy and resentment is, indeed, present at places in Doña María's life story. She frames one of her most potent critiques of the Catholic Church precisely in terms of the differential access to material goods embodied in the different quality of dresses young girls wear to their communions and the Church's role in facilitating this inequality:

> What happens when a daughter comes back from taking her communion, and she has worn her white school overall, but she says to her mother, "You saw Juanita, what a dress she was wearing, what needlework, what ribbons of silk," and the mother has to keep quiet and tell her to drink her milk and perhaps the overall was given to her at school, she didn't even buy it.

Associated with envy and resentment is the emotion of shame: shame that her children did not eat well, that their clothes were not good, shame at the sort of house they lived in. The story of the acquisition of her own home is, after all, in part also a story of desire for material improvements motivated by shame. Although Doña María at times speaks of the tenement rooms with nostalgia, at other moments she describes them as "ugly . . . , full of smells, with a filthy bathroom that you shared with many people."

In this sense, then, the stories of Evita function as vehicles to express elements of working-class female consciousness of dubious legitimacy within the dominant gender conventions. Steedman expresses the hope that "by allowing this envy entry into political understanding, the proper struggles of people in a state of dispossession to gain their inheritance might be seen not as sordid or mindless greed for the things of the marketplace, but attempts to alter a world that has produced in them states of unfulfilled desire." [21] The target of Steedman's criticism is the traditional parties of the British left. It may well be that part of Peronism's advantage over parties of the left was precisely its ability to articulate this gendered politics of envy. And if this is so, then the narrative figure of Evita plays a crucial role, providing a site within which grievance and desire can be narrated. Once more her life is exemplary and makes her a credible figure: shame and resentment are fundamental tropes in the story of Evita. She may be seen as a semantic figure metonymically representing her female public and its desires. Evita can possess the things of the world, rich dresses and jewels, without diminishing her spirituality.

Confronted with the power of available communal stories, public myths, and formal ideologies to shape contexts and set the parameters within which life stories such as Doña María's are constructed, how can we approach the problem of using such stories to better understand the issue of gender in working-class history? Is there a way to reconcile the two different sets of stereotypes about gender present in her narrative? One solution prevalent in much feminist scholarship is to emphasize the presence of counterdiscourses, expressive of oppressed and repressed women's voices in these sorts of texts. Faye Ginsburg argues, for example, that her pro- and anti-abortion activists used their testimonies "to reframe experiences they originally felt were dissonant with social expectations by constituting them as new cultural possibilities."[22] In such a way she suggests their life stories articulated a counterdiscourse that legitimized their adoption of "alternative life scripts" and led to a newfound harmony in their visions of themselves. In a similar vein Laurel Richardson has suggested that women can overcome their "textual disenfranchisement" embodied in cultural stories that are inadequate to their needs and experiences by creating new "collective stories" with new roles, stereotypes, and resolutions.[23] At the other extreme, a recent study by Spanish feminist historians found that the dominant public myth of the ideal woman as mother and homemaker had succeeded in obliterating the memory of women's role as fighters and production workers during the Spanish Civil War among women who had adopted such roles.[24]

Now, I think that it is possible to read important elements in Doña María's life story as a form of counterdiscourse challenging the authority of a dominant set of images about working-class women and their lives. It seems to me, however, that this plot and the tensions it engenders and expresses does not lead to a final resolution in favor of a new life script, a newly found harmony that blended personal history and socially legitimized roles. This ending seems to me to be too neat a resolution for Doña María's story, failing among other things to take into account the power and efficacy of communal and class narratives in working-class communities like Berisso. More helpful, it seems to me, is Carolyn Steedman's evocation of her mother's working-class story "told by tension and ambiguity, out on the borderlands"; a story that disrupted the central one but was not simply available in ready-to-use form waiting to be appropriated.[25]

Such stories, told out on the borderlands, inevitably involve unresolved contradictions, silences, erasures, conflicting themes. Within the conventions of written autobiography such lapses are often tidied up. Oral testimony is more messy, more paradoxical, more contradiction-laden, and perhaps, because of this, more faithful to the complexity of working-class lives and working-class memory. It would be possible to see the existence of contradictory versions of gender in Doña María's story in terms of the problems of memory, and this may certainly be the case, but it equally reflects, I think, the existence of genuinely unresolved tension between an official discourse concerning gender relations and one that is far less palatable and legitimate within the terms in which Doña María had to live out her life.

At some stage the oral historian has to make the leap of faith that direct historical experience will break through and find expression in an individual's testimony. This leap of faith is the basis for any belief in a referential pact that could be at the root of any distinction oral history might wish to claim for itself from, say, literary criticism. Within this perspective, then, I think that we must pay Doña María the respect of assuming that her recounting of her life faithfully reflects—mediated as her telling is by existing narratives and dominant ideologies—the way in which a working-class woman experienced gender and class relations in a particular historical era. Her adoption of forms of self-representation drawn from stereo-types of traditional female roles found in official discourse should not simply be taken at face value. They reflect both the power of dominant ideologies and myths but also the power of the storyteller to imbue these forms with her own meanings, her own subjectivity.

4

A POEM FOR CLARITA

Niñas Burguesitas and Working-Class Women in Peronist Argentina

A text is not a text unless it hides from the first comer, from the first glance, the law of its composition and the rules of its game.

A text remains, moreover, forever imperceptible. Its law and its rules are not, however, harbored in the inaccessibility of a secret; it is simply that they can never be booked, in the present, into anything that could rigorously be called a perception.

And hence, perpetually and essentially, they run the risk of being definitively lost. Who will ever know of such disappearances?

The dissimulation of the woven texture can in any case take centuries to undo its web: a web that envelopes a web, undoing the web for centuries. . . . There is always a surprise in store for the anatomy or physiology of any criticism that might think that it had mastered the game, surveyed all the threads at once, deluding itself too in wanting to look at the text without touching it, without laying a hand on the "object," without risking—which is the only chance of entering into the game, by getting a few fingers caught—the addition of some new thread.—Jacques Derrida, "Plato's Pharmacy"

Social Democracy thought fit to assign to the working class the role of the redeemer of future generations, in this way cutting the sinews of its greatest strength. This training made the working class forget both its hatred and its spirit of sacrifice, for both are nourished by

the image of enslaved ancestors rather than of liberated grandchildren. — Walter Benjamin, "Theses on the Philosophy of History"

On a winter's night in 1947 Doña María sat in her house and grieved
for Clarita, her friend and *compañera de trabajo* from the Swift meatpacking plant. Clarita had earlier that day died of tuberculosis in the
municipal hospital in La Plata. Unable to sleep, tormented by anger
and frustration, Doña María sat down and wrote a poem to commemorate her friend and to unburden herself. This was not something that Doña María was accustomed to doing. In fact, this was
the first time she had written a poem. Many years later, in the summer of 1987, she recalled for me the circumstances that had given
rise to this extraordinary action and recited the poem from memory,
having many years before lost the written version.

One day, pobrecita, she died, so we took her to Berisso, but we didn't
have anything to bury her with, and the mayor of Berisso, which still
wasn't a municipality, it was a delegation, was a man who is dead
now, Evaristo Anselmino, he gave us the coffin, and lent us the *cucaracha,* which was like a motor carriage with four wheels that used to
bear the coffin in full view to the cemetery . . . and we watched over
her in the house of a man who lent us his house in New York street,
without telling her mother or anything, because she was an old lady
and could die from the shock. . . . Well, so I felt very bad and I think
that we all felt bad, but I felt so bad that I had to get up from the
bed, and of course my husband saw that I was not returning to the
bedroom and he came to the kitchen and said to me, "What are you
doing?" and I was there with a pencil writing the verse to Clarita,
because I felt tired of crying without solving anything, and it seemed
to me that I was fulfilling my obligation to her, and I made her this
verse, which goes like this:

Ay, pálida obrerita que marchás apenada
al establecimiento antro de explotación
a ganarte la vida y enriquecer a viles
con caras de verdugos y frentes de reptiles
que llevan una lira de oro por corazón.

El ruido de las maquinas hace crispar tus nervios
histérica te vuelves y pierdes hasta el yo
ese yo de ironía que te hace alzar la frente
y aunque muerta caminás te agotás tristemente
dejando hasta el carácter en manos del patrón.

Las niñas burguesitas te observan con un dejo
de burla indiferente, con burlona intención
ignorando las pobres muñequitas burguesas
que cobre sobre cobre labraste la riqueza
del ladrón patentado que nada te dejó.

Y a esas artificiales y enfermas mujercitas
que viven cansadas de placer
díles que te hagan frente
ataviados andrajos
que tu pecho valiente presentás al pingajo
sangrada hija del pueblo, carnaza del taller.

Díles que ayer ha muerto una compañerita
una pobre explotada vencida por el mal
díles que a poco hermosa a la fábrica entraba
y que tuberculosa ayer agonizaba
en el último lecho de un mísero hospital
que tus labios marchitos tal vez de tanto encierro
se han deplorado en gritos y no besando perros
como los besan ellas en voluptuosa unión.

Clarita, amiga y compañera
te fuistes de este mundo sin decirnos adiós
y en un vuelo divino llegaste a Jesús
Y en un rincón del Chaco una viejita buena
masticando su pena esperándote esta.

[Ay, pale little worker marching sorrowful
off to the factory, den of exploitation
to make a living and enrich vile men,
with hangman's faces and reptile brows,
and the gold coins that take the place of their hearts.

The noise of the machines puts your nerves on edge:
you become hysterical, and lose your very self,
that ironic self that keeps your chin up,
even dead-tired, you walk on, wearing yourself out in sadness,
leaving even your character in the hands of the boss.

The little bourgeois girls watch you with a touch
of indifferent mockery, with a mocking intent,
not knowing, the poor little bourgeois dolls,
that cent after cent you minted the riches
of the licensed thief who left you with nothing.

And to those artificial and sick little women
forever exhausted from pleasure:
tell them to face you,
dressed-up tatters,
as you present your valiant breast to the shreds,
bloodied daughter of the people, cannon fodder of the shop floor.

Tell them that yesterday a comrade died
poor and exploited, defeated by evil
tell them that not long ago you entered the factory, beautiful,
and yesterday you lay dying, consumptive,
in the last bed of a miserable hospital
and that your lips, withered perhaps while locked away,
have condemned in screams, and not kissing dogs,
like the dogs they kiss in voluptuous union.

Little Clara, friend and comrade,
you left this world without saying good-bye
and in a divine flight you made it to Jesus.
And in some corner of the Chaco a sweet old lady
chews over her sorrow, waiting for you.]

This I dedicated to my friend Clarita, my dear friend Clarita. . . . I
felt better, I feel better when I say it because I loved her very much.

The emotion of the memory, the pain evoked by the tribute forty
years after the death were palpable and remain powerfully present
on the recording in the catch of her breath and the tone of her voice.

One principal question I wish to address in this chapter concerns the uses that a historian can make of such a text. The answers were not self-evident. For several years the poem remained in a state of interpretative limbo, a sort of anecdotal jewel to be displayed as a culminating gesture on my part, as I strove to exemplify a working-class woman's creativity and subjectivity in my analysis of her oral testimony. The very emotionalism of the performance and the immediate power of many of its rhetorical images seemed to make further analysis unnecessary. Doña María's own framing of the poem seemed to render more formal interpretation redundant: it was, self-evidently, an expression of personal anguish within a larger narrative of class bitterness.

What I want to do is to go beyond the immediacy of the performative impact of the poem and subject it to something like a sustained "reading" as a literary/historical text. This attempt is, of course, in part, a sign of the times, a reflection of the impact of the "linguistic turn" on social historians. In the previous chapter I suggested how Doña María's oral testimony should be regarded as a narrative, a form of storytelling that organizes events and gives meaning to personal experiences in the context of broader, more powerful narratives.[1] The reading strategies applied to the larger text of a life story can be applied to the narrative embodied in a particular text—in this case a poem. This application would imply being attentive to the rhetorical aspects of the text, with their exclusions and oppositions, inconsistencies and silences, and also to the use of linguistic devices such as metaphor and metonymy. It would also imply close attention to form and genre as crucial components of the contested construction of content and meaning.

Although there is now general agreement about the importance of textual readings of literary/historical documents, there are also several problems from the point of view of social and labor history in the way such readings are frequently executed. Perhaps the most prevalent problem concerns the tendency for the analysis of meanings within a text to stay within the universe of textual logic, to remain within the self-referential structures of the discursive system.

Now most social and labor historians wish to interrogate their texts to help them disinter hidden traces of subjectivity, agency, and consciousness. Yet a powerful implication of the "linguistic turn" is to deny that this can be done. Outside discourse, beyond language and its textual embodiment, there is nothing that is knowable; individual experience is constructed by and through discourse. An overly textualist reading can threaten to leave the entire project of a gendered social history of working-class women as a chimera, with women workers in history condemned to silence. Much of the women's history carried out under this impulse has involved the reconstruction of the discursive categories produced to address women and women's work. Women workers are present in this analysis as objects interpellated/produced by the discourses of the powerful whose textual logic has been decoded by deconstructive reading. Within this sort of analysis there has been little attention paid to the response of working women to these discourses, their struggles to construct meaning and identity within these discursive terms.

Yet to restrict the analysis of a poem such as Doña María's within such a framework would seem to be as willful a neglect of its interpretative potential as my original inclination to leave it as an anecdotal jewel. I want to argue that a poem such as this enables us to speak to issues of working-class women's subjectivity in the concrete historical context of Peronist Argentina in the 1940s. By subjecting a relative historical rarity—a direct example of a working-class woman's cultural text—to a reading "against the grain," we may be able to go from the individual to the social and ideological, following Fredric Jameson's notion that narrative conventions provide clues that "lead us back to the concrete historical situation of the individual text itself, and allow us to read its structure as ideology, as a socially symbolic act, as a prototypical response to a historical dilemma."[2]

At its most accessible level of meaning Doña María's poem can be read as a story of class injury, framed in a class-based language of exploitation. Indeed, Doña María provides an important initial story marker with her reference to the *cucaracha,* which carried Clarita to the cemetery. In Berisso the cucaracha had very clear social connotations of indigence. One of Berisso's local poets, Felipe Protzucov, describes it as "a kind of social charity, for every dispossessed soul on its final journey to the cemetery." In street parlance it came to represent the fate awaiting all those who were profligate and failed to care for their worldly goods.[3]

It was precisely this level of meaning that resonated so immediately and strongly with her neighbors and fellow Peronists to whom she recited the poem. Within Berisso the evils associated with working in the packing houses were part of the collective memory or direct personal experience of her listeners. It is this drawing on a common well of class-based experience that makes the poem's meaning so apparently self-evident. Yet it is still worth emphasizing the presence of a language that speaks directly of "explotación" and that personifies that exploitation in "verdugos" [executioners] and "viles" [vile ones] with "frentes de reptiles" [reptilian foreheads]. The poem also locates exploitation in the robbery associated with wage labor: "labraste la riqueza del ladrón patentado que nada te dejó" [you minted the riches of the licensed thief who left you with nothing]. The language also refers explicitly to the alienation associated with the impact of factory work on individual workers:

El ruido de las máquinas hace crispar tus nervios
histérica te vuelves y pierdes hasta el yo
este yo de ironía que te hace alzar la frente
y aunque muerta caminás te agotás tristemente
dejando hasta el carácter en manos del patrón.

[The noise of the machines puts your nerves on edge:
you become hysterical, and lose your very self,
that ironic self that keeps your chin up,
and even dead-tired, you walk on, wearing yourself out in
    sadness,
leaving even your character in the hands of the boss.]

This story of class exploitation is also expressed through imagery that speaks of the working-class woman as the "sangrada hija del pueblo, carnaza del taller" [bloodied daughter of the people, cannon fodder of the shop floor].

Beyond these accessible class references there is also what we might call an underlying sensibility of moral disgust and outrage toward the bourgeoisie. In part, this attitude is revealed in the un-flattering descriptions of the patrón. Perhaps more surprisingly, it is also directed at the "niñas burguesitas," who are constructed in images that emphasize their perverse and pathological natures. They are "artificiales y enfermas mujercitas que viven cansadas de placer" [artificial and sick little women forever exhausted from pleasure].

Let us shift the focus a little and try to deepen this class-based reading. We may start by stating the obvious. This poem is by a woman for a woman. If it is a poem of class bitterness, anger, and sorrow, such bitterness and anger are expressed through female fig-ures. Doña María invokes anger at the physical destruction wrought by the factory system on Clarita, and she focuses this anger largely on a female enemy, the "niñas burguesitas." These upper-class women do not simply represent a class enemy that exploits Cla-rita's labor. The "ladrón patentado" fulfills this function. Rather they are portrayed as figures who taunt and humiliate, and who gaze on Clarita with "un dejo de burla indiferente, con burlona intención." On the other hand, the poem can also be read as celebrating female friendship among working women, in symbolic opposition to those rich women who mock and betray. Values of female solidarity and friendship are implicitly affirmed in the poem, as they were indeed confirmed in Clarita's life story. In the absence of her family it was her friend who cared for her, buried her, and who finally reclaimed her memory and life in a poem.

If we contextualize the conditions of production of this poem, the presence of this class and gender sensibility becomes clearer. The sources of this sensibility were various. Doña María is in part draw-ing on a language and iconography of class available within popular and working-class discourse in the Argentina of the 1940s. Some of the poem's crucial images and icons are derived from the socialist, communist, and anarchist lexicon present in Argentina since the late nineteenth century and which in turn drew on the cultural tradi-tion of European republicanism and radicalism. The "sangrada hija del pueblo, carnaza del taller" is an image taken directly from this tradition, as is that found in the preceding line, which speaks of the

"daughter of the people" presenting her "valiant breast" to her ex-
ploiters. It seems likely that Doña María had had some exposure to
this repertoire of images and figures. We know that her father was a
man of anarchist sympathies; we also know that as a girl and young
woman, she was restless and sought to find out about various political philosophies. It is also likely that having lived in Berisso since
1930, she had come into contact with some left-wing propaganda.
Communists and anarchists had established a noticeable, if limited,
presence in the 1930s and early 1940s. Finally, we should also relate
the presence of this class discourse to the nature and intensity of
Doña María's own experience in the years immediately preceding
the writing of this poem. In the space of just over two years she had
entered the packing plant, she had become a shop steward and participated in strikes, she had helped organize the strike and march
of 17 October 1945 and had spoken that day in the Plaza de Mayo,
and she had been a founding member of the Partido Laborista and
traveled the country speaking on its platform during the February
1946 elections that brought Perón to the presidency.

One other likely source within the popular culture of the era that
may have provided Doña María with a repertoire of images of a
more mystical and religious sensibility was the work of the poet
Pedro Palacios, popularly known as Almafuerte. Almafuerte was
widely read among working-class audiences, and his work could be
found in many of the popular libraries of Berisso. Indeed, Almafuerte had spent most of his life in and around La Plata. The first
public square inaugurated in Berisso in 1937 had been dedicated to
his memory, and a statue of the poet was erected there in 1943. Doña
María recalls in her testimony that she was an enthusiastic reader of
his poetry.

Imbued with a messianic tone, much of his poetry invoked his
compassion for, and identification with, "la chusma" [the lowly
ones]. This identification was expressed at times in Christ-like
terms; at other moments his poems were framed in terms of the
wrath of an Old Testament prophet. Profoundly critical of the
Church, his poetry frequently sounded the tone of ethical outrage
at and moral condemnation of a corrupting and corrupt industrial
society found in the first decades of the century in a variety of anar-

chist texts. The claim for the religious redemption of the poor found in the last stanza of Doña María's poem may well speak of Almafuerte's influence, as would the general tone of moral imprecation that frames the whole poem. More precisely, there are, in some of his most socially critical poetry, a series of images similar to those we find in Doña María's poem. In one of his best-known poems, "Antífona Roja," a prophetlike figure speaks to the "doliente familia de parias" [a suffering family of pariahs] and provides them, in stanzas of increasing intensity, with an accounting of all the miseries visited on them by an unjust society. Among these miseries we find "brazos tranchados en el raudo voltear de las maquinas" [arms torn off in the rapid movement of the machines] and working women "arrojando el pulmón a jirones como una blasfémia sangrienta que estalla" [straining their lungs like a bloody blasphemy that explodes]. In another stanza Almafuerte speaks of the "abierta, insolente, triunfal carcajada" [the open, insolent triumphant chuckle] with which the rich mock the poor.

Although it is clear that the poem expresses an experience rooted in class conflict and uses a repertoire of images and symbols drawn from a class-based discourse, these were not transparently and directly available for Doña María to use. They are framed within, and mediated by, a particular genre—that of melodrama. This form and set of conventions was readily available in popular cultural expressions ranging from pulp fiction and domestic radio novellas to tango and popular theatrical productions. Much of the fiction produced within the anarchist and socialist tradition was also melodramatic in form. The conventions of melodrama establish a Manichaean divide in the world, a conflict between good and evil that is usually, but not always, resolved in ethical terms in favor of good. The aesthetics of melodrama express this conflict in sets of stereotypical figures, often described in stark and hyperbolic terms and embodied in plots structured around sets of opposing values. The appeal of melodrama is complex. Recent studies of its role in nineteenth-century British culture have suggested that it acted as something like an overarching popular cultural imaginary underlying several more specific literary/cultural projects. More specifically, particular attention has been paid to its appeal to women as a narrative vehicle that foregrounded gender and power and provided a textual space for expressing issues of sexuality.

Doña María's poem has a fundamentally melodramatic binary structure reflected in a series of crucial contrasts: Clarita, the factory girl/niñas burguesitas; Clarita/the factory; Clarita/the patron; good/evil with Clarita as the ultimate embodiment of good. She was, Doña María assures us, "a supernatural being." Laura Mulvey has noted how "ideological contradiction is the overt mainspring and specific content of melodrama." Indeed, its direct representation of such contradiction formed part of its attraction for working-class writers. Of all the opposing terms present in this poem perhaps the most important is that which contrasts the "sangrada hija del pueblo" [bloodied daughter of the people] with the "niñas burguesitas," the authentic "daughter of the people" with the "artificiales y enfermas mujercitas que viven cansadas de placer" [artificial and sick little women forever exhausted from pleasure]. Ultimately, this contrast is between healthy, natural working-class women deformed by exploitation and their inauthentic, unnatural oligarchical counterparts:

> que tus labios marchitos tal vez de tanto encierro
> se han deplorado en gritos y no besando perros
> como los besan ellas en voluptuosa unión.

> [that your lips, withered perhaps while locked away,
> have condemned in screams, and not kissing dogs
> like the dogs they kiss in voluptuous union.]

The melodramatic structure of the poem is also related more generally to Peronist rhetoric. Peronist discourse established a series of oppositions whereby the enemy, the other, was constructed and distinguished in terms of moral criteria. Susana Bianchi and Norma Sánchis in their book on the Partido Peronista Feminino point out that Evita Perón and official Peronism constructed a discourse around precisely the same sort of oppositions: authentic versus inauthentic; sacrifice versus egotism; austerity versus frivolity; perverse versus healthy; the true national versus antinational.[4] In fact, it may be that in order to understand the sources of Peronist discourse's power and resonance we should pay more attention to its use of a melodramatic form that drew on a popular imaginative structure steeped in such conventions and figures.

A large number of melodramatic plot variations were available in Argentine popular culture. One of the commonest—indeed perhaps *the* archetypal melodramatic story—involved a working-class woman who was the victim of a sexually rapacious rich male who seduced her away from family/husband/lover. This story and its many variations involved, therefore, a female victim, an outraged father or lover, and a rich villain. It was usually a story of loss, despair, abandonment of the woman, and finally redemption. The redemption of the fallen woman could come in spiritual terms often marked by death through illness, or suicide, with a deathbed reconciliation. This moral price had to be paid for the transgression implicit in a woman's following her sensual nature, going outside the natural boundaries of womanhood, and falling. The quintessential symbol of this fall was the figure of the prostitute. Alternatively, the struggle between good and evil was resolved through a return to a state of domestic bliss, with the home figured as the site of happiness where the natural place of women could be restored and the sexual honor of working-class males reinstated. Often this resolution implied the presence of the nostalgia so essential to this genre, the looking back to a golden age of domestic harmony and moral equilibrium.

There are clear echoes of this traditional melodramatic narrative in Doña María's poem. The death from tuberculosis of the heroine/victim is, perhaps, the most obvious. There are, however, some crucial reconfigurations that appear in the poem and that speak to a different sensibility than that which inhabits the more traditional popular cultural forms in Argentina. Beatriz Sarlo has commented on the symbolic role played in the weekly novels of the 1920s and 1930s by the city, the ultimate location and emblem of modernity, as a source of temptation and moral corruption in these narratives.[5] In Doña María's poem the city has been displaced by the factory as the signifier and location of evil, and this evil is defined in strongly sexualized imagery. In fact, the poem can be read as an extended metaphor equating the factory and factory work with prostitution. Within the poem's imaginative terms the woman worker is the whore, the factory is the whorehouse, and the boss is the pimp or customer.

The equating of factory labor with prostitution is established in the first stanza, where Clarita enters the "establecimiento antro de explotación" [den of exploitation]. Although *antro* can mean a cavern and can serve as a marker of the dark and inhuman quality of the factory as a work space, it also has the meaning in popular speech of a cheap bar where prostitutes go to ply their trade. This phrase is immediately followed by "ganarte la vida," which in addition to its literal meaning of earning one's living is also frequently a euphemism for working the streets. There is also the clear implication of the interchange involved between money and sex: "ganando la vida" she will "enriquecer a viles," and those who she will enrich will have a "lira de oro" [gold coins] instead of a heart—again, I think, a reference to the monetary exchange rather than any sentiment at the root of the relationship. Finally, the phrase "ladrón patentado que nada te dejó" [the licensed thief who left you with nothing] can be taken not only to refer to the robbery of wage labor but also to invoke the image frequently found in popular culture of the prostitute abandoned by the pimp after she becomes too ill or too old.

On one level the melodramatic imaginative structure of Doña María's poem reflects a formal discourse on female labor and the sexual division of labor that was prevalent in the working-class culture of communities like Berisso. The metaphorical linking of prostitution with factory labor in which the woman worker is metonymically transformed into the *puta* (prostitute) was widespread by the 1940s. Its expression in this text could be related to several sources. Once again I would suggest that the militant culture associated with Marxism and anarchism may be one such source. The equating of prostitution and wage labor has a long history within that tradition. Marx in the 1844 manuscripts had stated that "prostitution is only a specific form of the general prostitution of the laborer."[6] More generally, we find both Marxist and anarchist writings in Argentina profoundly critical of the position of women in industry. Although this critique was often expressed in terms of its ill effects on the employment and wages of male workers, it was also expressed in terms of the illegitimacy of factory work, which deformed the natural role of women as educators and nurturers within the home. The role of formal state rhetoric and policy was also important. Donna Guy has argued that already by the 1920s prostitution and factory labor had been placed in the same discursive space in Argentine society, and that by the 1930s the factory was rapidly replacing the bordello as a site of danger and contamination.[7]

Popular attitudes within communities like Berisso toward female factory work reflected both formal state discourse and long-standing anxieties over gender roles expressed in popular cultural forms. The issue was certainly complex. Women had since the opening of the frigoríficos played an important part in the workforce, dominating certain sections, such as the picada where Doña María worked, which were defined as specifically female forms of work. By the 1930s the wages of women had become an essential part of the survival strategies of working-class families in Berisso. Mirta Lobato has also shown how work in the plants became a crucial part of the life-cycle strategies of working-class women in Berisso.[8] Yet a profound element of working-class culture seems to have questioned the very presence of women in the plants. Oral testimony collected in Berisso offers many examples. Some women recall fathers and brothers who informed them that only loose women worked in the plants; there were others who recalled the frequent invocation of the working-class adage that factory work was for putas. Within this folk wisdom the only legitimate work for women outside the home was as *enfermeras* (nurses) and *maestras* (schoolteachers). Beba Anzolini spoke of her own experience of this attitude:

> My mother worked in the *conserva* section of Swift. . . . when I got to the age when I was finishing school I began to dream of working in the plant; it seemed exciting and I knew the money would help. I spoke to a foreman who worked there, and he said that he could get me in. I didn't say anything to my father. At that time you had to buy your own overalls and boots, and I saved up and got them.

The night before I was to start I had my things laid out for the next day, I was really excited, but when my father got home and saw the overalls he asked, "What's that for?" When I told him, he said that no daughter of his was going to work in the plant. He said that I didn't have any idea of what the atmosphere was like inside with so many men. My father said that if I was going to work I could go and work in a government office in La Plata. As I got older, my mother told me of many stories of how the foremen took advantage of young women in the plants.[9]

I think that it is important to contextualize this issue in order to understand its weight in Doña María's text. It has been argued that melodrama as a genre had its roots in the upheaval wrought by an increasingly secular and commercialized society. Peter Brooks in his classic work on the subject, *The Melodramatic Imagination,* maintains that "melodrama comes into being in a world where the traditional imperatives of truth and ethics have been violently thrown into question, yet where the promulgation of truth and ethics, their instauration as a way of life, is of immediate, daily concern."[10] Drawing on this insight, Judith Walkowitz argues that melodrama possessed a form and content particularly suitable for the working class, evoking in simple and immediate terms the vulnerability and instability of life in an industrializing market culture in which the traditional patterns of deference and paternalism were being eroded.[11]

I wish to suggest that working-class communities like Berisso in the 1940s were undergoing a similar experience of upheaval and instability related in part to the influx of internal migrants into the plants from the 1930s onward. There is much that we still do not understand about this process. However, a plausible hypothesis is that the new migrants had an especially disruptive impact on traditional notions of working-class respectability and gender codes. This impact was intensified in the 1940s when the packing plants, in response to wartime demand, dramatically expanded their labor force, drawing more migrants into the community and more women into the plants. Both Swift and Armour ran continuous shifts twenty-four hours a day in this period.

The tensions generated within the community can be read in oral testimony, though they are frequently indirect and in conflict with a community narrative that told of the harmonious blending of different ethnic groups. They are present, for example, in the way in which the European immigrant families of the first generation of Berisso workers are frequently figured as models of domesticity, even though many of the women worked outside the home. Their houses are described as neat and clean with colorful gardens. The European women are good homemakers who conform to the ideals of the domestic sphere when not in the plants. In contrast, the Correntinas and Santiagueñas are not infrequently represented as having unstable or inadequate family lives with unattractive homes and inadequate domestic skills.[12] More specifically, there are references to male perceptions at the time of the increased sexual availability of these "negritas." One male worker recalled both their innocence and the immediacy of their unsophisticated response to affection and kindness: "They were different and they sometimes seemed lost in the frigorífico. . . . They dressed in cheap clothes in what they thought was fashion. They put a sort of paraffin-based pomade on their hair. They'd give themselves to you if you just stroked their cheek."[13] The perception of sexual threat and disruption, the breaching of older codes of gender behavior, was also associated with the increase in consuming power and economic independence of factory women of this era. A communist woman organizer who worked in the mid-1940s in the packing houses of Avellaneda described the situation outside the plant gates on payday:

> They'd come running out of the gate as soon as they'd got paid at midday, and across the street in front of the plant would be dozens of vendors who had spread their wares out on the sidewalk. It was mostly cheap things, clothes, scarves, cheap jewelry. But it was as though they couldn't get enough of it, like they had a thirst to buy things. . . . And, well, it was logical; they'd never had any money in the provinces, never before in their lives had they had so much money and the chance to buy things for themselves.[14]

Melodrama as a genre, embodied as it was in a number of popular cultural forms, provided Doña María with a narrative vehicle within which to express her anxiety and concern over this disruption.

There is a sense, therefore, in which Doña María's poem uses the imaginative structure of melodrama to express the formal discursive construction of female labor that emanated from various sites within Argentine popular culture and state rhetoric. I wish to argue, however, that the poem can be read as doing far more than this. She does not simply internalize elements of the dominant discourse and then replicate them in her text. The ideology to be uncovered in the poem is not simply the state's; but it is not simply a pure product of creative agency. Neither the text nor the subjectivity contained within it are transparent or unambiguous. I wish now to try and uncover the elements of a counterdiscourse present in the poem.

Paula Rabinowitz in her study of the proletarian fiction of the 1930s in the United States, *Labor and Desire,* makes the point that women's narratives that attempt to construct working-class women's subjectivity within their texts show signs of what she calls "genre instability."[15] Doña María's poem shows clear signs of such instability. There are several ways in which the poem violates the genre conventions within which it is framed. It is clear that in this plot women are not presented as responsible for their ultimate fall. There is no fundamental individual transgression brought about by female nature. Women are not constructed as sources of pollution, as they are frequently in both the pulp fiction and the tango of the era. Although prostitution is a key image, it is kept at the level of a metaphoric image. The actual heroine, Clarita, is consistently portrayed in terms of her purity, beauty, and goodness. Another significant divergence concerns the role of men. They are, except for the patron, largely absent in this plot. Certainly, there are no grieving working-class heroes—or lovers—who will attempt a reclamation of the female victim/fallen woman. Indeed, there is no one who will rescue Clarita from the abuse of factory labor. This absence signals another skewing of the genre. There is no happy ending possible here. Melodramatic plots usually offer a depiction of a moral drama and a cathartic resolution in a nostalgic return to an order in which traditional values are recovered. In Doña María's poem there is no nostalgia and no room for the melodramatic fix for "the hurt of history."[16]

What can these genre violations tell us? I think that they are testimony, as Rabinowitz suggests, to the attempt to write about working-class female subjectivity within a cultural formation whose dominant genre conventions, repertoires, and figures were ultimately inadequate for the task. As Jameson indicates, such genre deviations can provide clues to the deeper ideological meaning of a text. Perhaps the most significant deviation in this respect is the presence of the female body and the representation of female sexuality in the narrative.

Yet this representation was not an unalloyed accomplishment, directly expressive of a self-revelatory acquisition of consciousness. This terrain was indeed difficult for Doña María to negotiate, crisscrossed as it was by existing discourses and subjectivities. Certainly, the female body and the experience of industrial labor formed an almost obsessive preoccupation of medical and legal discourse in Argentina from 1910 onward.[17] The relationship between women and modern industrial work had also appeared in earlier cultural expressions. In some of the novels dealing with life in the packing plants, for example, we find a similar obsession on the part of the male authors with the physical ravages of factory work. As a counterpoint to the trope of sexual danger present in these texts, there is a concern with the inevitable loss of physical beauty and femininity. "Mujeres hombrunas" [mannish women] people these texts. In *Pobres Habrá Siempre,* one of the best known of this genre published in 1943 and reedited frequently in the Peronist era, one female character is distinguished precisely because "los años de trabajo rudo parecieron no haberle curtido y deformado del todo su femininidad, como a las otras" [the years of brutal work seemed not to have hardened her and completely deformed her femininity, as it had the others].[18]

Ismael Moreno, author of *El Matadero* (1920), a novel explicitly set in Berisso, fills his narrative with images of what poverty and factory labor do to women. Women in the packing houses are "andrajos de mujeres, despojados prematuramente de su juventud, no les restaba de su sexo mas que el vientre fecundo" [scraps of women, prematurely despoiled of their youth, nothing remained of their sex but their fertile bellies]. In one of the novel's climactic scenes Moreno describes with almost Zolaesque intensity his "Venus del Trabajo": "Her squalid, arched chest; her melancholic gaze; her elongated little face, sprinkled with freckles; her flagellated breasts; slippery stomach; her dark brown, tortured thighs." If, as we have seen, the factory was figured in many of these texts as a space of sexual danger and promiscuity, it was no less a place where women were desexed, where they lost the physical qualities that defined them as women who could be desired by men.[19]

Doña María, therefore, has access to certain cultural models dealing with female sexuality, the female body, and factory labor. Yet these were of dubious value to her. She was aware of the dominant perceptions of women workers in the packing plants. The fact that Clarita was from the Chaco, a "cabecita," a "negrita," is of no small importance to her when she writes her poem. Later in her testimony an interesting exchange concerning Clarita took place. I asked Doña María a question as to whether migrants from the interior had arrived in Berisso "con diferentes pautas de cultura" [with different stages of culture]. She replied in what was almost an aggressive interruption:

> No, no, but they were accepted, they adapted immediately, like the girl who died, *pobrecita,* who I wrote the poem to; she was a girl who almost didn't know how to read and write, but she had a tremendous education with respect to her elders, she was going to bring her mother, she didn't want to mess around with any boy, she said, the day I have a fiancé it will be to get married, a girl, no, no, very educated people came, the people from the north are very respectful.

It would seem that Doña María protested too much; my question to her had been a very general one about "pautas de cultura." I had not mentioned Clarita, nor had I suggested anything about the sexual morality of migrants from the interior. Yet Doña María chose to define education in terms of Clarita's sexual probity. Why this concern, forty years later, to emphasize Clarita's innocence and purity?

I think the explanation lies precisely in the continuing hold on

Doña María's mind of a traditional narrative of female sexuality and factory labor. Forty years earlier its hold must have been even stronger. Yet it is a narrative that she instinctively resisted at the time she wrote the poem and continued to resist many years later. She insists on portraying Clarita as innocent and pure precisely because of her awareness of the dominant imagery embodied in those narrative conventions. She wants to write about what the factory did to her friend and her friend's body without using that imagery. Yet what other repertoire of images existed? She clearly felt, as we have suggested, that those derived from melodrama and popular romance were inadequate, but to portray Clarita in more realistic, flesh-and-blood terms meant entering the domain of the dominant male-centered imagery of women and factory labor.

The effect of this dilemma and Doña María's attempt to resolve it can be seen in her handling of the presence of the female body in her poem. Clarita's body is destroyed by factory labor, but this destruction is not expressed in the same terms as those derived from the voyeuristic male gaze of the meatpacking novels. Although the contrast between her beauty before entering the plant and her death in a squalid hospital is noted, it is not dwelt on; the details are left largely unspoken. There is no inventory of bodily woes such as we find in both the meatpacking novels and the medical discourse of the era. The novelty of her handling of this theme can be appreciated if we contrast it with a well-known poem dealing with working women, physical decline, and tuberculosis: "La dactilógrafa tuberculosa" written by Nicolás Olivari in the 1920s and published in his collection, *La musa de la mala pata*:

Esta doncella tísica y asexuada
esta mujer de senos inapetentes
—rosicler en los huesos de su cara granulada
y ganchuna su nariz ya transparente—.

Esta pobre yegua flaca y trabajada,
con los dedos espatulados de tanto teclear,
esta pobre mujer invertebrada,
tiene que trabajar

Esta pobre nena descuajeringada,
con sus ancas sútiles de alfiler,
tiene una alma tumefacta y rezagada
¡y se empena en comer!

Yo la amé cuatro meses con los ojos,
con mis ojos de perro triste y vagabundo,
cuando la miraba los pómulos rojos,
¡qué dolor profundo!

Un día juntamos hombro a hombro nuestra desdicha,
—vivimos dos meses en un cúchitril—
en su beso salivoso naufragó la dicha
y el ansía de vivir.

Una tarde sin historia, una tarde cualquiera,
murió clásicamente en un hospital.
(Bella burguesita que a mi lado pasás, cambia de acera,
    porque voy a putear.) [20]

["The consumptive typist"
That young miss, tubercular and asexual,
that woman whose breasts had no hunger
—rosy the bones of the pimpled face
and already transparent her hooked nose.

That poor mare, thin and worn out,
with her fingers turned to spatulas from so much typing,
that poor woman without a backbone
has to work.

That poor girl falling to pieces
with her razor-thin rump
has a soul swollen and left back
and insists on eating!

I loved her for four months with my eyes,
with these eyes of a sad wandering dog,

when I looked at her red cheeks
what pain so deep!

One day we joined shoulder to shoulder
our misfortune
—we spent two months in a hovel—
and in her kisses heavy with drool she drowned
the joy and hunger for life.

One forgotten afternoon, one afternoon like any other
she died in a hospital, classically
(lovely high-class girl walking by,
better cross the street,
because I'm about to curse.)]

There are some similarities of tone and sensibility, but this is a poem with no love for the victim, only pity and disgust. It is a poem written exclusively from a male perspective with images that could only have been written by a man—in particular, the terrible second stanza with its images of "esta pobre yegua flaca y trabajada, . . . esta pobre mujer invertebrada."

These observations do not, however, exhaust the topic. The relating of physical attractiveness and factory labor was not simply a male invention, part of a fantasy provoked by the male gaze. Industrial work and working women's notions of self-worth and identity were closely related. Working women's subjectivity was closely linked to their sense of their bodies and the physical and aesthetic stigma attached to factory labor. As Mirta Lobato has suggested, there was a clear hierarchy of acceptability in working-class culture attached to different forms of labor for women.[21] Meatpacking had a uniquely low status within this hierarchy precisely because of its impact on the female body.

Women who worked in the plants were acutely aware of this issue. Those who worked for any length of time with knives in sections such as the picada bore the marks for the rest of their lives. Their fingers were stunted and their nails permanently cracked. Constant contact with cold or semi-frozen meat also contributed to deformations of the hands. Doña María herself frequently commented about the ugliness of her own hands. Work in other sections involved chemicals that produced unsightly skin rashes. Perhaps even more stigmatizing from the point of view of sexual attractiveness was the odor associated with meatpacking. Some sections of the plants where women were concentrated, such as tripería, were precisely those where the smell was the most intense. Beba Anzolini recalled:

> My mother worked in the conserva section of Swift, on a line putting food in jars. She developed calcium deposits in her elbows from doing the same thing over and over again. But what she hated most was the smell. She used to shower at work, but the smell was still with her when she got home, and she used to shower again. A neighbor of ours worked in the tripería, and she would try everything to get the smell off her. She would squeeze lemons over her hands. Some people would never lose the smell, it would be on their clothes when they died. . . . I've been on the tram from Berisso to La Plata when people would hold their noses to keep out the smell of people returning home from the plants.[22]

Within this context we can begin to appreciate the figure of the niñas burguesitas and their complex role in the text. They would seem, in part, to embody for Doña María a sexuality that is threatening and illicit because it is signaled by the possession of fine clothes, sexual protection, and sensuality. Yet the very attribution of such illicit sexuality to the niñas burguesitas should command our attention. Such attribution involves the undermining of the very metonymic logic that she has posited, in particular that which entails the linkage between prostitution and the female worker. The feminine as a cultural image was a bourgeois category defined precisely by the possession of physical, social, and aesthetic attributes that working women were felt to lack, and this image of bourgeois femininity was constructed precisely in opposition to the image of morally debased working women, as expounded in medical discourse and other fields of cultural representation.

Doña María undermines this metonymic logic by inverting the traditional terms used to represent the difference between bourgeois women and women workers. All the traditional signifiers used to define working women's social and sexual status are inverted; the carnality, sensuality, and immorality ascribed to the niñas burguesitas are the exact analogue of terms usually attached to factory women. This was a formidable discursive obstacle course facing Doña María, as she attempted to articulate a working woman's subjectivity. Working women were aware that they were differentiated from, and constructed by, the gaze of other, bourgeois women. Doña María knows that, as Cora Kaplan argues for nineteenth-century women writers, visual appearance played an important role in the setting up of moral hierarchies between women.[23] But her rhetorical solution of inverting the normative trope of the working woman and the debased, sexualized other had to confront a powerful loading of the discursive dice.

Olivari's poem should already have alerted us to the powerful sexualized symbolism attached to tuberculosis. Diego Armus has recently argued that by the 1920s the link between tuberculosis and sexual excess was a staple of discourses ranging from the strictly medical to the anarchist and that such a linkage was primarily embodied in the figure of the working woman.[24] The nature of Clarita's disease was, therefore, not an incidental factor for Doña María. The very inhabiting of the public space by working women was itself part of a normative coding that invoked vice and licentiousness.

The cost of attempting to speak of a working woman, factory labor, and the female body within this discursive landscape was a high one. Its principal effect was to exclude the possibility of presenting Clarita as a desired and desiring subject. To enter the realm of desire would be to enter the domain of the niñas burguesitas, their explicit sexuality, their promiscuity, and their mocking betrayal of working-class women. There is, moreover, a final rejection, a further undermining of the "logic of metonymic entailment."[25] The move, fundamental to the meatpacking novels, whereby the female body and its woes are projected onto and come to represent the working woman's sense of herself, her subjectivity, is ultimately rejected by Doña María. The final logic of the poem would seem to be that Clarita is unknowable by the bourgeois women who cannot know her thoughts, her past, her self, her "yo de ironía." In a gesture reminiscent of one mentioned in chapter 1, which Doris Sommer attributes to contemporary women testimonialists in Latin America who construct "resistant texts,"[26] this poem seems to argue that neither we the listeners nor the niñas burguesitas can derive a very complete sense of Clarita's self from the marks of class and sexual oppression inscribed on her body.

If the cost of Doña María's refusal to accept the logic of metonymic entailment is that Clarita remains in a profound sense unknowable, we still need to register the fact that for all her ambivalence and reluctance Doña María *does* inscribe the female body at the core of her poem and expresses its experience of factory labor in what are ultimately sexualized terms, though a sexuality signaled as coercion and not as desire. The stanza that begins "El ruido de las maquinas" can be read as not only a generalized statement about the alienation of modern factory work but indirectly about what exploitation and machinery *do* to female bodies. "Hysterical" Clarita will lose "hasta el yo," and "exhausted" she will leave "hasta el carácter en manos del patrón"; later she describes the thief/patron as he who "nada te dejó." Within the moral economy of the poem I would suggest that this description can be read as referring to the loss of virginity. Having exploited her economically, the system takes the one thing that she has left, her sexual honor—"hasta el carácter." The poem, therefore, recognizes very clearly that women do not only exchange their labor power for money. After all, in terms of the labor contract it is not true that the thief/patron leaves her nothing. Yet behind the wage contract there is another, the sexual contract, which involves something more fundamental—a claim to control over and access to the female body.[27] In a fundamental way, although expressed indirectly, Doña María is staking a claim for a recognition of difference; factory labor is not experienced equally by men and women, and that difference is ultimately a sexual one.

This interpretation is reinforced by another feature of the poem. There are strong references to rape. Once more we need to be aware of the complexity of the discursive landscape within which Doña María was operating. The trope of rape and working-class women was to be found in many sites within Argentine popular culture. Almafuerte in "Antífona Roja" had warned that working-class daughters would have to "rendir sus tributos de carne sin suenos ni amores, ni vírgenes ansías" [render their tributes of flesh without dreams or loves, or virginal concerns] if they entered the factory. In general terms the theme was intimately connected with the genre conventions associated with melodrama, with its invocation of lost sexual honor and its subsequent redemption. More specifically, within these conventions rape was figured as an indicator of bourgeois rapacity and perversity. Typically, the female victim suffered at the hands of the boss or the forces of law and order. The symbolism attached to rape was multifold. On the one hand, in texts such as the meatpacking novels, it could serve as a metaphor for class exploitation. In the more politically committed of these texts such as Raúl Larra's *Sin Tregua* (1953),[28] the female victim comes to metonymically represent, as Rabinowitz suggests for the U.S. male proletarian fiction of the 1930s, the working class before its acquisition of consciousness. Female vulnerability and weakness in the face of bourgeois sexual depravity is thus equated with the vulnerability of a working class without consciousness and organization. In these plots rape, or attempted rape, will be avenged by politicized male protectors. On the other hand, we also find rape frequently associated with transgressive female behavior in male-authored texts. In particular, participation in picketing and rape are frequently linked. In Bernardo González Arrili's *Los Charcos Rojos*,[29] for example, during the strike that forms the climax of the novel we are offered a scene describing the actions of women picketers. With clothes torn and with sexually explicit language they taunt the troops sent to repress the strike. Their actions and words render them as animals. The scene culminates with their capture and gang rape by the soldiers.

Doña María's handling of the theme of rape takes the poem beyond the general metaphorical linking of prostitution and female labor or rape and class exploitation. Absent, too, is the redeeming and avenging working-class male protector. The subtext of the poem gives it a far more concrete grounding in the female body and the violence visited on it. The most significant line in this respect is: "que tu pecho valiente presentás al pingajo" [as you present your valiant breast to the shreds]. As we have already suggested, at one level this is an image taken from traditional working-class iconography: Maríanne, the Republic, is frequently pictured bare breasted in nineteenth-century French republican imagery. Yet the line makes no literal sense, since "pingajo" means rag or tatter. It seems likely that what Doña María has done is to elide two separate words, "pinga," which means "prick"/"cock" in slang, and "vergajo"—the penis of a bull that, after it has been cut and dried, is used as a whip. The image is immediately transformed from one celebrating female proletarian virtue to one of violent rape, with the female body presenting itself, face forward, breasts exposed, to the instrument of sexual violence. This reading also offers another meaning for the line that follows: "sangrada hija del pueblo." "Sangrada" could now be interpreted as the blood caused by the rape.

The elements that we have been discussing can be seen as expressing what Raymond Williams called an emergent "structure of feeling."[30] Williams developed the concept of structure of feeling to address the problem of relating cultural and artistic forms to changes in the social formation without recourse to the base/superstructure model of traditional Marxism. A structure of feeling implies not a formal ideology or worldview expressed in a text but rather what Williams calls "meanings and values as they are actively lived and felt," "a particular quality of social experience and relationship." An emergent structure of feeling is directly related to the tension between received interpretations available in the dominant discourse and the practical, lived experience of social actors. Such tensions are often, Williams argues, difficult to express within existing fixed forms and conventions, and in the absence of alternative vehicles they remain present as "an unease, a stress, a displacement, a latency." Often, indeed, there are experiences "to which the fixed forms do not speak at all, which indeed they do not recognize," and whose traces can only be located in the structure of feeling of a text. In this case the structure of feeling refers to "characteristic elements of impulse, restraint, and tone; specifically affective elements of consciousness and relationships." The social ideals and particular quality of social experience embodied in a structure of feeling produce their particular narrative forms, their typologies of conflict and resolution, their repertoires of personalities, which form what Williams defines as their characteristic "semantic figures."

In Doña María's poem we can disinter traces of the tension between a received interpretation of female labor and the actual lived experience that Doña María wished to express. The result is that we can read traces in the poem of what could be described as an emergent, seminascent structure of gender feeling among working-class women. This gender feeling is reflected in a new semantic figure — the working woman who bears the marks of factory labor on her body and whose experience is expressed in sexualized language. It is also, however, reflected in a characteristic tone and impulse of bitterness and anger — a stance not usually associated with poor women in traditional forms. The voice that embodies this anger is ultimately that of Doña María, not Clarita's. Doña María as narrator is the "absent presence" that seeks to express itself in the poem, and this absent presence is figured in what is perhaps the most novel of the semantic figures that emerge from the poem — an aggressive, threatening female presence. Again, I want to emphasize that this is a question of tone, implication, nuance rather than direct embodiment. The presence is not that of the nurturing, maternal figure of classic melodrama or the passive female victim. The absent narrator is rather a mother figure, and the story that she tells can be seen as a gesture toward men, at once both angry and threatening. Indeed, it may not be too far-fetched to suggest that there are echoes of that most threatening of archetypal female symbols: the woman with a gun, the red riflewoman, the phallic mother who will also castrate.[31]

I wish now to return to the question of voice in this poem, since despite its importance it is far from straightforward. If, on the one hand, we can say that Doña María's is the voice that attempts to speak through Clarita, it is also true that the form of the poem indicates a desire to give Clarita back her own voice. The dominant rhetorical trope that frames the poem is that of apostrophe. We encountered this literary figure in the "Requiem for a Frigorífico" in chapter 1. Barbara Johnson's definition cited there can serve us now: it is "a form of ventriloquism" whose primary poetic function is "to call up, animate, the absent, the lost, the dead." [32] The poetic device primarily used to place this ventriloquism in motion is prosopopeia. Let us also recall Alberto Moreiras's definition of prosopopeia, offered in chapter 1, as referring to a "mask through which one's own voice is projected onto another, where that other is always suffering from an inability to speak." [33] In the second half of the poem Doña María insistently calls on Clarita to speak: "Díles que te hagan frente"; "díles que ayer ha muerto"; "díles que a poco hermosa" [tell them to face you; tell them that yesterday a comrade died; tell them that not so long ago]. Yet despite these frequent injunctions Clarita cannot speak, and indeed she even leaves the world, as Doña María tells us in the last stanza, without speaking. It is her friend, María Roldán, who will speak through her and for her.

This projection is, however, bounded by the frailties of human beings and the relentless march of time. As Barbara Johnson notes, a poet using apostrophe is always in a sense saying "be thou me" to the addressee, but this gesture also implies that a poet has animation to give. The particular emotional power embodied in Doña María's rendering of her poem in 1987, when she was old and dying of cancer, may well reflect her despair that she has little voice left to give.

There may be another source for this emotion, deriving from the singular link that Johnson suggests exists between motherhood and apostrophe. In virtually all the references to her in Doña María's testimony Clarita appears as little more than a child; we have commented, too, on her insistence on Clarita's childlike purity and lack of sexuality. Doña María's relationship with Clarita seems to have had a strong maternal component, and her death may well have been felt as much as the death of a child as that of a compañera de trabajo. In this case it would represent the second such loss, since her son had died of polio only the previous year. Johnson suggests that when women speak about the death of children, they are moving beyond the conventionally figurative use of apostrophe to metaphorically give voice: "When a woman speaks about the death of children . . . a powerful taboo is being violated . . . (the notion) that any death of a child is . . . something a mother ought by definition

to be able to prevent." The pain invoked in this poem would, therefore, seem to be far more than the pain deriving from nostalgia or
the anger sparked by class exploitation.

The formula that Doña María is the "absent presence" in this poem
is, therefore, only partially adequate. Clarita is not simply the convenient vehicle, the ventriloquist's puppet, who serves to voice Doña
María's subjectivity. What is ultimately at stake in the poem is as
much Clarita's fate in history as Doña María's anger. In this sense the
poem has a profoundly redemptive intention. It wishes to represent its object, Clarita, and make her speak in much the same way as
Walter Benjamin's angel of history wishes to awaken the dead.[34] On
the surface it would seem that within the poem's imaginative terms
this redemption can only come through Jesus; there is no rescue for
Clarita in this world, and the poem's last stanza offers the image of
Clarita standing before Jesus. Within these terms death would be the
ultimate liberation and redemption: "que ya era liberada por Jesus,"
Doña María had said when speaking of Clarita's death.

Without diminishing the plausibility of this religious reading, or
understating the depth of Doña María's religious convictions, I do
find reasons to question the convenient nature of this sort of narrative closure. In part, this question arises because of the poem's apparently overly simplistic resolution. It is possible that having avoided
the melodramatic fix for much of the poem, Doña María could not
resist it in the final stanza, which offers us both redemption in Jesus
and the figure of the "viejita buena," both staples of the melodramatic imagination. Yet this resolution smacks of a fake solution that
does not in fact succeed in silencing the questions and criticisms
provoked by the poem's evocation of the "hurt of history." This
sense is strengthened by what we know of Doña María's life at the
time she wrote the poem, which would seem to indicate that she did
not intend to advocate the passive waiting on religious redemption.

There is another redemptive vehicle present in this poem: the redemptive power of language itself, of words and of poetry. If we
go back to her testimony introducing the poem, we will see that
Doña María had placed the liberating power of the poem very much
on the same level as the redemptive power of Jesus. She wrote the

poem she says because by doing so she would liberate both herself and Clarita. The redemptive power claimed for the written word in this formulation is made even more striking if we bear in mind the phrase that introduces it. When her husband asks her what she is doing, she tells us that she was sitting writing the verse because she was tired of "crying without improving anything." She had, one supposes, simply cried too many times by 1947 over the hurts of history, over the deaths of children and working girls who were little more than children. Apparently political and union activism had not changed things; writing a poem could do what they could not, or at least so it seemed in the middle of that sleepless night waiting to bury her friend.

This is, of course, to cede to literature an awesome power, to make of a poem an extraordinarily effective speech act capable of intervening in history. Yet it is, I would argue, the key to understanding the redemptive urge of this poem. It is also one reason for its ambiguities and tensions, for in the end what can a poem do to redeem the victims of history? In purely literary terms this operation is problematic. As Barbara Johnson notes, apostrophe as a trope nearly always places in question the effectiveness of its own rhetorical strategies: "The final question becomes can this gap be bridged; can this loss be healed, through language alone."[35] There is a sense, indeed, in which the poem can be read as a sort of metacommentary precisely on the difficulty of using language to "awaken the dead," on the difficulty of speaking from the subject position of working-class women. In this sense, therefore, in one and the same gesture the poem both affirms and calls into question the very redemptive power of poetry claimed by Doña María. Faced with this tension, we could perhaps read the final stanza and its overt invocation of religious redemption as a partial solution to an insoluble dilemma.

The dilemma is inherent in the notion of awakening the dead through language alone. In a letter written to Walter Benjamin in 1937, commenting on Benjamin's insistence that "the work of the past is incomplete," Max Horkheimer had argued that "past injustice is done and finished. Those who have been beaten to death are truly dead. . . . the injustice, the pain, the terror of the past are irreparable." [36] For Benjamin the angel of history who would complete the tasks of the past was, possibly, the historical materialist who could tap into "the weak messianic power" of each generation and offer the hope of redeeming each generation's debt to past generations, of thereby completing the work of the past. This solution was not available to Doña María. In its absence, and after calling desperately on Clarita to give voice in the previous stanzas, she offers a religious resolution. Such a resolution had been the essence of Horkheimer's comment to Benjamin: the thesis of the incompleteness of the past must lead, he warned, ultimately to a belief in the Last Judgment.

It is worth pausing to consider this resolution more closely. The standard representation of this dilemma at the time would have been to have invoked the name of Perón and Peronism as a secular solution capable of resolving the injustices of the past. There were, indeed, many examples of this sort of "realist" solution in the emerging genre of regime-inspired poetry. The Peronist press was full of this sort of poetry. Yet for Doña María this is no easy solution. There may be several explanations for this. In part, it may speak of the difficulty of dealing discursively with working women's oppression, which was beyond the reach of solutions immediately available for class oppression. In part, too, as we have already intimated, it may well have been that at this moment the pain was too great, the injustice too insistent, for her to believe that salvation could simply come from the hands of Perón.

There is, finally, another redemptive sense to the poem. Walter Benjamin had not directly replied to Horkheimer's claim that the injustices of the past were irreparable, but he would write in his notes shortly before his death in 1940 that "history is not only a science but a form of remembrance. What has been established by science can be modified in remembrance. Remembrance can make the incomplete (happiness) complete and render the complete (suffering) incomplete." [37] In this sense Doña María's poem can be viewed as an act of remembrance, permeated by the hope—fragile and uncertain—that the past can be modified. Each time she recited the poem over the years to her listeners in Berisso, she reaffirmed the hope that the dead had not died in vain, that the angel of history who wanted to awaken the dead could also "make whole what had been smashed."

I have up to now been offering an interpretation of Doña María's poem, and as with any textual interpretation this inevitably raises epistemological and ethical issues. Such issues have haunted the difficult relationship between historians and literary critics and, within history, between those who have followed the poststructuralist path and those who have not. Although it might be possible for most historians to accept the notion of the radical indeterminacy of meaning in literary and historical texts, it is far more difficult to accept the explicit questioning of referentiality, the fundamental cutting loose of the sign from signified universe advocated by some practitioners of the linguistic turn. Derrida's claim that there is nothing outside the text is clearly impossible for most historians to accept at face value. Similarly, though from a rather different position, Umberto Eco has recently insisted on the primacy of the text and its logic. For Eco a proper interpretation, which he distinguishes from an abusive "overinterpretation," seeks to arrive at the "intentio operis." This line of analysis implies that personal, historical contextualization is illegitimate: "We have to respect the text, not the person in flesh and blood." [38]

From the historian's point of view there would seem to be at least two sorts of problems related to this approach. First, in a fundamental way historians must look beyond the text, to referents buried in particular social, cultural, and political universes. As William Sewell has noted, the historian's object of study is different from that of literary critics in that "the historian's ultimate goal in reading texts is to understand a world that is manifested, reflected, refracted, or referred to in the texts but that is different from and not homologous with the texts." [39] It is precisely an attempt to bridge this divide that seems to inform Jameson's notion of the political unconscious as the repository of historical meanings repressed by ideology and which characterizes all texts. Appropriately historicized readings can recover these meanings; these readings must be aware of current and former ideological attempts to contain meanings and contradictions.

Beyond this epistemological problem there lies a fundamental ethical issue that is especially acute for those dealing with oral texts. Although it is true that transcribing oral discourse into written text involves what Paul Ricoeur calls a form of "distanciation" that may emancipate a text from its "ostensive references," we need to be aware of the limits of this process and the specificity of particular types of text. As John B. Thompson argues in an essay on Ricoeur, the autonomy of the written text is limited; it is always the case that a text is written for an audience and the expectations of its reception are embedded in the conditions of production of the text itself.[40] In the case of Doña María's poem the speech community to whom she implicitly addresses the poem is apparent. Indeed, she explicitly contextualizes the poem within the parameters of a particular discursive community. The poem was offered to me as part of an extended life story; it is embedded within that broader text. On one level this implies that issues of intent and contextualization are far more concrete, offering the possibility of clarifying the referential connotations of the text. Although we cannot reduce the poem's meanings to its extratextual conditions of production, Doña María's text is clearly not as unknowable as Wordsworth's Lucy poems or Keats's "moving hand" fragment—two oft-quoted examples of the ultimate undecidability of textual meaning.[41]

On the other hand, our ability to contextualize a poem such as Doña María's also means that the ethical issue of avoiding bad faith on the part of the interpreter is especially keen. I did not know Wordsworth; I had no implicit bargain with him in terms of "faithfully" rendering the meaning of a life or a poem. My compact with Doña María is of a different sort and certainly involves more than a purely intellectual relationship. Derrida attempts to address these ethical issues with his notion of a "responsible reading." He distinguishes between two levels of reading: a general level focused on an accepted minimal consensus with relatively stable meanings; and a second moment of interpretation proper that calls into question some of the elements of consensus found at the first level.[42] This movement between levels of interpretation, which involves the notion of "reading against the grain," is probably what the historian can most productively take from literary theory. Implicit in this is an understanding of the plurivocality of meaning, a recognition that rhetorical/textual assertions are precisely that rather than unalloyed historical and social truths. It is this understanding that underlies my own attempt in this chapter to go beyond the first level of the poem's meaning, to question the consensus embodied in a "class-based" reading.

And yet, in the end, the interpretation of any text is a profoundly personal issue of reading, involving intellectual and emotional elements that I personally bring to a particular interpretative encounter. I have, for example, spoken frequently of tone, and tone is very much a question of hearing and at bottom a personal matter. Raymond Williams attempted, by subsuming "tone" within his notion of structure of feeling, to give it a broader, transpersonal quality, but I can never be sure that the tone I have chosen to hear in a given work is the "right" one. I cannot claim to have empathetically entered Doña María's mindset as it existed on that winter's night in 1946 and to have uncovered the meaning encoded in the "tone" of her poem. It would be possible to place the meaning elsewhere, to hear a different tone, to perform a different reading, to risk in the terms of Derrida's metaphor cited in the epigraph to this chapter "the addition of some new thread."

In the end the basic gesture behind my interpretation in this chapter has been the decision to go beyond the meanings immediately available to the community to whom the poem was addressed, to uncover its subtext. This gesture has implied a double maneuver of historical and cultural contextualization and of close attention to literary and linguistic form. It is this maneuver that I take to underlie Gabrielle Spiegel's concept of the social logic of the text predicated on a "relational reading of text and context, of overt and supressed meanings, of implied and articulated purposes, together with the variety of literary and discursive modes in which they are given voice."[43]

Clearly, there is a risk involved in such a strategy. Yet it would seem to be a reasonable one to take in order to undertake the sort of gendered reading I have attempted here. Terms such as *palimpsest* and *double-voiced text* have for some time been accepted critical tools in the arsenal of feminist critics in their interpretations of the formal literary products of women writers to signal the "hidden meaning" behind the conventional narratives these writers are forced to adopt.[44] Applying the same critical strategies to the interpretation of Doña María's poem ultimately pays it the sort of respect normally reserved for "higher" forms of cultural production.

It also points us toward a recognition of the extraordinarily difficult task Doña María had embarked on as she wrote the poem. As we have already argued, the attempt to express female subjectivity within established forms tended to deform the available narrative conventions. Faced with the inadequacy of existing semantic figures, the absence of either an appropriate language or plot models, she struggled to invent new ones, reconfigure old ones, and make use of indirection and tone. The endeavor was made all the more difficult, of course, by the dubious legitimacy—if not outright illegitimacy—of the experience and feeling she was trying to convey. In the Argentina of 1946 it was extremely difficult to raise the issue of the female body and female sexuality at a time when they had not entered the arena of the public sphere and working-class politics. In this absence it was extremely difficult for a working woman to speak legitimately of the body as a defining element of her subjectivity. Existing narratives of class experience of factory labor were exclusively masculine. Doña María herself was already marked within the community as a "mujer atrevida" for her activism. In this context, at a moment of profound anguish and grief, in a cold house in the middle of the night, Doña María Roldán sat down to express herself in a poem. It was, I think, an extraordinary achievement, and one not without significance for the historian.

Some years ago I suggested in an essay that the emergence of Peronism as a mass movement in the years 1945–46 was a unique conjuncture that gave expression to a whole range of tensions and conflicts within Argentine society that had been repressed up until then.[45] I had in mind, in particular, issues of cultural and symbolic power. For a brief period the eruption of these conflicts—which were of a different tenor to more specifically economic class conflicts—threatened to go beyond the ability of the Peronist state to channel them. It may be that the tone of gender relations and anxieties expressed in Doña María's poem should be added to the elements that potentially threatened to disrupt the harmony of Peronist Argentina. In that case, it may be necessary to think of the role of Evita Perón, the Partido Peronista Feminino, and many of the social policies of the Peronist state not only in terms of their mobilizing power but also as forms of disciplining. In this sense they might be viewed as ways to impose the "melodramatic fix" that Doña María's poem had so resolutely refused.

IV

EPILOGUE

EPILOGUE

Why bother to remember a past that cannot be made into a present?
— Søren Kierkegaard, *Fear and Trembling*

Doña María Roldán died on 3 July 1989. She died of a heart attack in her home on the Calle Czechoslovakia while playing with her great-granddaughter, Sol. I had last seen her five weeks before. At that time Argentina was racked by a wave of supermarket lootings brought on by the profound economic crisis and hyperinflation that accompanied the last weeks of the government of Raúl Alfonsín. Doña María was busy with other Peronists in Berisso organizing a food distribution network to provide the basic necessities among the poorer sections of the community. Rumors were rife about violent crowds fueled by desperation. She was worried that I would have trouble returning to Buenos Aires, since the police were stopping buses looking for "agitators." I joked that my English passport would save me. I also told her that I was more worried about her and about what would happen in Berisso. She assured me that nothing would happen in Berisso. It was, she said, "a community that has suffered much but is very disciplined." We said our good-byes, and I returned to Buenos Aires with little difficulty. In retrospect her assessment of what would happen in Berisso proved prophetic. The bonds of communal solidarity and social and political networks saved Berisso from the upheaval that afflicted other localities.

I spoke to her briefly by phone a few weeks later to say good-bye. Our farewells were usually a little emotional. We were genuinely fond of each other, and she, with the wisdom of old age, knew that there are no guarantees of future meetings. I later learned that she had been suffering from cancer for several years. This was something that I think I knew at some intuitive level but had been unwilling to confront. A mixture of diffidence and reluctance to recognize the presence of illness and death had kept me from broaching the topic with her. I do not know if a certain presentiment that we would not speak again added an extra emotional charge to our last conversation. I suspect not, for she ended with her usual wish that God might bless me and my family, and that we meet again the following year, "si Dios quiera." The blessing had become so familiar to me that it scarcely registered. Now, thinking back on it, it seems entirely appropriate that her last words to me expressed a profoundly religious sentiment that underlay her life, but which I, the atheist, had been hesitant to hear.

I returned to Berisso the following May. I had brought a down comforter as a present for Doña María, to help ward off the cold of her cement-floored bedroom. I decided to visit another friend, Miguel Sánchez, first. It was lunchtime, and I didn't want Doña María to feel obliged to make me a meal. As we sat around the table after eating, Miguel casually remarked that it was "a shame about the old lady." It took me several seconds to realize what he was talking about. "What old lady?" "You know, your old lady, what's her name? la Roldán." "Why, what happened?" "She died, didn't they tell you?" "No, I haven't heard anything for a year." "Well, she must have died almost a year ago." I was stunned at first and then a little relieved that I hadn't gone directly to her house with the gift. It turned out that her family had not been able to find my address in the papers left in her house, and none of my other friends had thought to mention it in the sporadic correspondence we kept up. Beyond my sadness at her death, I also felt a certain bewilderment. I had returned primed with new questions concerning themes that needed elaboration, threads of her life that needed tying up, previous evasions and inconsistencies on her part that needed, finally, to be resolved. I was initially overwhelmed by a sense of panic. How could I complete a history of a life, if the subject had departed without giving me all the facts or offering the real key that would decode the transcript of the many hours of conversations we had taped? How was intellectual closure concerning this incomplete project possible in these circumstances?

Eventually, I would come to a sort of terms with this conundrum. In the short term I researched the historical context of her life and interviewed others whose lives had intersected with hers in some way. I was like a playwright developing his plot by coaxing out the minor characters in the absence of his heroine. Gradually, too, Doña María's narrative settled into the background, as I concentrated over the ensuing years on a long-term history of Berisso with my colleague Mirta Lobato. However, it was never completely subsumed within the larger project. I have frequently taken it out to reread it and to puzzle over it, driven by a sense of personal obligation to Doña María and by a sense of intellectual fascination.

Of the many things concerning Doña María that fill my shelves —tapes, transcripts, photos, notes—there was one item that I had never taken down in my frequent reengagements with Doña María's life story. It is a videotape, and it sat unviewed for almost ten years. As I was leaving Berisso in 1990, Miguel offered me the tape. It was, he said, shot by a local journalist in 1988, and it contained scenes of the campaign of Carlos Menem to win the Peronist nomination for president in the elections of 1989. I thanked him without much enthusiasm and put it in my bag without further comment. Miguel, his wife Emilce, and his children Lito and Mónica, are all fervent, orthodox Peronists, and we had had many arguments about politics. As they well knew, Menem was hardly, to use a favorite phrase of Miguel's, "santo de mi devoción." Our friendship had survived, based on a fundamental decency and hospitality that characterize working-class culture in places like Berisso. As though reading my mind, Miguel looked right at me and told me that it had several scenes in which "the old lady" was featured. This time I knew who the "vieja" was. "Take it," he said, "it can be a memento, something to remember her by."

Why had the video sat on my shelf for eight years? In part, I think, it was because I did not need it to help me remember her. I had spent too long with her, I had her words, her voice, and, if those were not sufficient, I also had photographs, a few of her as a young woman and many more I had taken myself. I hesitated to view her image for much the same reason I refused the offer to view my mother after she had died. In part, too, it was because I instinctively resisted the mnemonic charge that video brings; its ability to add to the visual representation, movement, and sound and thereby to enhance the "carnal quality" that mere photos already possess.

When I came to write the epilogue to this book about Doña María and her life story, however, it seemed clear that I should at last watch the video. It was a piece, perhaps a very small piece, of the much larger mosaic of evidence and representations that I possessed and from which I was trying to fashion the written text of her life story, and my analysis of it. I had no illusion that it would be the symbolic piece that brought together the many strands of her life in a final synthesis. I hope that the previous chapters have registered my skepticism regarding this sort of transcendent claim for oral history. Epilogue in its most common sense does refer to a concluding section that "rounds out the design of a literary work." One of its more basic senses is, however, to simply say something in addition. Perhaps, the video would provide a way of doing this. The video was also a recording, I knew, of her final public political performance, and as such it might indeed stand as a "rounding out," "a summary" of what had been conceived as a profoundly public life.

The video is, indeed, a telling document. It is on one level an extraordinary view of working-class Peronism as a social and political movement. The first event recorded is the launching of Carlos Menem's campaign in the province of Buenos Aires on 23 April 1988. The fact that he chose Berisso to begin his campaign was itself significant, drawing on Berisso's reputation as a bastion of Peronism "of the first hour." He also chose, significantly, to ask Doña María to be present alongside him as a representative of that generation, as one of those who had led the workers of Berisso on the sacred day of 17 October 1945. A minute's silence was also offered to the memory of Hipólito Pinto, another figure associated with that day and that generation of Peronists in Berisso and who had recently died. After Menem's speech a roll call of other "históricos" was called as they approached the table to receive diplomas of recognition from Menem.

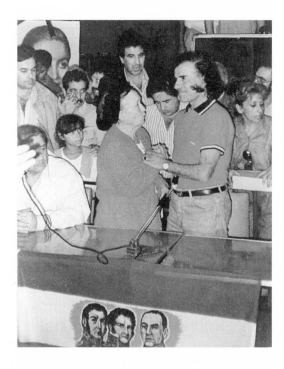

Doña María Roldán
and candidate Carlos
Menem, Berisso,
23 April 1988. *Courtesy
of María Roldán.*

The events in the hall are framed by illustrations of the controlled chaos that I had come to recognize as distinctive of Peronist political events. Menem was, at times, drowned out by the constant din of loudspeaker trucks broadcasting Peronist slogans outside the hall. At times the sound system inside the hall failed. After the speech, as the meeting broke up, general pandemonium reigned as everyone approached to embrace the candidate and bend his ear with political advice. Afterward in the street itself, the Avenida Montevideo, the video journalist captures the mixture of political rally, carnival parade, and street fiesta characteristic of Peronism in its heyday and much imitated by other political groups in Argentina. Political slogans, marching bands, banners, balloons, parents, kids, and political militants all come together in a cacophony of sound and color.

Menem's speech itself articulated many of the standard themes of traditional Peronist political rhetoric. He and his partner for the Peronist ticket, Eduardo Duhalde, represent a "national project" that will complete the work begun by General Perón. The underlying principles of this project are summed up, Menem asserts, in the classic Peronist slogan, "A socially just, free, sovereign nation." Social justice must be guaranteed by the state as the basic reward that labor can claim in a nation where "trabajo" is seen as a fundamental mark of identity and virtue. Menem argues for a moratorium on the foreign debt, a debt that the "Argentine nation did not contract." Although he is not against the free enterprise system, he is against "the absurd modernization" that Argentina has suffered and that has led to the dire social situation that Argentine workers are experiencing.

The next event captured by the video journalist takes place two weeks later, across the Grand Dock from Berisso, in the city of Ensenada. This occasion is more somber. Duhalde and several local Peronist political and union leaders have come to the local of the State Oil Workers' union. It is nighttime, and the first signs of winter are apparent. The meeting takes place in the hall of the YPF Merchant Fleet branch of the union. This is a time of crisis for the union, as talk of privatizing the state oil company, and in particular its tanker fleet, is in the air. As the camera moves around the hall, the atmosphere of crisis is palpable. Behind the platform there are huge banners proclaiming, "¡NO al Vacimiento de la Flota Petrolera de YPF!," "NO al Vacimiento del Petroleo Argentino!"

To the side is another large poster showing a huge gorilla dressed in a stars and stripes shirt and grasping in its enormous hand an Argentine oil tanker that it is apparently going to confiscate. The gorilla is perhaps the most potent of Peronist symbols, representing the essence of the antinational, the antipopular, the antiworker, and the anti-Peronist. It is closely related in the Peronist imaginary to another crucial rhetorical figure, the oligarchy. Other fundamental Peronist icons are also present on the bare concrete walls of the union hall. Posters of the general and Evita are clearly visible. The general is in his military uniform from the 1940s, and Evita is the rather gaunt figure of her last years as protectress of the humble, her hair brushed straight back and bound tightly behind in a bun. Signs everywhere proclaim "El Poder de la Humildad" [The power of humility]. Another Peronist symbol, the drum corps, which is dominated by the huge bass drum, the bombo, whose insistent throbbing beat had been a staple of Peronist events since the 1940s, is also present.

On the stage as the camera zooms in for a close-up are local union figures, Duhalde himself and the mayor of Morón, Juan Carlos Rousselo. Also there, beside the master of ceremonies, is Doña María. The meeting starts with the singing of the Peronist anthem, the Marcha Peronista. As the camera moves from the stage to the several hundred members of the public, it is clear that this audience is overwhelmingly working class and that it consists nearly entirely of men. The Marcha is sung with a passion that goes beyond the strength of the singing to engage the whole body. The public is standing—there are no chairs—and they do not simply sing the words; their bodies lean forward rhythmically and the right arm is extended with palm facing upward imitating the characteristic, beckoning gesture of Perón. As I watch this on the video, I am reminded again of what I had felt many times before when I had been present during the singing of this anthem. The singing of this song is more than a simple act of political identity, it is also a form of communion for this working-class audience that bears an intensity that both moves and frightens me.

After several short speeches by union leaders denouncing the Radical government and its economic policy, Doña María is introduced as someone who had been in the vanguard of the historic movement that rescued Perón and launched Peronism. The speech she gives is a short one. It lasts ten minutes. Her function was, after all, to help set the scene for the two main speakers, Rousselo and Duhalde. I was, however, transfixed as I watched it. I had never seen her speak in public before, though I had been told by others that in her prime she had been a powerful orator. She had told me herself that she had an instinctive ability to speak in public. Seeing the diminutive figure now on the videotape confirmed all this. She stands quite still, squarely facing the audience, with her hands slightly apart on either side of the microphone. Her hand bag hangs down from one forearm. As she speaks, she rarely moves her arms. Instead, her voice provides the dynamic movement, as she changes its tone and rhythm to suit her purposes, to convey emotion, to reach crescendos, and to communicate with her audience. The public gives her its rapt attention.

What was it that she chose to convey to this public of Peronist

Singing the Marcha Peronista at a rally for Eduardo Duhalde, State Oil Workers' Union, Ensenada, 4 May 1988.

Doña María Roldán speaking at a rally for Eduardo Duhalde, State Oil Workers' Union, Ensenada, 4 May 1988. Both film stills from untitled video, property of author; videographer unknown.

workers in this, her last public performance? Interestingly, she does not choose to continue the denunciations of the Radical government, though she would have been perfectly capable of doing so, as I could confirm. Instead, she casts her talk in terms of an evocation of certain crucial moments in the collective memory of Peronism. After offering her conviction that Menem and Duhalde will win the Peronist primaries and the subsequent presidential elections, she gets to the heart of her concerns. "I recalled the other night at a meeting where we spoke of the divine Evita . . ." From this point she launches into a detailed evocation of October seventeenth. As I watched and listened, the words had a familiar ring. I realized that I had heard this story almost word for word before in our personal

conversations. Her overall intention is the same. She wishes to re-
mind her audience of the fundamental moral point that in those
October days the workers of Argentina mobilized to support someone they scarcely knew: "Casi no conocíamos a Perón" [We barely
knew Peron]. They were driven to do this by "miserias morales y
materiales" [moral and material miseries] that they could no longer
endure. They had no guarantees of what would happen: "We didn't
know what would become of us." All of this meant that October
seventeenth was "una noche incierta" [a night of uncertainty], a leap
in the dark, or, perhaps more fittingly, a leap of faith. For this is the
point Doña María wishes to make. It is this element of faith, of risk
with no guarantees of success, that provides the moral underpinning
of the unique relationship of the workers with Perón, a relationship
inscribed in the Peronist lexicon in the word "fe" [faith].

As I listen, I am also struck by how this speech functions as a mnemonic performance. Doña María takes her public, most of whom
had not lived those days, through the days leading up to the seventeenth. In staccato, almost shorthand form, she enumerates the days,
"The twelfth . . . the thirteenth . . . the fourteenth . . . ," building to the crescendo of the seventeenth. She then elaborates on the
essential details of that night: the crowd, the weather, the mood, her
own role. She places her listeners on the platform, she recalls what
the president de facto, General Edelmiro Farrell, said, and Perón's
reply. There is a ritualistic quality to this evocation. If the words
and phrases were familiar to me, they were also familiar I suspect
to many of her listeners from family, union, political, and communal settings. By repeating them and performing them she is both
instigating and inscribing memory and in the process effecting the
transmission of collective memory from one generation to another.

What is captured on this video is a powerful example of memory work. For Doña María this is far from an academic exercise.
It embodies a contemporary political lesson. October seventeenth
was "a night of triumph for the Argentine workers," which led them
to victory over the oligarchy, the armed forces, and other forces in
Argentine society. It is the re-creation of such a movement and the
unity that underlay it that can now lead, God willing, to a victory
for Menem. She ends her speech with vivas to Perón, to Evita, and

to Menem. The public responds with thunderous applause as she is embraced by Duhalde.

Doña María's final speech raises in a powerful way the issue of memory and the past. Yet after viewing the video several times, I am strengthened in my conviction that she did not dwell in the past. She very much inhabited the present. In order for her to function in the present she needed to come to terms with the past and bring it into the present. Peronism has frequently been associated with nostalgia, and, indeed, as a social and political movement its rhetoric and ideology were peculiarly predicated on access to past symbols and historical experiences. Indeed, its constant internal battles have been articulated in an idiom of authenticity and loyalty, defined ultimately by rival claims to have access to the symbols and memory of the past.

Although this rivalry had always been a feature of Peronism, it became particularly intense after the death of Perón in 1974 and its echoes are captured in the 1988 video. Menem and Duhalde make a point of defining their movement as orthodox, by which they meant that they had the legitimate claim to represent and embody the values and memories of the Peronist past, particularly its proletarian past. This claim to authenticity was intended to distinguish them from their rivals, who openly proclaimed themselves the "Renovators" of Peronism. Such a claim may be expressed in a nostalgic register, but it should not be simply reduced to this. Nostalgia has been defined as "memory without the pain," and yet it is clear that Doña María's speech is no tranquil summoning up of a lost paradise. She is well aware that there is no new Perón waiting in the wings, nor a second Evita.

Rather, it seems to me that she is engaged in a symbolic struggle over the content and control of memory. Indeed, the events captured on the video can be interpreted on one level as a ritual ceremony centered on the evocation of traditional symbols and the performance of a political identity founded in memory. This explains the heavy weight of Peronist icons visible in the video, and the constant references to the classic symbols of Peronism. The speaker who followed Doña María to the podium, the mayor of Morón, Juan

Carlos Rousselo, explicitly recognized the importance of such ceremonies. He urged his listeners to "return to the history of Peronism" as a way of "transmitting to our children and grandchildren" the essence of Peronism, which for him was embodied in the words of Perón but also in the fundamental "feeling" that separates Peronists from non-Peronists. Finally, Rousselo expressed the desire that his audience reclaim "our slogans, our songs, our bombos, our photos, our anthems, our symbols, this great wealth that embodies our history."

Viewing the video after these speeches, and nine years after Doña María's death, its ironies are not lost on me. Memory can be a powerful mobilizing tool capable of energizing political identities, but it cannot guarantee political and ideological outcomes. Doña María and many others present at these events in 1988 thought they were witnessing the rebirth of a more appropriately working-class Peronism, but that rebirth was not to occur. Within five years most of the economic and social evils attacked from the platforms in Berisso and Ensenada had in fact been implemented by the very people who occupied the podium that night. Menem and Duhalde have presided over the dismantling of what was left of the Peronist social welfare state and inaugurated a wave of privatizations that have undermined the traditional strength of Peronist unions and decimated the workforce. By the mid-1990s YPF had essentially been sold off to private, foreign buyers, and its tanker fleet had been scrapped. The massive refinery in Ensenada was a mere shadow of its former self. The Merchant Marine branch of the union local where the impassioned meeting of 1988 had taken place now exists simply as a clearinghouse for pension and severance claims.

In Berisso the hopes for the future were ill-founded. The deindustrialization begun under the military dictatorship has been accelerated by the neoliberal policies of the Menem years. Real levels of unemployment hover around 35 percent. Within Berisso itself the municipality is now the largest employer, and the wage bill for these workers eats up 80 percent of the city's budget. The social costs of such an economy are evident. Berisso now has one of the highest indices of infant mortality in the province of Buenos Aires. Unofficially, social workers will tell you that family violence has increased dramatically. All the social ills that Menem and Duhalde laid at the door of "an absurd modernization" as they launched their campaign in Berisso and Ensenada in 1988 have been intensified in the ensuing years under their government.

The undoing of the world of labor that this betrayal has entailed must have profound implications for a working-class political identity centered on the emotional bonds generated by a shared memory and tradition. I began this book by analyzing the memory landscape offered by the Centro Cívico in Berisso. It is an important memory site—one of a declining number in Berisso—but its ability to embody living memory is problematic at best. Whatever the intentions of the muralists and monument makers, their power to call up memory and to offer meaning is arbitrary and fragile. In part, this may be due to the very nature of such memorialization. Robert Musil considered that "there is nothing in this world as invisible as a monument. They are no doubt erected to be seen—indeed to attract attention. But at the same time they are impregnated with something that repels attention."[1] The high school kids who socialize among the monuments in front of the murals may well have other, more immediate concerns; the icons of this plaza may have acquired a taken-for-granted status that defeats the memorialist's best intentions.

We must also consider the problem of generational memory. In the video I recognized the face of one of my best friends in Berisso, Nestor Juzwa. Since 1995 he has been mayor of the city. In 1988 he was one of a handful of younger Peronist militants who persuaded Menem and Duhalde to launch their campaign from Berisso. In the video he can be seen hurriedly getting people seated, offering the microphone to Menem, ushering people forward. Later, buoyed by the success of the Berisso launching, he would play an active role in the presidential campaign of 1989, and in 1990 he became a local Peronist counselor. In 1995, as efforts to organize an official commemoration of the fiftieth aniversary of October seventeenth got underway in Berisso, I spoke to him often about the memorialization of the October days. He told me that, although his father had never spoken to him of the events, it was as if he had participated in them. He had a memory of them that related the events to specific sites in Berisso—the places where the workers had first congregated, the streets they had marched along, the slogans they had chanted. "It is as though I know that at such and such a corner this happened on that day." Partly this memory may be due to a surviving communal folklore about the days. In part, too, it owes something to the memory work associated with Nestor's political initiation in the late 1960s in Peronist youth formations who obsessively sought legitimation by assuming as their own the movement's glorious past. The larger panorama of events in Buenos Aires in front of the Casa Rosada on the legendary night were transmitted to him in a similar fashion. I suspect that he found Doña María's recitation of the story in the union local in Ensenada very familiar, though he had never heard it from her mouth before. In a word, Nestor had been able to assume as his own personal memory the collective memory of the October days.

The week before the official celebration of October seventeenth representatives of the Peronist movement in Berisso inaugurated a plaque that was placed under the bust of Perón in the Centro Cívico. As I stood watching the proceedings from the other side of the Avenida Montevideo and listening to speeches from representatives of the "históricos" and the younger generation of leaders like Nestor, I saw his elder son, Emiliano, walking toward me. After our greetings I gestured across the road and asked him why he was not over there participating. He paused and smiled wryly and with a hunch of his large shoulders said, "Este, no me dice nada" [This doesn't mean anything to me].

Emiliano wears his hair long and loves American rock music and fashionable clothes. He is also concerned for the state of his country and its working people. He has access at home to the activist Peronist tradition of his father and his mother, Elsa. But the gesture of his head and shoulders across the Montevideo referred to far more than the group commemorating 17 October 1945 in front of the busts of Perón and Evita. It encompassed, I suspect, virtually all of the symbols and embodied memories present in the plaza, including the immigrant past of his Ukrainian great-grandparents, who had arrived to work in the frigoríficos in the 1920s.

For Emiliano and his generation of Berissenses the meanings

of the past still available to their parents have been rendered increasingly opaque by historical and cultural change. Even for an older generation of Peronists in Berisso October seventeenth seems to have an increasingly tenuous hold on collective memory. At a national level the Peronist government did all in its power to rob the fiftieth anniversary celebrations of any significance. Duhalde left the country on an official visit to avoid committing himself to any commemorative act, and Menem retired to his home province of La Rioja to view the events from afar. In Berisso the celebrations had a muted tone, even among that generation who had direct experience of the events of 1945. As a collective memory, it would seem to have become increasingly decontextualized, robbed of its raison d'être. There is a clash between the values of a Peronist government committed to the logic of global capitalism and the meanings and values traditionally taken to inhere in the October days. The memory of those events had first been sustained by an experience of mobilization and agency; later, in the period after the fall of Perón in 1955, the memory was kept alive in communities like Berisso by social practices of resistance that were crucial to sustaining and conveying knowledge of the past. Such practices and their accompanying memories were centered above all on the workplace. In the era of deindustrialization and the accompanying social and economic marginalization that has ended the work careers of many older Berissenses and that has condemned many of Emiliano's generation to a future of temporary work on the periphery of radically reduced labor markets, the memory of 17 October 1945 may simply be unsustainable in the long run, robbed of any relevance in the contemporary social context. It will cease to be the living memory of a community and will become reduced to the formal status of a historical fact.

In contemporary Berisso it is hard to imagine a political event like the one videotaped in 1988 being reenacted with the vibrant commemorative charge I found so transfixing in Doña María's speech. This is not to say that Peronism has lost its ability to convoke large sections of the working class and the poor in Argentina. Doña María had an investment in validating her own and her generation's struggles. Although she shared with me some of her private doubts and although I, playing the oral historian's role of part inquisitor, part confessor, have sought to uncover other paradoxes and tensions in her personal testimony, in her public persona she honored the demands of collective memory. She wanted her legacy to be a source of optimism for Emiliano and her great-grandchildren's generation of Argentine workers.

NOTES

Prologue

1 Lia M. Sanucci, *Berisso: Un reflejo de la evolución argentina* (La Plata: n.p., 1983) is the only formal history of the community.

2 For a general interpretation of Peronism as a social and political movement see Daniel James, *Resistance and Integration: Peronism and the Argentine Working Class, 1946–1976* (Cambridge: Cambridge University Press, 1988).

1. Listening in the Cold.
The Practice of Oral History in an Argentine Meatpacking Community

1 Paul Thompson, *The Voice of the Past* (Oxford: Oxford University Press, 1990); Raphael Samuel and Paul Thompson, *The Myths We Live By* (New York: Routledge, 1990).

2 Luisa Passerini, *Fascism in Popular Memory: The Cultural Experience of the Turin Working Class* (Cambridge: Cambridge University Press, 1987); Ronald Grele, "Listen to Their Voices: Two Case Studies in the Interpretation of Oral History Interviews," *Oral History* 7, no. 1 (1979): 33–42; Alessandro Portelli, *The Death of Luigi Trastulli and Other Stories: Form and Meaning in Oral History* (Albany: State University of New York Press, 1991).

3 Samuel and Thompson, *Myths We Live By*, 2.

4 Portelli, in *Death of Luigi Trastulli and Other Stories*, 2.

5 The phrase is Ronald Grele's, in "La historia y sus lenguajes en la entrevista de historia oral: Quién contesta a las preguntas de quién y porqué," *Historia y Fuente Oral* 20, no. 3 (1989), 63–83.

6   See James Clifford and George Marcus, *Writing Culture: The Poetics and Politics of Ethnography* (Berkeley: University of California Press, 1986); George E. Marcus and Michael M. J. Fischer, *Anthropology as Cultural Critique: An Experimental Moment in the Human Sciences* (Chicago: University of Chicago Press, 1986).

7   See, for example, Theodore Rosengarten, comp., *All God's Dangers: The Life of Nate Shaw* (New York: Knopf, 1974); and Jacquelyn Dowd Hall et al., *Like a Family: The Making of a Southern Cotton Mill World* (Chapel Hill: University of North Carolina Press, 1987).

8   See especially John Beverley and Marc Zimmerman, *Literature and Politics in the Central American Revolutions* (Austin: University of Texas Press, 1990).

9   See Passerini, *Fascism in Popular Memory,* and Portelli, *Death of Luigi Trastulli and Other Stories.*

10 Henry Glassie, *Passing the Time in Ballymenone: Culture and History of an Ulster Community* (Philadelphia: University of Pennsylvania Press, 1982), 620.

11 Quoted in James Clifford, *The Predicament of Culture: Twentieth Century Ethnography, Literature, and Art* (Cambridge, Mass.: Harvard University Press, 1988), 75.

12 The twenty truths of Peronism refer to a set of basic maxims that were meant to guide the social and political behavior of Peronist affiliates.

13 The concept of a Great Tradition and a Little Tradition was originally developed by the anthropologist Robert Redfield. For its usage in an oral interview context see Barbara Myerhoff, *Number Our Days* (New York: Simon and Schuster, 1978), 256.

14 See Barbara Johnstone, *Stories, Community, and Place: Narratives from Middle America* (Bloomington: Indiana University Press, 1990), 99–101.

15 Glassie, *Passing the Time in Ballymenone,* 651.

16 See Gillian Bennett, "Narrative as Expository Discourse," *Journal of American Folklore* 99, no. 394 (October–December 1986): 415–35.

17 James Fentress and Chris Wickham, *Social Memory* (Oxford: Blackwell, 1992), 101.

18 Glassie, *Passing the Time in Ballymenone,* 664.

19 Grele, "La historia y sus lenguajes en la entrevista de historia oral," 74.

20 On the notion of symbolic violence see Pierre Bourdieu, *Outline of a Theory of Practice* (Cambridge: Cambridge University Press, 1983).

21 Philippe Lejeune, *On Autobiography* (Minneapolis: University of Minnesota Press, 1989), 22.

22 Gelya Frank, "Anthropology and Individual Lives: The Story of Life His-

tory and the History of the Life Story," *American Anthropologist* 97, no. 1 (March 1995): 145–49.

23 Charlotte Linde, *Life Stories: The Creation of Coherence* (Oxford: Oxford University Press, 1993), 21. See also George C. Rosenwald and Richard L. Ochberg, eds., *Storied Lives: The Cultural Politics of Self-Understanding* (New Haven, Conn.: Yale University Press, 1992).

24 Alberto Moreiras, "The Aura of Testimonio," in *Testimonial Literature and Latin America,* ed. George M. Gugelberger (Durham, N.C.: Duke University Press, 1996).

25 The phrase "redemptive ethnographer" is Ruth Behar's, in *Translated Woman: Crossing the Border with Esperanza's Story* (Boston: Beacon Press, 1993), 269.

26 Clifford Geertz, " 'From the Native's Point of View: On the Nature of Anthropological Understanding," in *Local Knowledge: Further Essays in Interpretive Anthropology* (New York: Basic, 1983), 58.

27 See Linde, *Life Stories.*

28 See Geertz, "From the Native's Point of View."

29 Doris Sommer, "Resistant Texts and Incompetent Readers," *Latin American Literary Review* 4 (1992): 104–8.

30 Marc Kaminsky, introduction to *Remembered Lives: The Work of Ritual, Storytelling, and Growing Older,* Barbara Myerhoff (Ann Arbor: University of Michigan Press, 1992), 13.

31 Pierre Bourdieu, "Understanding," *Theory, Culture, and Society* 13, no. 2 (1996): 24. Translation of Bourdieu, *La Misère du Monde* (Paris: Seuil, 1993), 903–25.

32 James Agee and Walker Evans, *Let Us Now Praise Famous Men* (New York: Houghton Mifflin, 1988), xlvi.

33 Portelli, *Death of Luigi Trastulli and Other Stories,* 59.

34 Glassie, *Passing the Time in Ballymenone,* 707.

35 *Webster's New World Dictionary of the American Language,* 2d ed., s.v., "requiem."

36 Barbara Johnson, "Apostrophe, Animation, and Abortion," *Diacritics* (spring 1986): 30.

37 Paul Connerton, *How Societies Remember* (Cambridge: Cambridge University Press, 1989), 40.

38 John Berger, "The Uses of Photography," in *About Looking* (New York: Pantheon, 1980).

39 Christian Metz, "Photography and Fetish," 51 *October* no. 34 (fall 1985): 85; Sigmund Freud, "Mourning and Melancholia," in *The Freud Reader,* ed. Peter Gay (New York: Norton, 1989), 584–89.

40 Annette Kuhn, *Family Secrets, Acts of Memory, and Imagination* (London: Verso, 1995), 13.

41 John McCole, *Walter Benjamin and the Antinomies of Tradition* (Ithaca, N.Y.: Cornell University Press, 1993), 253–79.

42 Walter Benjamin, "On Some Motifs in Baudelaire," in *Illuminations: Essays and Reflections* (New York: Schocken, 1969), 159.

43 Ruth Behar's conception of herself as Benjaminian storyteller in *Translated Woman*, 13.

44 See Lejeune, *On Autobiography*, 210.

45 Kaminsky, introduction, 66.

46 Myerhoff, *Number Our Days*, 74.

47 See Kaminsky's critical comment on Myerhoff's essay, "Life History as Integration," in Myerhoff, *Remembered Lives: The Work of Storytelling, Ritual, and Growing Older* (Ann Arbor: University of Michigan Press, 1992), 254.

48 Myerhoff, *Remembered Lives*, 240.

49 Andreas Huyssen, *Twilight Memories: Marking Time in a Culture of Amnesia* (New York: Routledge, 1995).

2. "The Case of María Roldán and
the Señora with Money Is Very Clear, It's a Fable"
Stories, Anecdotes, and Other Performances in Doña María's Testimony

1 Richard Bauman, *Story, Performance, and Event: Contextual Studies of Oral Narrative* (Cambridge: Cambridge University Press, 1986), 6.

2 Charlotte Linde, *Life Stories: The Creation of Coherence* (Oxford: Oxford University Press, 1993), 99–127.

3 Bauman, *Story, Performance, and Event*, 8.

4 Marie-Françoise Chanfrault-Duchet, "Narrative Structures, Social Models, and Symbolic Representation in the Life Story," in *Women's Words: The Feminist Practice of Oral History*, ed. Sherna Berger Gluck and Daphne Patai (New York: Routledge, 1991), 77–93.

5 Ibid., 80.

6 Kenneth J. Gergen and Mary M. Gergen, "Narratives of the Self," in *Studies in Social Identity*, ed. Theodore Sarbin and Karl E. Scheibe (New York: Praeger, 1983), 263.

7 Chanfrault-Duchet, "Narrative Structures, Social Models, and Symbolic Representation in the Life Story," 79.

8 Alessandro Portelli, *The Death of Luigi Trastulli and Other Stories: Form*

and Meaning in Oral History (Albany: State University of New York Press, 1991), 65.

9 Chanfrault-Duchet, "Narrative Structures, Social Models, and Symbolic Representation in the Life Story," 80.

10 Kevin Murray, "Drama and Narrative in the Construction of Identities," in *Texts of Identity,* ed. John Shotter and Kenneth J. Gergen (London: Sage, 1989), 176–205.

11 *The New Princeton Encyclopedia of Poetry and Poetics,* ed. Alex Preminger and T. V. F. Brogan (Princeton, N.J.: Princeton University Press, 1993), 634.

12 Gergen and Gergen, "Narratives of the Self," 269.

13 Barbara Johnstone, *Stories, Community, and Place: Narratives from Middle America* (Bloomington: Indiana University Press, 1990), 34–35.

14 *Webster's New World Dictionary of the American Language,* 2d ed., s.v., "anecdote."

15 See Bauman, *Story, Performance, and Event,* 54–78.

16 See William Labov and Joshua Waletsky, "Narrative Analysis: Oral Versions of Personal Experience," in *Essays on the Verbal and Visual Arts,* ed. June Helm (Seattle: University of Washington Press, 1967), 12–44; William Labov, "The Transformation of Experience in Narrative Syntax," in *Language in the Inner City* (Philadelphia: University of Pennsylvania Press, 1972), 354–96.

17 Bauman, *Story, Performance, and Event.*

18 Frank Lentricchia, "In Place of an Afterword—Someone Reading," in *Critical Terms for Literary Study,* 2d ed., ed. Frank Lentricchia and Thomas L. McLaughlin (Chicago: University of Chicago Press, 1990), 429.

19 Chanfrault-Duchet, "Narrative Structures, Social Models, and Symbolic Representation in the Life Story," 81.

20 Ibid., 81.

21 Luisa Passerini, *Fascism in Popular Memory: The Cultural Experience of the Turin Working Class* (Cambridge: Cambridge University Press, 1987), 29.

22 Johnstone, *Stories, Community, and Place,* 66–76.

23 See Carol Gilligan, *In a Different Voice: Psychological Theory and Women's Development* (Cambridge, Mass.: Harvard University Press, 1982); Nancy Chodorow, "Family Structure and Feminine Personality," in *Women, Culture, and Society,* ed. Michelle Z. Rosaldo and Louise Lamphere (Stanford, Calif.: Stanford University Press, 1974), 43–66.

24 Portelli, *Death of Luigi Trastulli and Other Stories,* 134–35.

25 Passerini, *Fascism in Popular Memory,* 27–28.

26 See Johnstone, *Story, Community, and Place,* 77.

27 Ibid.

28 Erving Goffman, *Forms of Talk* (Philadelphia: University of Pennsylvania Press, 1981), 128.

29 Penelope Eckert, "Co-operative Competition in Adolescent Girl Talk," *Discourse Processes* 13 (1990): 92–122.

30 Bauman, *Story, Performance, and Event*, 77.

31 Erving Goffman, cited in Nessa Wolfson, *CHP: The Conversational Historical Present in American English Narrative* (Dordrecht: Floris Publications, 1982).

32 See Wolfson, *CHP.*

33 Ibid.

34 Barbara Myerhoff, *Remembered Lives: The Work of Storytelling, Ritual, and Growing Older* (Ann Arbor: University of Michigan Press, 1992), 233.

35 Ibid., 235.

36 Linde, *Life Stories*, 98–127.

37 Alasdair MacIntyre, "Epistemological Crises, Dramatic Narrative, and the Philosophy of Science," *The Monist* 60 (1977): 453–71.

38 Linde, *Life Stories*, 93–94.

39 Portelli, *Death of Luigi Trastulli and Other Stories*, 21.

40 Gergen and Gergen, "Narratives of the Self," 269.

41 See Johnstone, *Stories, Community, and Place*, 94–102.

42 Portelli, *Death of Luigi Trastulli and Other Stories*, 112.

43 Victor Turner, *Dramas, Fields, and Metaphors: Symbolic Action in Human Society* (Ithaca, N.Y.: Cornell University Press, 1974), 23–60.

44 Haroldo Gutiérrez, interview with author, Berisso, 16 December 1995.

3. "Tales Told Out on the Borderlands."
Reading Doña María's Story for Gender

1 See Sherna Berger Gluck and Daphne Patai, eds., *Women's Words: The Feminist Practice of Oral History* (New York: Routledge, 1991); and Personal Narratives Group, ed., *Interpreting Women's Lives: Feminist Theory and Personal Narratives* (Bloomington: Indiana University Press, 1989).

2 Julia Swindells and Lisa Jardine, *What's Left? Women in Culture and the Labor Movement* (London: Routledge, 1990), 118.

3 Joan Scott, "The Evidence of Experience," *Critical Inquiry* 17, no. 3 (summer 1991): 773–97.

4 Gayatri Chakravorty Spivak, "The Rani of Sirmur: An Essay in Reading the Archives," *History and Theory* 24 (1985): 247–92.

5   Gyan Prakash, "Subaltern Studies as Postcolonial Criticism," *American Historical Review* (December 1994): 1475–90.

6   See Myra Jehlen, "Gender," in *Critical Terms for Literary Study*, ed. Frank Lentricchia and Thomas L. McLaughlin (Chicago: University of Chicago Press, 1990), 273.

7   James Fentress and Chris Wickham, *Social Memory* (Oxford: Blackwell, 1992), 126.

8   Luisa Passerini, *Fascism in Popular Memory: The Cultural Experience of the Turin Working Class* (Cambridge: Cambridge University Press, 1987), 42.

9   For an analysis of the nature of Peronist discourse directed at women see Susana Bianchi and Norma Sánchis, *El Partido Peronista Feminino* (Buenos Aires: Centro Editor de América Latina, 1987).

10 See Beatrix Campbell, *Wigan Pier Revisited: Poverty and Politics in the 80s* (London: Virago, 1984).

11 Irma Pintos, interview with author, Berisso, July 1992.

12 See Marcela Nari, "La mujer obrera: Entre la maternidad y el trabajo," Research report, Facultad de Filosofía y Letras, Universidad de Buenos Aires, 1995.

13 Faye Ginsburg, "Dissonance and Harmony: The Symbolic Function of Abortion in Activists' Life Stories," in Personal Narratives Group, *Interpreting Women's Lives*.

14 Michael Herzfeld, *Anthropology through the Looking Glass: Critical Ethnography in the Margins of Europe* (Cambridge: Cambridge University Press, 1987), 95–122.

15 David Carr, *Time, Narrative, and History* (Bloomington: Indiana University Press, 1989), 158.

16 See Carr, *Time, Narrative, and History;* Barbara Johnstone, *Stories, Community, and Place: Narratives from Middle America* (Bloomington: Indiana University Press, 1990).

17 Prakash, "Subaltern Studies as Postcolonial Criticism," 1488.

18 Passerini, *Fascism in Popular Memory*, chapter 4.

19 Kenneth Burke, *The Philosophy of Literary Form* (Baton Rouge: Louisiana State University Press, 1941), 293–304.

20 Ernesto Laclau, *Politics and Ideology in Marxist Theory: Capitalism, Fascism, Populism* (London: New Left Books, 1977).

21 Carolyn Steedman, *Landscape for a Good Woman* (New Brunswick, N.J.: Rutgers University Press, 1989), 123.

22 Ginsburg, "Dissonance and Harmony."

23 Laurel Richardson, "Narrative and Sociology," *Journal of Contemporary Ethnography* 2, no. 1 (1990): 117–35.

24 Elena Cabezali et al., "Myth as Suppression: Motherhood and the Historical Consciousness of the Women of Madrid, 1936–39," in *The Myths We Live By*, ed. Raphael Samuel and Paul Thompson (New York: Routledge, 1990).

25 Steedman, *Landscape for a Good Woman*, 65.

4. A Poem for Clarita.
Niñas Burguesitas and Working-Class Women in Peronist Argentina

 1 See Daniel James, "Historias contadas en los margenes: La vida de Doña María: historia oral y problemática de género," *Entrepasados*, no. 3 (1992).

 2 Fredric Jameson, *The Political Unconscious: Narrative as a Socially Symbolic Act* (Ithaca, N.Y.: Cornell University Press, 1981), 84.

 3 Felipe Protzucov, *Vivencias Berissenses* (Berisso: Felipe Protzucov, 1995).

 4 Susana Bianchi and Norma Sánchis, *El Partido Peronista Feminino*, 2 vols. (Buenos Aires: Centro Editor de América Latina, 1987).

 5 Beatriz Sarlo, *El imperio de los sentimientos* (Buenos Aires: Catalogos, 1985).

 6 Karl Marx, *Economic and Philosophical Manuscripts of 1844* (New York: International Publishers, 1964), 133.

 7 Donna Guy, *El sexo peligroso: La prostitución legal en Buenos Aires, 1875–1955* (Buenos Aires: Sudamericana, 1994).

 8 Mirta Lobato, "Mujeres en la fábrica: El caso de las obreras en el frigorífico Armour, 1915–1969," *Anuario IEHS* 5 (1990).

 9 Beba Anzolini, interview with author, Berisso, June 1990.

10 Peter Brooks, *The Melodramatic Imagination: Balzac, Henry James, Melodrama, and the Mode of Excess* (New Haven, Conn.: Yale University Press, 1976), 88.

11 Judith R. Walkowitz, *City of Dreadful Delight: Narratives of Sexual Danger in Late Victorian London* (Chicago: University of Chicago Press, 1992).

12 Migrants from the interior provinces of Corrientes and Santiago del Estero.

13 Alejandro Chible, interview with author, Berisso, July 1993.

14 Irma González, interview with author, Buenos Aires, 1987.

15 Paula Rabinowitz, *Labor and Desire: Revolutionary Fiction in Depression America* (Chapel Hill: University of North Carolina Press, 1991), 62–96.

16 The term is Catherine Crosby's, in *The Ends of History: Victorians and the "Woman Question"* (New York: Routledge, 1991), 39.

17 See Mirta Lobato, ed., *Política, médicos y enfermedades: Lectura de historia de la salud en la Argentina* (Buenos Aires: Editorial Biblios, 1996).

18 Luis Horacio Velazquez, *Pobres Habrá Siempre* (Buenos Aires: Editorial Kraft, 1953), 92.

19 Ismael Moreno, *El Matadero* (Buenos Aires: Editorial Selecta, 1921), 124.

20 Nicolás Olivari, *La musa de la mala pata* (Buenos Aires: Centro Editor de América Latina, 1986).

21 See Mirta Lobato, "Women Workers in the 'Cathedrals of Corned Beef': Structure and Subjectivity in the Argentine Meatpacking Industry," in *The Gendered Worlds of Latin American Women Workers: From Household and Factory to the Union Hall and Ballot Box,* ed. John D. French and Daniel James (Durham, N.C.: Duke University Press, 1997).

22 Anzolini interview.

23 See Cora Kaplan, "'Like a Housemaid's Fancies': Representations of Working Class Women in Nineteenth Century Writing," in *Grafts: Feminist Cultural Criticism,* ed. Susan Sheridan (London: Verso, 1989).

24 Diego Armus, "Salud y Anarquismo: La tuberculosis en el discurso libertario argentino," in Lobato, *Política, médicos y enfermedades,* 75–92.

25 Wai Chee Dimock, "Gender, Class, and a History of Metonymy," in *Rethinking Class: Literary Studies and Social Formations,* Wai Chee Dimock and Michael T. Gilmore (New York: Columbia University Press, 1994), 86.

26 Doris Sommer, "Rigoberta's Secrets," *Latin American Perspectives,* no. 3 (summer 1991): 32–51.

27 The concept of the "sexual contract" is developed in Carole Pateman, *The Sexual Contract* (Stanford, Calif.: Stanford University Press, 1988).

28 Raul Larra, *Sin Tregua* (Buenos Aires: Editorial Boedo, 1975).

29 Bernardo Gonzalez Arrili, *Los Charcos Rojos* (Buenos Aires: Colección Eden, 1922).

30 Raymond Williams, *Marxism and Literature* (New York: Oxford University Press, 1977), 130–32; for further elaboration of "structure of feeling" see Williams, *The Country and the City* (Oxford: Oxford University Press, 1973).

31 On the issue of the figure of the red riflewoman as a male fantasy see Klaus Theweleit, *Male Fantasies* (Minneapolis: University of Minnesota Press, 1987).

32 Barbara Johnson, "Apostrophe, Animation, and Abortion," *Diacritics* (spring 1986): 30.

33 Alberto Moreiras, "The Aura of Testimonio," in *Testimonial Literature and Latin America,* ed. George M. Gugelberger (Durham, N.C.: Duke University Press, 1996), 192–224.

34 See Walter Benjamin, "Theses on the Philosophy of History," in *Illuminations: Essays and Reflections* (New York: Schocken, 1969), 257–58.

35 Johnson, "Apostrophe, Animation, and Abortion," 31.

36 For the Horkheimer-Benjamin exchange on the incompleteness of the past see Rolf Tiedemann, "Historical Materialism or Political Messianism? An Interpretation of the Theses 'On the Concept of History,'" in *Benjamin: Philosophy, History, and Aesthetics,* ed. Gary Smith (Chicago: University of Chicago Press, 1989), 181.

37 Walter Benjamin, cited in Tiedemann, "Historical Materialism or Political Messianism?" 182.

38 Umberto Eco, *Interpretación y sobreinterpretación* (Cambridge: Cambridge University Press, 1995), 70.

39 William Sewell, review of *Gender and the Politics of History,* by Joan Scott, *History and Theory,* no. 3 (1990), 71–82.

40 See John B. Thompson, *Theories of Ideology* (Berkeley: University of California Press, 1986).

41 For a discussion of these issues see Gerald Graff, "Determinacy/Indeterminacy," in *Critical Terms for Literary Study,* 2d ed., ed. Frank Lentricchia and Thomas McLaughlin (Chicago: University of Chicago Press, 1995), 163–77.

42 Jacques Derrida, "Afterward: Toward an Ethic of Discussion," in *Limited, Inc.* (Evanston, Ill.: Northwestern University Press, 1988), 153.

43 Gabrielle M. Spiegel, "History, Historicism, and the Social Logic of the Text in the Middle Ages," *Speculum* 65 (1990): 59–86.

44 The fundamental texts here are Sandra Gilbert and Susan Gubar, *The Madwoman in the Attic: The Woman Writer and the Nineteenth-Century Literary Imagination* (New Haven, Conn.: Yale University Press, 1979); and Nancy K. Miller, "Emphasis Added: Plots and Plausibilities in Women's Fiction," in *The New Feminist Criticism,* ed. Elaine Showalter (New York: Pantheon, 1985).

45 Daniel James, "17 y 18 de octubre, 1945: El peronismo, la protesta de masas y la clase obrera argentina," in *El 17 de octubre 1945,* ed. Juan Carlos Torre (Buenos Aires: Ariel), 1995.

Epilogue

1 Robert Musil, cited in James E. Young, "The Biography of a Memorial Icon: Nathan Rapoport's Warsaw Ghetto Monument," *Representations* 3 (1992): 33–66.

INDEX

Page numbers in italics denote pages with photographs.

Daniel James is Bernardo Mendel Professor of Latin American History at Indiana University. He is the author of *Resistance and Integration: Peronism and the Argentine Working Class, 1946–1976* (1988), and the editor (with John D. French) of *The Gendered Worlds of Latin American Women Workers: From Household and Factory to the Union Hall and Ballot Box,* which was published by Duke University Press in 1997.

Library of Congress Cataloging-in-Publication Data

James, Daniel, 1948-
Doña María's story : life history, memory, and political identity / Daniel James.
p.   cm. — (Latin America otherwise)
Includes index.
ISBN 0-8223-2455-5 (alk. paper) — ISBN 0-8223-2492-x (pbk. : alk. paper)
1. Roldân, Doäa Marââ.   2. Packing-house workers—Argentina—Berisso.
3. Working class women—Argentina—Berisso.   4. Women labor leaders—Argentina—Berisso.   5. Women in politics—Argentina—Berisso.   I. Title. II. Series.
HD6073.PI52 A74   2000
331.4'8649'0092—dc21
[B]   00-035457